W9-CFR-560

FIGHTER FOR FREEDOM

"Hertha Pauli has done a masterful job in recording the picture of an individual who should not be forgotten in our history."—*Eleanor Roosevelt*

"A stunning book. The first page is enough to make one want to drop everything and read it straight through. . . . A fascinating and stirring story."
—*Langston Hughes*

"Recreates vividly the indomitable spirit of one of our civil rights pioneers who devoted her entire life to the fight for full freedom."—*Dr. Martin Luther King, Jr.*

HERTHA PAULI was born in Vienna, into a family of scientists and writers. She had written two novels in Austria before its annexation by Hitler in 1938; as a known anti-Nazi she had to flee that country immediately. After two years in France she was rescued and was brought to America with a group of noted authors sponsored by Thomas Mann. She is the author of many books, among them I LIFT MY LAMP, the story of the Statue of Liberty, and CRY OF THE HEART, the story of Bertha von Suttner, the woman who founded the world peace movement. She lives with her husband in Huntington, New York.

Her Name Was Sojourner Truth

Hertha Pauli

CAMELOT BOOKS / PUBLISHED BY AVON

AVON BOOKS
A division of
The Hearst Corporation
959 Eighth Avenue
New York, New York 10019

First Camelot Printing, September, 1971

CAMELOT TRADEMARK REG. U.S. PAT. OFF. AND
FOREIGN COUNTRIES, REGISTERED TRADEMARK—
MARCA REGISTRADA, HECHO EN CHICAGO, U.S.A.

Printed in the U.S.A.

Contents

Her Name Was
Sojourner Truth

A Woman Discovered

"MR. LINCOLN," the woman said, "I never heard tell of you before they put you up for president."

"But I heard of you," the President said, smiling.

It was in a public library, years ago, that I chanced upon this conversation. The White House visitor was a former slave called Sojourner Truth. I could not leave her there, bound in a book; she came with me. And she has not left me since.

Reading more about her, I found that mine was not an unusual reaction. In the nineteenth century Sojourner Truth was known from the eastern seaboard to the western frontier, and none who ever met her could forget her. If not many know of her now, it is because her work was intangible. She never learned to read or write. She left no concrete achievements. The one practical plan of her life did not even reach the discussion stage. She worked in the most perishable of materials, the human heart. Her creative endeavors died with the multitudes that had thrilled to her invariably greeting: "Chillun, I talks to God, and God talks to me."

She survives in other ways, as I learned when I put down the books, the old newspapers, the yellowed records of a hundred years ago, and went traveling in her steps, driving where she had journeyed on foot or by horse and buggy, from her birthplace in the Hudson Valley—still owned by the family that owned her—to her grave in the prairie city that proudly calls her its "first national figure." Wherever I went, her spirit was fresh and alive, though her memory had faded. Young people were stirring, joining up for the ventures once undertaken alone by the forgotten woman. New leaders were calling for action in a key

of Christian love, the key Sojourner struck in her day, all
by herself.

She never heard the slogans of nonviolence, but the way
of life that marks the fight for freedom in America today
was her way of life. She never saw a Greyhound bus, but
every Freedom Ride recalls the trolleys she struggled to
board, having her arms wrenched rather than forgo her
cry of triumph, "I've had a ride!" She could not read a
letter, but every child now walking a gantlet of hate into a
Southern school takes her advice to "get behind the law."
The students now filling Southern jails carry out her threat
to Copperheads during the Civil War: "If you put me in
the guardhouse, I'll make the United States rock like a
cradle!"

Historians have had a difficult time with Sojourner
Truth. She would not fit their categories. If you called her
a revolutionary, you came into conflict with virtually
every word she ever spoke. If her faith impressed you as
a compound of "witchcraft, necromancy, and superstition,"
you had to ignore the contrary opinions of all who knew
her in an age when religion was a main fact of American
life. If you arraigned her for neglecting her family and
singled out her favorite grandson as "the only blood kin
she was ever known to love," you could not mention the
decades she spent surrounded by affectionate daughters,
sons-in-law, and grandchildren.

She does not lend herself to timely interpretations. She
defies psychoanalysis and economic determinism. It is on
her own premises only that she rings true and speaks as
clearly now as when she was sojourning up and down the
land.

She was the stuff of legend, even in her time. At fifty
she was said to be seventy, at seventy, "above a hundred."
In 1875, when Americans had the next year's Independence Centennial on their minds, a friend referred to her
in flowery language: "She stands beside the closing century
like a twin sister"—and soon there were printed reports
that Sojourner Truth had a twin sister nicknamed The
Century. Sometimes she encouraged the myths. But what

she told for a fact, however incredible, is usually borne out by other sources.

Oddly enough, her story is better documented than almost any other former slave's. For the early lives of all those pieces of property without vital statistics we depend on personal memories; Sojourner related hers in middle age, with details, of which quite a few are verifiable, and not one has proved false. Besides, the small volume published in 1850 as *The Narrative of Sojourner Truth, a Northern Slave,* was not her first appearance in print. She already had a unique past. Just out of bondage, she had resorted to the law to free her son from an Alabama plantation; later, as a domestic in New York, she had been the first Negro to file and win a suit for slander against prominent whites. The latter case, involving a much-talked-about religious scandal, had occasioned two books —one grossly abusive of Isabella, as Sojourner was originally called, the other championing her and incidentally supplying us with such material as the full employment record of her first years in freedom.

The material changes radically about the time her *Narrative* came out. In the 1850's we keep reading of her in anti-slavery papers, and soon in others. She starts showing up in the biographies of noted men. Her picture seems familiar across the country. A veritable tide of letters to her, and about her, has left deposits in the manuscript collections of libraries from coast to coast. She was controversial: jibes at the "crazy black mummy" are scattered through the homilies to "the most singular and impressive figure that has appeared in modern times"—this from an editorial in one of the nation's leading journals. In the 1870's there was no major Northern newspaper that did not carry occasional items on Sojourner Truth.

A curious aspect of the accounts of her rise from obscurity to publicity is her way of speech. According to the sources, it developed abnormally: grammatical in her youth, colloquial in middle life, and a caricature of Negro slang in her time of renown. It seems hard to believe. Most likely, she did later stress the folksy manner she found so effective on the platform, but we need not doubt that it was further exaggerated by the reporters, just as it had been played down by the prim lady who penned the *Narrative* of Sojourner's early years. The only liberty I have taken with her recorded sayings is to quote them in a fairly consistent language.

Inwardly she never changed. Experience matured her; there is growth in her story, but no shift in character from the maltreated slave child to the old woman whom thousands loved and revered. It is as though an inner compass had held her to her true course, never letting her veer from her one guiding relationship—not with people but with something above them, above herself.

There is but one unanswerable argument against race prejudice: that mankind has one Father. Sojourner was sure of it, and she communicated her assurance to her brothers and sisters, however white, however unbrotherly. Instead of feeling superior, they grew humble in the presence of a favored child of God.

Her life was a dialogue with God and a portent of what would in time become the way of her people. Sojourner knew it. "Being a sign unto the people," she called her mission.

In the spring of 1961 a prayer meeting in a mob-ringed Southern church appeared on American television screens. "God is not dead," the minister told the beleaguered. It was the answer to a question made famous by Sojourner Truth—a question she put to a Negro leader of her time, breaking the spell of despair he had cast over a mass meeting—a question that shines from a stone in a Michigan graveyard:

IN MEMORIAM
SOJOURNER TRUTH
Born a slave in Ulster
County, New York ...
"IS GOD DEAD?"

A Northern Slave

IN ULSTER COUNTY, New York, the name of Hardenbergh is magic to this day. Dutch descendants of German nobility, the Hardenberghs were patroons in the seventeenth century, colonial lords of the manor in the eighteenth. Their grant from Queen Anne, some two million acres of fertile fields and wooded mountains between the Hudson and Delaware rivers, was farmed on feudal terms by hundreds of tenants. They commanded the Ulster militia and sat in the Colonial Assembly and in the Provincial Congress. When George Washington visited Ulster in 1783, it was Hardenberghs who entertained the General and Mrs. Washington and Governor and Mrs. Clinton of New York.

The Hardenbergh house at Hurley, Ulster County, still stands. The stone walls and tall chimneys and huge fireplaces, the oaken floors, the rough-hewn beams exposed in garret and cellar—all are as they were when the house was built.

In the beginning the cellar housed the slaves, about a dozen colored men, women, and children. Separate quarters for the sexes were not customary, no more than separate kennels for bitches and hounds. Modesty did not require it; there was not much the eye could see in the cellar that was the first memory of Bell, the slave child who was to become Sojourner Truth. What windows there were opened on wells below ground level, so that the only brightness filtering through dingy, broken panes was a pale reflection of daylight. The floor consisted of boards laid loosely on the sloping earth. Underneath were mudholes and occasionally pools of stagnant water, which made the boards rot swiftly and kept the straw on them damp at all times.

Bell's father was named James but known as "Baumfree," which meant "straight as a tree" in the Low Dutch spoken by the Hardenberghs and their slaves. He had been tall and erect as a youth, and the nickname had survived the posture. Bell's mother, Elizabeth, was called "Mama Bett"—"Mau-Mau Bett," the Dutch pronounced it. She was Baumfree's third wife. Bell never knew whether only one or both of his earlier ones had been sold away from him.

The first master Bell knew of, according to her own narrative, was named Hardenbergh. Years later, telling her story to people, she pronounced the name so that it sounded like "Ardinburgh." Thus garbled, the first family of Ulster County appeared and reappeared in printed items on their onetime slave throughout the nineteenth century.

Bell could remember hearing Hardenbergh's father, the colonel, referred to as "the Old Master." She remembered how fortunate her parents had been after the Old Master's death, to come together into the possession of Master Hardenbergh, who was the best of the family. He prized the devoted couple. To reward their fidelity, he gave them a plot of land on a mountainside for their own use, and by cultivating it on Sundays and fair summer evenings they managed to raise some corn, flax, and tobacco, which could be bartered for extra food and clothing for their children.

They had ten or twelve—Bell was never quite sure of the number. All had been sold before her recollection, except for the youngest boy, the only one she knew who had been with her in the cellar at Hurley. She recalled a winter morning when the sun shone on the snow so dazzlingly that their eyes hurt as they raised the trap door. Bell was little—about five, she guessed later. The two children crawled out, blinked at the glittering whiteness, and started playing in the snow until the merry tinkle of bells made them look up. A sleigh with two men perched high on the box drew up to the manor house. It was a

thrilling sight, and the little boy got to his feet and headed
for it, squealing with joy.

Suddenly his squeals grew terrified. Bell saw him turn
and run back as fast as his short legs would carry him,
followed by the men who had jumped off the sleigh.
Crouched in the corner of the trap door, the child saw
them chase her brother down the cellar steps. She saw him
try to hide in the straw and saw their own parents point
him out to the strangers.

"Go," shouted their father.

"Obey," cried their mother, tears streaming down her
face.

Bell saw her brother dragged past her, up the steps, and
into the blinding light. He disappeared, but she kept hearing
his screams, shrill, then muffled, until the lid of the sleigh
box fell shut. The silvery tinkle of the bells resumed, grew
fainter, and also ceased.

Somebody closed the trap door. Darkness enveloped Bell.
But, she thought, trembling, if it's dark they may not see
us . . .

Her father tried to comfort his wife. It was better this
way, Baumfree whispered. Did they not know what had
happened when a small boy on a neighboring estate had
not quietly followed the trader?

Bell knew what had happened. She had heard it whenever Mau-Mau preached obedience: the boy's master had
taken him by the legs and dashed out his brains against a
wall. And Baumfree would tell of the Indian who had met
the mother in the woods, on her way to bury the poor
little corpse; the redskin, on hearing the story, had said
that if he had been there he would have buried his toma-
hawk in the white man's head. Baumfree did not bring that
up now. He begged Mau-Mau to stop crying. It was time
for her to go upstairs and fix dinner, and they disliked it
upstairs if mothers "made a fuss."

That night, after Mau-Mau came down from the kitch-
en, Bell sat with her on the cellar door. When she saw her
mother's folded hands, she folded hers, although she did
not know the meaning of the gesture. She tried to repeat

what Mau-Mau was mumbling: "Our Father which art in
heaven . . ."

Bell shivered a bit, not with cold, but with fear. What if
the sleigh came back for her? "Don't be scared, child,"
said Mau-Mau, stroking the small dark head. "There is a
God who sees and hears everything."

"A God?" asked Bell. "Who's he? Where does he live?"

"In the sky," said Mau-Mau, pointing upward. "When
you're sold away from me, child, and you don't know
where I am and I don't know where you are—up there
will be always the same moon, and the same stars, and
the same God. And if you're whipped, or if you get in
any trouble, you just ask God and he'll help you."

Bell looked up into the starry winter night. They sat
like this for a while; then they went into the cellar, where
a blazing pine knot warded off the chills.

In the end it was not the trader's sleigh that parted Bell
from her parents; it was an auction. The master died, and
the "slaves, horses, and other cattle of Mr. Hardenbergh,
deceased," went under the hammer. From all over the
valley people came in carriages and on horseback, from
the township and from the neighboring Palatines, from
Kingston, the county seat, and from Dutchess across the
river. The paddock at Hurley looked like a fair ground
with ladies and gentlemen, townsmen and farmers milling,
chatting, joking, renewing acquaintances, counting their
cash, and inspecting the livestock for sale.

There was a last-minute change when the heirs, after a
hasty conference, withdrew Bell's mother. Her father was
not even listed; he was rapidly going blind, half-paralyzed
by rheumatism contracted in the cellar, and could not
honestly be put on the market. The fellow who had been
straight as a tree in his prime was worthless and would
only burden his owner. Mau-Mau might still fetch a price,
but hardly what it would cost to keep Baumfree. Why not
do the kind thing, suggested one of the heirs, and give
them both their freedom?

All agreed that it was well worth sacrificing Mau-Mau's
price if she would be responsible for the cripple who could

not be freed alone—not without posting bond with the authorities, lest he become a public charge. Someone wondered how the pair might live, and it was decided to let the two faithful servants stay in the cellar, for the love of God. No one else would want to use it, anyhow. For food, in addition to what Mau-Mau earned by her labor, they could have the windfalls from the apple orchard and whatever fruit they could knock off the trees.

The decision came as joyful news to the couple who had not expected to see each other again.

Meanwhile, the auctioneer had trouble with Bell. He could not get a price for her. The Hardenbergh horses, famous from New York to Albany, had been sold first, for good money; the slaves had also done well, except for this last one. And it was time to get on to the sheep and the cows. . . . "What, no more for this strong girl? She's only about nine, folks! When she's full grown, she'll do a man's work. Come on, now. What am I bid?"

Nothing happened. The auctioneer had an idea. He called for a half dozen sheep to be brought into the paddock. "What am I bid for *both* this strong girl and this fine lot of sheep?"

Bidding became brisk. "A hundred dollars from John Neely—do I hear more? Going—going—gone!"

Bell stood among the sheep, trying not to tremble. "Obey," her mother had warned her once more, before the auction. "Don't lie—don't steal—and don't be scared. God will see that you're treated right. Just obey."

Bell looked up at the sky. Up there, Mau-Mau had said, would always be the same moon and the same stars, and the same. God But it was high noon now, and the sun shone mercilessly.

Her new master came and said something, in English. Bell knew only Low Dutch. Neely understood Dutch but disliked to speak it; when the child asked about her parents, he merely shook his head, motioning to her to come along with the sheep.

It was a long walk, up and down hills and along the banks of a small river, to the place where she would now belong. John Neely was new in the county; he had only

recently come from New York to open a new landing and
store at Twaalfskill, some two miles up Rondout Creek
from Kingston Landing and half as far from Kingston
Village. Advertising a "General Assortment of European
and West India Goods, American and German Steel,
Swede's and common Iron, etc., at uncommon low prices,"
it had seemed a promising venture. Yet it turned out badly.
The only vessels in the creek were Indian canoes and
skiffs taking a bag or two of grain to the mill, and the
Dutch farmers would walk an extra mile rather than shop
where they could not get the news in their guttural tongue.
Neely's stock was going to waste. His cash dwindled. Sheep-
raising was his last hope.

He had never owned a slave and bought Bell only because she went with the sheep; if he had waited for other
sheep, not so encumbered, they might have come in lots
too big for this purse. He already rued the deal by the
time he came home, and his wife's nagging did not make
him feel better. That scrawny slip of a girl, she said, would
never earn her keep.

Mrs. Neely did not know a word of Dutch and was inept
at sign language. She would shout, on the theory that if
the girl heard a command it must be stubbornness that
made her fail to obey. It was irksome enough when your
neighbors refused to speak English; you did not have to
take that from a girl you owned. Breaking a slave, the
Neelys felt, must be like breaking a horse. Bell got
enough food to keep her in good working order, and
enough whippings to keep her on the alert. When winter
came, she worked outdoors with frozen feet—horses had
to be shod, but slaves could go barefooted.

Bell remembered Mau-Mau's advice to seek help from
God. It was not easy, with the sky so high; one must surely
cry very loudly for God to hear. The opportunity to do so
without being overheard by master or mistress did not
present itself often.

One Sunday Bell knelt in the barn, her hands tied before
her. She knew why: there had been no chance to ask God
to spare her the whipping. . . . Blood ran down her back.
She knew why: she could not understand her orders.

Missus had sent her for the frying pan, and she had brought the pothooks. Then Missus had told her to go to the barn. . . . John Neely kept laying on with rods made supple in the embers. He did not tire for a long time.

Bell staggered through the fields, crying to God. The landing was far; the Neelys were far; there was nothing around her but the open fields, the open sky, and God.

"God, you know how I'm treated—you think that's right, God? You must give me another master! You must help me, God!"

Soon after, a fisherman came to Neely's landing and bought her for $105.

His name was Martin Schryver, and aside from fishing, he kept a tavern at the forks in the road from Kingston to Kingston Landing. It was a rough place. The customers were lumberjacks, boatmen, and such, all as crude and profane and honest and good-natured as were the host and his family. Schryver also owned a farm but did not work it, did not even get around to clearing the land. Bell enjoyed the work she was given to do; it seemed more fun than work to carry fish, hoe corn, fetch roots and herbs from the woods for beers, go to "the Strand"—as people called the row of storehouses at the Landing—for a jug of molasses or liquor, or to help at the tavern or just to "browse around." She learned to ride a horse and to row a boat. She watched the sailing ships come and go at the Landing, and once or twice she got a glimpse of the new ship that did not enter the creek but went up and down the open river without any sails, moving like a huge two-wheel cart, the wheels half-covered with water.

At the tavern Bell was cuffed and slapped on occasion, but more in jollity than in anger; while Schryver owned her, she was never whipped hard. She even got permission to visit her parents and was about to start for Stone Ridge when her father came, asking for her.

Baumfree looked like a broken man. The day before, he had been raking leaves for the people who were now renting the house—they were not rich, held no slaves, and were kind to the old couple in the cellar—and Mau-Mau had gone to ask the woman to bake her a loaf of bread she had made. He had poled off a few apples and heard Mau-Mau pick them up for baking. When the horn blew for dinner, he had stowed the rake and cart and groped his way down the cellar steps, his mouth watering for the baked apples. Suddenly the stick he pushed ahead of him had hit something. It was soft and made a gurgling sound. . . .

His voice failed. Bell understood. It was her mother who had lain there without stirring, between two loose planks of the cellar floor. Mau-Mau was dead.

Bell's master allowed her to stay with her father for a few days after the burial. Baumfree, crippled and blind, unable to fend for himself, was inconsolable. "I'm good for nothing any more," he cried when Bell had to leave; "my children are all gone, and I'm left helpless and alone— what's to become of me?"

With a heavy heart Bell returned to Kingston. The next time she was allowed to go to visit the invalid at Hurley she found the cellar empty. The neighbors said that the Hardenberghs had taken pity on their old servant and were taking turns keeping him at their homes—a few weeks at one, a while at another, and so forth. It was on such a journey from one "Ardinburgh" house to another that Bell saw him again. He sat alone on a rock by the roadside, miles from any place, gripping a staff in his gnarled, palsied fingers. His hair was white as wool, his eyesight almost gone, but he recognized Bell's voice.

His pitiful joy wrenched her heart. "You've come, you've come," he said and promptly started again to bewail his loneliness. "Why should I live and not die? They're all taken away from me. Why should I live and not die?"

Bell tried to comfort him. At the tavern someone had said that every slave in the state would go free in ten years. She begged her father to wait just this little while till she could take care of him. "I'll take as good care of you as Mau-Mau would, if she was here," she promised.

"Oh, child, I can't live that long," said the old man.

"Do," Bell insisted. "Do live, and I'll take such good care of you!" She felt sure he could live if he would; she became quite angry when he shook his head and repeated that he could not live ten more years.

She promised to see him again, never doubting that she would be able to get permission, for most of the time the Schryvers seemed not to care where she was or went. But one day, when she had been with them about a year and a half, a stranger came to the tavern, a well-dressed gentleman who would buy round after round. Picking up an armful of mugs, Bell heard her master point out the man as a rich landowner from New Paltz, John J. Dumont, who had apparently just closed a profitable deal in town. Bell took the mugs to the drinkers, and John J. Dumont of New Paltz followed her with his eyes.

Bell was twelve or thirteen, slim and long-limbed, moving with an angular grace. Dumont beckoned to the innkeeper. Would he take seventy pounds for the wench?

Seventy pounds equaled over three hundred dollars, three times her purchase price. "Sold," said Martin Schryver.

Bell stared at her new master. His shoulders were broad, his features like an eagle's, his eyes like the sunny sky. That's how God must look, Bell thought as she walked behind his horse.

John J. Dumont lived on a hillside on the Newburgh road, in the town of New Paltz but several miles east of the old Huguenot village. His neighbors and friends were of English stock, and he himself, although descended from French Huguenots, sent his children to the English school in Kingston. Only one daughter was still at home in 1810, the year he bought Bell.

Dumont owned 750 acres of land, one of the largest properties in New Paltz, and enough slaves to go with it. His house was of stone, with successive extensions and dormers added to an original structure two stories high, thirty-five feet long, and ten feet wide. No manor house such as the Hardenberghs owned at Hurley, this ancient narrow core was a wilderness homestead built for defense against firearms-carrying Indians as much as for shelter. The windows were few in number and small, less than four feet high and barely two feet wide. From the outside they looked like embrasures in the fortresslike masonry. The barn was huge, larger than the house, and square, and the hilltop behind it overlooked the land for miles around. The river was not far, and in winter, when the trees stood bare, one could see all the way across the broad valley.

This was the place where John Dumont made his home, and where Bell spent the remainder of her time in bondage.

Mrs. Dumont disliked the new slave girl from the start. Born and raised in a non-slaveholding family, she did not feel at ease with Negroes, thinking far more of her two white hired girls. The hired girls agreed, and one named Kate in particular made a point of putting Bell in her place. "Trying to grind me down," Bell called it. Only the master seemed pleased with his acquisition. Dumont had always held slaves; he knew them, liked them, showed them at least as much consideration as his other animals, and thus was seldom disappointed.

The first storm in the house broke over the breakfast potatoes, which Bell had to boil before doing the milking. One day they looked dirty. The next day Bell washed them extra carefully. In vain—when she returned from the barn, the family sat round the breakfast table and the mistress was holding a potato under her husband's nose. "There's a fine specimen of Bell's work," she said. "It's how all her work is done."

Dumont scowled and said Bell was doing all right otherwise; she would surely be more careful in the future.

Bell worked her fingers to the bone, for a good reason. Word had come of her father: the Hardenberghs, tired of shifting him around their homes, had given the old man a cabin in the Catskill forest and freed two other old slaves, Caesar and Betty, to look after him. Unfortunately, Caesar had long been ailing with fever sores, and Betty with jaundice. Neither had been fit to survive in the woods, much less care for Baumfree. They had died in short order, leaving him blind and immobile in his lonely mountain shack.

The bearer of the news, an aged freedwoman who had lately passed the cabin, told how Baumfree was suffering from filth and vermin, how he had pleaded with her to stay a while and wash and tend him so he might feel half-way decent once more—and how, fearful of being stricken herself and dying, unaided, out in the wilderness, she had been reluctantly obliged to leave him to his fate.

Bell worked and worked, for the master had said she might visit her father next Sunday. On Saturday she scrubbed each potato spotlessly clean before putting them on to boil; she milked as fast as she could and ran back, to peer into the kettle. The potatoes were dirtier than ever. Near the fire the cat sat, purring.

The cat must have been at them, Bell thought, and in her despair she lashed out at the animal just as the master came in. Wordlessly John Dumont took his slave girl out for a whipping. The blows were lighter than Neely's had been, but they hurt more, coming from him who seemed justice itself, like God. "You'll not visit your father," Dumont said and left her crumpled on the floor.

The day's chore was tending the sheep in the upper pasture. Bell liked sheep ever since she had been sold with them; somehow she felt that she and they belonged together. The sheep were grazing along a stream when she saw the bellwether cross a natural bridge to an islet shielded by willows. The flock followed, and Bell followed the flock. A waterfall cascaded noisily over rocks; the willows formed an impenetrable curtain. It was a place to be unheard and unseen, a place to cry to God.

"God," she shouted, "if you was in trouble and I could help you, you know I would! I'll be good if you help me, God!"

The waterfall chattered on, and the sheep kept grazing under the willows until the sun set. On the way home, Bell met the master's daughter, Gertrude. "I've been looking for you," said the blonde girl who was Bell's age but smaller, with skin like apple blossoms. "Wake me up early tomorrow, and I'll tend to your potatoes while you milk. Let's see if we can't have them nice."

They herded the sheep home together, and in the morn-

ing little Gerty came into the kitchen while Bell was still
wondering whether she dared awaken her. The white child
looked on as the dark one drew water, washed each potato, drew more water, washed the kettle, drew water
again to fill the kettle, dropped the potatoes in, and put
them on to boil. "I'll watch your fire," Gerty told Bell and
sat down in the chimney corner.

In the hall, Kate was sweeping. As Bell went past, the
hired girl kicked her broom so the handle hit Bell on the
shins. Bell went to the barn.

She had just finished milking when she heard Gerty
screeching in the house, "Poppy! Oh, Poppy!" Bell picked
up the bucket of milk and ran back to the kitchen, arriving
just as Gerty dragged her father through the other door.
The mistress followed on their heels. Kate was sweeping in
the far corner.

Bell glanced at the potatoes. They were black. She felt
wretched as Gerty drew the master to the fireplace.

"Poppy," cried the child, "Kate's been putting ashes in
the potatoes! I saw her do it. Look at those here, on the
outside! Now you see why they were soiled every day,
though Bell washed them clean."

The mistress looked blank and said nothing as Kate disappeared. But the master gave Bell a look that wiped out
all memories of the whipping. "I always knew you were a
good girl," Dumont said. "You may go to see your father."

There was a small crowd around the mountain shack
when Bell got there, and four strong men were about to
carry Baumfree down into the valley, in a fine, painted
coffin. It was a gift from John Hardenbergh, a grandson of
the Old Master and a nephew of Master Charles; at the
news that Baumfree had been found dead in his cabin,
starved or frozen or both, John had vowed to give the
faithful slave a good funeral. As good as his word, he had
sent a pot of black paint for the coffin and a jug of whisky
for the mourners.

Bell stood by the open grave. An old man who knew
how to pray mumbled, "Our Father which art in heaven,"
while the coffin was lowered. "And forgive us our debts,

as we forgive our debtors," Bell repeated after him, as once after Mau-Mau. Behind her, John Hardenbergh's whisky made the round.

"Forgive?" someone whispered into Bell's ear. "They let us croak, and then we get a coffin. . . ."

She turned and looked into the boyish face of Bob, one of the slaves from the Catlin place near Dumont's. She knew him only by sight; he was older than she, taller and handsomer than he seemed at a distance. The other mourners were still passing the jug; it seemed to cheer them up. Bob took Bell home. It was dark by the time they got to Dumont's gate and said good-by.

Bob kept coming over secretly, at night. To be safe from discovery, they would go to the islet by the waterfall. Bob knew much. He knew about the law that Bell had heard discussed at Schryver's tavern, the law for the abolition of slavery in the state of New York—abolition was a big work, but Bob pronounced it fluently. It was still some years off under the law, and even then it would apply only to old people over forty. The rest would go free ten years later.

Free, Bell thought—what would it mean to be free when you were young? To Bob it meant you would have to take no more whippings. If a freeman was struck, he could strike back. It meant you could go anywhere without permission, with no one coming after you to bring you back.

Returning a blow had never entered Bell's mind. When she was whipped, she thought it was because she had been bad, or beause she had not called to God in time. But if she had been free now, she could have cared for her father.

"If I was free, I could marry you," said Bob, whose master had forbidden him even to see Bell. Mr. Catlin was an Englishman or Scotsman who could not see why his goods should serve to augment John Dumont's. There were wenches enough on his own place, Catlin thought, for the rascal Bob to father little blacks on.

Bob and Bell lay in the grass under the willows. The

cascade roared in the night, and Bob murmured into Bell's ear, "What's a slave marriage, anyhow? . . ."

Dumont's slave quarters were in the hayloft over the barn, and when Bell came down with a fever one day, he went up to look after her. "Have you seen Bob today?" he asked.

She had not.

"If you see him," Dumont said, "tell him to watch out. The Catlins are after him."

Bell was too shocked to answer. After the master left, she huddled by the barn window that overlooked the yard. Suddenly she saw Bob in the gate, and at the same instant she saw the Catlins, father and son, rush up cursing.

"Knock down the damned black rascal," the elder yelled at his son, swinginging his cane.

Bell clasped the crossbars of the window as she saw Bob crumple. They beat him with the heavy ends of their canes, knocking aside his raised arms. Blows rained on his head and face. Blood was all over him. Bell heard a cry, "Jesus!" and a sound as from a dying animal.

Who is Jesus? it flashed through her mind. Could he help? Bob looked like a slaughtered beast, but they went right on hitting him.

"I'll have no niggers killed here!"

It was her master's voice. Bell stared at the yard: Dumont had come to the gate and stood by as the Catlins got out the rope they had brought to secure their property. When they had Bob trussed up, Dumont intervened again. "No brute is going to be tied like that on my premises," he said and made them loosen the cord.

Bob was kicked to his feet and led off staggering, blood-spattered, his head dangling on his chest. Dumont followed them down the road.

Bell sank to the floor. "God——" No answer. "Don't forsake us, God!" She felt lost, like Bob. What was the name Bob had cried when they knocked him down? "Jesus." Who was that? A mighty one such as the white folks talked about?

Someone was speaking to her. "He's alive. I went with him," her master said, lifting her up. . . .

Bell did not see Bob again. She had to be good, to keep her promise to God, to do everything for the master who saw all and knew all, who was as just as God. The hours formerly spent with Bob were given to her master's service. She started working not only all day but all night, snatching brief naps in a chair; sometimes, afraid of sleeping too long in the chair, she would rest standing against the wall. Her hands and feet kept working when her eyes fell shut.

John Dumont began to point her out to his friends. "That wench is better to me than a man," he boasted. "She'll do a good family's washing in the night, and in the morning she'll be ready to go into the field and do as much raking and binding as my best hands."

The other slaves called her "the white folks' nigger." One named Thomas knew that Bob had married a slave girl on his master's place; the Catlins had broken him good, Tom said, leering at Bell. She did not answer. Tom had been married twice; after his second wife was sold he had run off to look for her. He had not found her, but he had gone as far as New York and remained there a year or two before being picked up. The master himself had gone all the way after him, Tom said with a touch of pride. Bell did not answer.

All that, she thought, must have happened long ago, when Tom was young. With his gray hair and dull eyes he looked almost as old as her father had; she was astonished to hear him grumble about being too young to be set free with the first batch, those forty or over. Tom thought he must be old enough—he certainly felt old enough. But the master said it was written differently in his papers. "If I could read," Tom muttered, "I'd know if he's lyin'."

Bell could tell without reading that the master would not lie. And what would Tom do if he was freed? Go to New York again?

For a moment, the dull eyes brightened. "New York," Tom said longingly. Then he shook his head; he was through running away.

Bell asked the master whether Thomas really was too

young to be freed with the first batch. Dumont nodded. "But if he hadn't put me to so much trouble looking for him, I'd let him go anyway. I want servants who want to work for me," he said. Bell's heart beat higher.

The first spring thaw found her with the sheep in the upper pasture, on the islet she had been shunning since her last night with Bob. There was ice in the stream and snow under the willows, but her bare feet did not feel it. "God—who's Jesus?"

No answer. Kneeling in the snow, Bell said Mau-Mau's prayer. "Thy kingdom come . . ."

Her head was stroked as by a gentle breeze. All the tears she had been choking down in her life seemed to well up at once and to flow freely down her cheeks. "I love, God—I love," Bell sobbed. "I can love even the white folks. . . ."

Happiness filled her on the way home with the flock. John Dumont watched her approaching the sheepfold, striding with her head held high, her long legs moving swiftly, her lithe body molding the shapeless tunic. Bell was six feet tall, a dark, young giantess with a curious dignity and strange, deep-set eyes.

"She might fetch a good price now," Mrs. Dumont suggested.

"She's not for sale," Dumont replied.

So the mistress gave Bell a new duty. Since Gertrude's recent marriage John Dumont had moved into her room, and his wife did not sleep well, alone in the big four-poster. She had heard about the Southern custom of having trusted slaves sleep under one's bed, in case some such service as bringing a blanket or a glass of water was required during the night. Bell would do for the purpose.

Bell did not mind. The rug she slept on now was softer than the straw in the barn, and being roused by her mistress' whims was less trouble than pushing Tom away all night. The new arrangement worked well until Mrs. Dumont went to see Gerty one day and sent a message that she would stay overnight. Bell, looking forward to a night's peace, was fast asleep when the door opened.

It was the master. Bell crawled out from under the four-poster, to await his bidding.

"Get into bed," Dumont said.

She stared at him. "Missus' bed? That's not for me. . . ."

There is a break at this point in the *Narrative of Sojourner Truth*. It was not her memory that had failed; she could recall conversations of long ago in graphic detail, and whatever confusions there are concern chronology, not facts. But here her amanuensis put down only a cryptic hint at "events which we must pass over in silence, some from motives of delicacy, and others because the relation of them might inflict undeserved pain on some now living."

The *Narrative* appeared in 1850; anyone living then has long since died. But the dead are silent. The uncorroborated hint remains our only explanation for John Dumont's rather unusual relationship with Bell and her family, both in slavery and then in freedom.

Bell was married to Thomas. It was the master's decision; he said the wench should start bearing. The slaves had but to obey. They were pronounced man and wife by a colored man named King, who frequently performed this office—for, of course, no minister of God would bless a union that the master could dissolve at will. "What's a slave marriage anyhow?" Bell muttered in the barn.

Before the year was out, she gave birth to a girl whom the master named Diana. If he came home and found the infant crying, since Bell could not always attend to its wants and to the commands of her mistress at the same time, Dumont would rebuke his wife. "I can't bear this crying," he said bluntly. "I will not hear any child cry so. Take care of this child, Bell, if no more work is done for a week." And he would stay to see that his orders were not countermanded.

It was about this time that the old people went free. On July 4, 1817, New York abolished the condition of involuntary servitude for all persons then forty years old or over. Nobody doubted the ages of the men and women who came shuffling off mansions and farms all over the state; the youngest of the livestock that became humankind on that magical Fourth of July looked a good sixty. And the remainder, destined to stay property for another decade, began to have unaccustomed thoughts: how to live after ten years, and what to do about one's family after ten years, and how long ten years might be. Some even wondered why they should wait ten years.

Bob was dead; he had not long survived the beating that Bell had seen. Thomas was reconciled to waiting, content to serve out his time with Bell and forget his dreams of New York. He felt he was getting too old for New York, especially when the master promised him a bit of land—in ten years, Dumont said, Tom could settle there with Bell and go on working on the place as a hired hand, with no need to worry about the responsibilities of freedom.

In the ten years Bell bore four more children, three of whom lived. A boy was named Peter, for one of the brothers Bell had heard so much of but had never seen; a second girl was called Elizabeth, which had been Mau-Mau's name. The youngest, also a girl, was named Sophia, for a sister rumored to have gone free somewhere near Newburgh.

When she went to work in the fields now, Bell would put her infant in a basket, tying a rope to each handle and hanging the basket from a branch of the tree. Thus the baby was safe from rattlers and other beasts, and at the same time it could be tended and rocked to sleep by Diana or some other child too young for labor. Bell's concern for her children pleased the master, who took an almost personal pride in the increase of his black flock and stoutly resisted his wife's advice to sell the little niggers while the law would still let him.

Bell taught her children the Lord's Prayer and trained them to rigid honesty, letting them go hungry rather than secretly take the bread she would not ask for. She never seemed to think of freedom, never seemed to hear the taunts of other slaves. She was known as the most faithful servant in New Paltz. Her children stayed.

There was a new restlessness among the others as the

ten years rolled by. Escapes multiplied. Authority itself was questioned. Unheard-of things happened: promises made to a slave—which used to be like slave marriages, revocable at the master's will—were suddenly taken at face value. New Paltz was stirred by the case of one Ned, whose wife had been sold twenty miles away: "I'll see if you can go visit her after the harvest," his master had said at the time. When the harvest was in, the master saw that Ned could not go, and he so informed the slave when he found him cleaning his shoes for the trip. Ned went right on cleaning his shoes.

"You mean to go?" asked his master.

"Yes," Ned said simply, and this impudence so outraged the master that he broke a sled stick over Ned's skull, killing him on the spot. There was a good deal of head-shaking in town and wondering what some nigger would think of next.

When Bell's son was five and she was again with child, Mrs. Dumont persuaded her husband to sell the little boy to their friend Dr. Gedney. The doctor had seen Peter around the house and been much taken with him; he was planning a trip to England and thought it charming to travel with that engaging black scamp in his entourage. Dumont, unable to say no but feeling quite embarrassed before Bell, promised her that if she did her work well, he would set her free a year ahead of time, on the next Fourth of July.

Bell worked faithfully, but Sophia's birth and an injury to her hand slowed her down. When the Fourth came and she asked Dumont for her "free papers," he refused to sign them because of her indisposition. He had sustained actual losses on account of it, he told Bell.

"I've worked all the time," she protested. "I know I wasn't as good as before, but I've done a lot that I wasn't up to."

"Don't argue," he said. "I need you another year."

Bell went back to the barn. She decided to stay until Dumont's wool was spun—there was a good hundred pounds of it, which ought to redeem his losses—but the rest of the year was hers. It had been promised her; it was

unjust to deny it to her. She kept her decision to herself,
and having spun the wool, she stayed on till the heavy
fall's work was done; then she thought of leaving. How to
go about it, though? "God," she said, "I'm afraid to go in
the night, and in daylight everybody'll see me. What can I
do?"

"Go at dawn," came the answer.

"Thank you, God," she cried. "That's a good idea."

It was at the break of day, one of the beautiful late
autumn days of the Hudson Valley, that she left her master's house. In one arm she carried Sophia, in the other
hand a cotton kerchief with food and all the clothes she
was not wearing. The road lay in darkness. No light
showed behind the shuttered windows, no life stirred in
the yards. Bell took a trail to the woods that emerged
from the night, their glorious colors shrouded in the gray
of dawn.

The trail led uphill. The forest, shadowy and menac-
ing, closed in right and left, but the birds were beginning
to twitter, lifting all fear from Bell's heart. She walked
swiftly, without looking back. On top of a high hill she
paused. Across the valley the sun rose in blinding splen-
dor. It had never been so light.

She looked back now; there were no pursuers. She sat
down to feed the baby, wondering where to turn. It was a
question to which she had given no thought, and already
the day was almost too bright for comfort. "Well, God,"
she said, "you've started me out; now please show me
where to go."

Virgin forest spread all round the hilltop. But suddenly
Bell saw a house; there she would find help. Then, as suddenly as it had appeared, the house vanished again.

Bell took up her child and her bundle and walked down-
hill after the sunbeams. She did not expect to have a long
walk, for she felt it would be wrong to go far—if Dumont wished to go after her, he should be able to find her
without the trouble it had cost him to find Tom. She
walked until a village came in sight, and when she took a
good look at the first house, it was the one she had seen

on the hilltop. "That's the place for me," Bell said and
knocked.

An old woman asked her to enter and said that her
children, Mr. and Mrs. Van Wagener, were absent but
would return shortly. When they arrived, Bell truthfully
related her story and was told to feel safe and at home.
She should eat and rest now; tomorrow one would see
about employment for her. Mrs. Van Wagener led the way
to a clean bedchamber with a huge, white, beautiful bed
and bade the guest good night.

Bell stared at the bed. It could not possibly be meant for
her! As soon as she was alone she crawled underneath the
bed and slept there with her baby until sunrise.

In the morning, as she had expected, Dumont came
looking for her. "Well, Bell," he said, reining in his horse
before the tall, dark figure on the Van Wageners' front
porch, "so you've run away from me."

She stoutly denied it. "I did not run away. I walked
away by daylight, and all because you promised me a year
of my time."

"You must come back with me," he said.

"No, I won't."

"Well," he said, dismounting, "I'll take the child then."

"No!" she cried.

Mr. Van Wagener came out of the house, weighing a
purse in his hand. "Friend," he told Dumont, "I have never
been in the practice of buying and selling slaves—I do not
believe in slavery—but rather than have this woman taken
back by force, I'll buy her services for the remainder of
the year. I'll pay twenty dollars, and five more for the
child."

Dumont looked at Bell and the child. Then he nodded,
accepted the money, remounted, and rode away.

Her heart overflowing, Bell turned to her benefactor.
"Master—"

He shook his head. "I am Isaac Van Wagener. Your
Master is mine."

The Law

IN TIME ONLY, step by step, Bell came to grasp the change in her situation. She was now called by her full name, Isabella, and by the last name of Van Wagener, acquired from her last master in the eyes of the law. In the Hudson Valley, emancipation customarily turned "Miller's Jack" and "Brown's Chloe" into Jack Mill and Chloe Brown.

Isaac Van Wagener, of Wagondale, gave Bell her name and her freedom at the same time. "Before God," he explained to her, "all of us are equal." God had always told Bell what to do, had always helped her in need, yet she had no more been a white person's equal than God's. She could scarcely believe it when Van Wagener described God as "no respecter of persons or colors." But when he read to her, from a well-thumbed black book, and came to the words, "I am the Way, the Truth, and the Life," she clapped her hands in wonder.

"Is that in there? I knew that! God told me."

The book, she learned, came from God. Next, she learned that there was a house of God; she had never been to church until the Van Wageners took her to theirs. It was full of whites, so she dared not enter but remained outside, unable to see but happy to hear the soaring choir of voices. Listening, she learned hymn upon hymn and forgot none as long as she lived.

One day she heard one that made her think of her own walk out of bondage.

> "It was early in the morning,
> It was early in the morning
> Just at the break of day,
> When He rose—when He rose—when He rose
> And went to heaven on a cloud."

Bell felt as if the sun were rising again before her eyes, on the hilltop.

She understood that she had to look forward, not to think back. She must forget the master who had sold her services for the rest of the time she would have been his under the law; it was Mr. Van Wagener who had paid money for her, only to tell her that she was now free. Freely, by her services, she must give him back his money's worth.

He would not have her call him "Master." What then should she say? she asked. "Call me Isaac Van Wagener," he replied, "and my wife is Maria Van Wagener."

For the first time, Isabella felt like a person rather than an appendage to somebody's household. She had chores given to her and was on her own otherwise. Nor was she part of a family. She had her infant to care for, of course, but nothing tied her to Tom, her so-called husband. It was the master who had joined them, not God, nor her heart. The master had made the match, with the comment that it was time for her to start bearing, and she had obediently lived with Tom through her child-bearing years. It had served the master's purpose, but a free woman need have no more to do with the creature she had been ostensibly bred with.

Now and then she might feel homesick for her older children. She did not worry about Diana and Elizabeth, who would be serving Dumont until they were twenty-five, but Peter's case was different. No one she could ask knew his whereabouts. Dr. Gedney had planned to take him to England—where was that? Overseas, said Isaac Van Wagener. Isabella could imagine neither the seas nor what lay beyond them. She knew only that it was far, too far away.

Peacefully the weeks passed in the small village of Wagondale, from Sunday to Sunday. After a while Isabella ventured inside the old stone church, pressing into a dark corner to stay unnoticed, submerged in the crowd like the dark, bell-like sound of her voice that softly joined the choir. One Sunday she saw a new face in the congregation. It was a lady she knew, a Miss Gear from New York, who had come to visit the Dumonts on occasion.

Isabella held her breath. Might she go and beg for news from home? For so long it had been punishable "insolence" to speak unasked to any white man or woman.

After the service Miss Gear stopped to talk to the Van Wageners while Isabella stood waiting by the roadside. When they beckoned, she ran to them and stood with her head lowered humbly, slave-fashion. Miss Gear had news from New Paltz, said Isaac Van Wagener.

"Well, Bell . . ." The lady seemed to find it hard to begin. Dr. Gedney, it seemed, had not taken Peter to England. About to embark from New York, he had found the boy too small for his service and sent him back to his brother Solomon in New Paltz.

In New Paltz! Bell's heart leaped. But in Miss Gear's face were only regret and compassion. Solomon Gedney, she said, had not kept Peter, either. He had sold him to his brother-in-law, an Alabaman named Fowler—Bell had surely seen him in New Paltz last year, courting Eliza Gedney. Now the boy was down South, on the Fowler plantation.

Bell's lips turned gray. She remembered the planter; he looked cruel. She remembered Mau-Mau, weeping for her children who had been sold down South. She could not utter a sound while Mr. Van Wagener said the sale was illegal and Miss Gear confirmed that John Dumont thought so too—he claimed to have sold the boy with the express understanding that he would soon be brought back to New York and emancipated in due time. Dumont should turn to the law, Van Wagener insisted. Miss Gear shrugged; Dumont did not know where to turn. The Gedneys were his friends. They were people of weight in New Paltz.

The law, Van Wagener repeated, forbade selling slaves out of the state. The law was bigger than people.

Isabella straightened up. "The law is?"

"It is," said Van Wagener.

"I'll go get my child," said Isabella, heading for the road.

They looked at her as if she were a madwoman, but she would not even take the time to go once more to the Van Wageners' house. She made them promise to care for little Sophia; then she set out alone, barefooted, still in the old cotton dress of a slave and with the old colored kerchief on her head, to retrace her steps to freedom. It was near dusk when she turned into the gate she had left at dawn, months ago. The slave quarters were empty. Her girls, said the hired maids in the yard, were still in the fields, and the master had gone to town.

"I must see him," she cried.

The noise brought the mistress to the door. "Bell! What are you doing here?"

Isabella approached her, lamenting the loss of her son. Mrs. Dumont saw the maids hang about curiously and wrinkled her nose. "Ugh—a fine fuss to make about a little nigger! Haven't you more of them left than you can see to take care of? A pity 'tis the niggers aren't all in Guinea! Making such a hullabaloo about the neighborhood, and all for a paltry nigger!"

Isabella heard her out and said, "I'll have my child again."

Mrs. Dumont sneered. "Have your child again? How? Have you any money?"

"God has money," Isabella said and turned to go. From the road she could still hear the mistress screaming after her to get out.

She walked another mile to call on Mrs. Gedney, whose son had sold hers to his Southern brother-in-law. Her fears made the old lady smile. "Dear me, what a disturbance to make about your child! Is your child better than my child? My child is gone down there—and yours is gone to live with her, to have enough of everything and to be treated like a gentleman."

"Yes," Bell said, "your child is gone there, but she's married, and my boy is gone as a slave. Oh, I must have my child!"

Mrs. Gedney had to laugh aloud. It did not sound human to Bell; this was devilish laughter, she thought and withdrew, frightened. "God," she said outside, alone under the first stars, "show them that you're my helper!"

It was cold under the stars. Bell saw a man walking

toward her; it was Dumont. "What did you come back for?" he asked as they stood facing each other.

"My boy," she replied. "You must ask the law to get him."

John Dumont shrugged. "I'm sorry, Bell. I can't help you."

She blocked his way. "God will help me."

He took her hand and pointed at two specks of light on a hill, halfway to the next village. "The people up there are Quakers. They live by the gospel, and they're already concerned about your boy. They may help you. But don't let on that I told you—you'd be doing me no kindness."

And before she could thank him, he vanished like a shadow under the trees on the way to his home, where Mrs. Dumont was waiting.

Bell thanked God and headed for the specks of light in the gloom.

The Quakers had never seen her but did not ask who she was or whence she came. They lodged her for the night in a room with another nice, high, clean, white bed even finer than the Van Wageners', and again she sat down to regard it, in wonder that such a bed should be for one like herself. When she decided finally to get in, it was for fear that leaving it untouched might offend her hosts' feelings. In the morning she told them her story, omitting only the name of John Dumont. "A man" had told her to come here, she said as if the man had been a stranger.

Names did not matter to the Quakers. Finding a neighbor about to drive to Kingston, they saw to it that she was given a ride in his chaise and set down in the village, with directions to go to the county courthouse and lay her complaint before the grand jury.

Everyone around the building was white. A man on the steps impressed Isabella as very grand, so she walked up to him and began complaining. Once he grasped her purpose, he advised her that the grand jury did not sit in the street; she would have to go inside and upstairs.

With difficulty she made her way through the courthouse crowd. At the top of the stairs she turned again to the grandest-looking man in sight: "Sir, be you a grand jury?"

"What's it to you?" he chuckled.

She resumed her complaint, only to hear that this was not the place for it, either. "Go in there," said the grand one, pointing out a door at the end of a hallway.

Behind the door, some twenty or more men sat around a long table. "What do you want?" they demanded, and for the fourth time that day she described the wrong that had been done. Some of the white men grinned; others scowled. One of them rose, cutting her off. "Follow me," he said and led the way to a room in which some clerks with goose quills in their hands sat bent over sheets of paper.

The quills stopped dancing as Isabella came in. The man who had brought her seated himself at a desk. "Can you swear," he asked, "that the child you speak of is your son?"

"Yes," she cried, "I swear it's my son—"

"You must swear by this book," the man said.

He gave her a book like the one Van Wagener used to read from, and she touched it with her lips. "I swear—I swear—"

The clerks guffawed. One of them turned to the man who had put the book into Isabella's hands: "Squire Chipp, what can be the use of swearing her?"

"It will answer the law," Squire Chipp said and made her place her hand on the Bible and repeat the legal words after him. Then he gave her a piece of paper: "This is a writ. Take it to the constable at New Paltz and have him serve it on Solomon Gedney."

Clutching the precious paper, Isabella ran downstairs and started walking—or trotting, rather; it was some eight miles to New Paltz, and she ran all the way. The constable promised to serve the paper and sent Isabella back to Kingston, where Mr. Gedney would have to return the writ in court. "And my child?" she asked.

The child also must be produced in court, explained the constable.

She decided to remain in Kingston, where the court was. Squire Chipp arranged it with a friend who had his office just around the courthouse corner and could always

use another domestic to oblige the squire, who sat with
him on the board of village trustees. A. Bruyn Hasbrouck
was a former congressman and future president of Rutgers
College; his family owned half of Kingston. Isabella was
sent to his mansion at Fair Street and Maiden Lane, a
more elegant home than she had ever seen, and assured of
a place on his household staff for the duration of her case
—a case not without legal significance, which Mr. Hasbrouck and his law partner, Judge Ruggles, would be following with interest.

Mr. Hasbrouck praised Isabella's choice of an attorney,
and yet, on her next trip to court Squire Chipp had bad
news for his client. The constable had served the writ on
the wrong Gedney, enabling the culprit to escape by boat
across the river before the mistake was discovered. "And
my boy?" she asked.

The lawyer told her to be patient. If Solomon Gedney
was found anywhere in the state and could not produce the
boy, it might cost him fourteen years in prison and a
thousand dollars in cash. The mills of the law ground
slowly but exceeding small, Mr. Chipp said.

Isabella had no conceptoin of a thousand dollars and
did not care whether Mr. Gedney was jailed. She wanted
her son. At the Hasbrouck house she waited, worked, and
prayed while her story spread like wildfire. The whole
town was talking of "Dumont's runaway nigger." What
was the world coming to, if one of her stripe could force
gentlemen into hiding? Solomon Gedney's own family
seemed not to know where he had gone. "And all for a
paltry nigger," many said, in the words of Dumont's wife.

It was spring again in the valley and apple blossoms
covered the hillsides like rosy snow when word arrived of
Gedney's return to New Paltz. Mr. Hasbrouck heard at
the courthouse that he had traveled all the way to Alabama for the little black there was so much to-do about.
Squire Chipp rubbed his hands gleefully; patience had its
rewards, he told Isabella. His writ had already made the
offender put up six hundred dollars bond for his appearance in court with the boy he had brought back from the
Fowler plantation; he still claimed him as his property, but

the lawyer felt sure that the court would award him to the mother. The next session was only a few months away.

"What? Wait months?" she cried. "Why, long before that he can go clear off and take my child along, nobody knows where! I must have him while he's to be had!"

"Well, if he puts the boy out of the way, he forfeits the six hundred dollars. Half of it will be yours," Chipp said in a tone implying that this should be plenty.

Isabella did not want money. She wanted her son. Now.

"You should appreciate what we've done for you," the lawyer rebuked her. "It has been a great deal." The only reasonable course, he said, was to wait patiently for the court session. And now Isabella must leave his office, for he was a busy man.

She left, not patiently, and went to pour out her heart to Mr. Hasbrouck. He cut her short; if she refused Squire Chipp's advice, he had nothing better to offer.

Aimlessly Isabella walked the streets around the courthouse. She realized that those who had helped her thus far were wearied of her. She greatly feared that God was wearied also. "God," she prayed, "who will lend me a helping hand?"

"Hallo, there," said a voice nearby. She looked up hopefully, but the man was a perfect stranger. "How are you doing with your boy? Will they give him to you?" he inquired.

Isabella told him the sad story. "They're all tired of me, and I've none to help."

"I'll tell you what you'd better do," said the stranger. "You see that house yonder? Lawyer Romeyn lives there. Go to him and lay your case before him. Stick to him; don't give him peace till he takes it. I'm sure if you press him he'll do it for you."

The house was across the street from Ruggles and Hasbrouck. An old man opened and would have closed the door again if she had not begun to talk at once, crying out against the injustice of it all and begging him to make lawyer Romenyn save her child.

The old man shook his head at the barefooted figure in the slave dress. "I'm Romeyn," he said finally. "If you give me five dollars, I'll get your son for you in twenty-four hours."

She was crestfallen. Five dollars? She had never had a dollar in her life.

A smile crossed the withered face. "If you go to those Quakers in Poppletown who brought you to court, I've no doubt they'll help you to five dollars. And you will have your son in twenty-four hours from the time you bring me that sum."

For Herman M. Romeyn was just a country lawyer with a single standard. He did for the poor what he did for the rich, and he did nothing for free.

It was ten miles to Poppletown, but Isabella got there by sundown. The Quakers gave her money—more, they pointed out, than the lawyer wanted—and invited her to spend the night, but she merely thanked them and trotted back, the money clutched in her hand. Arriving at Romeyn's house in the dead of night, she lay down on the stoop and slept until the sun had risen and a surprised servant found her and summoned the lawyer.

Isabella unclenched her fist and gave Romeyn what was in it. He asked why she had slept on his stoop, and when he heard that she had been staying at Mr. Hasbrouck's but was afraid she was no longer welcome there, he sent her to a friend of his, John Rutzer, who also had a large establishment.

Mr. Rutzer heard her story and wanted to know what she had done with the extra money from the Quakers. "Why, I got that for lawyer Romeyn," she answered. "I gave it to him."

"You're a fool," said Rutzer, with a glance at her feet. "You should have kept all over five dollars and bought yourself shoes."

"Oh," she said, "I don't want money or clothes now. I just want my son, and if five dollars will get him, more will surely get him."

Having no idea of the length of twenty-four hours, she kept running to Romeyn's all day to ask for her son. "Why, she's here again!" snorted the servant. At last, Romeyn made it clear that twenty-four hours would last till the following morning; then she was to see her son.

In the morning she knocked when Romeyn was still in bed. He came out in his nightshirt, growling that it would be morning till noontime and that she need not come again—he would let her know. "Don't worry," he said, relenting. "I've sent someone after the boy who won't fail to have him in court, dead or alive."

Dead or alive . . . The words rang in her ears all the way to Mr. Rutzer's. She cooked the family's dinner but could not swallow a bite. After dinner the bell rang. She ran to open. Romeyn stood outside, alone.

"Your son has come," he said.

She lifted up her eyes. Told that she had to go and identify him, she tied her kerchief round her head and followed the lawyer to the courthouse and to the room where she had sworn her first oath. The same clerks were there, not laughing this time. Romeyn opened another door, and Isabella saw Solomon Gedney and, hiding behind him, her child.

"Pete—" Her voice caught in her throat, for at the sight of her the boy screeched in fear. "Pete, don't you know your mammy?"

Peter clasped Mr. Gedney's coattails, screaming that she was not his mother, that his mother did not live in a place like this—and he fell on his knees and begged to stay with his dear master who had been so good and brought him back from the dreadful South.

"Come here, boy," said a calm voice.

A black-robed gentleman rose from behind a table. Through her tears Isabella saw Peter cling to his master until Mr. Gedney gently pushed him toward the judge. The judge inspected him. "How did you get that scar on your forehead?"

Peter glanced at Mr. Gedney. "Fowler's horse hove me," he said then.

"Forget your master and attend to me," the judge said sternly. "How about the scar on your cheek?"

He had got that running against the carriage, the boy replied with another glance to the rear.

The judge turned to Mr. Romeyn. "Is your client ready to identify the child as hers?"

Isabella was brought forward to look at the scarred, tear-stained little face, at the terrified eyes. "He's my child," she said and repeated the words of the oath.

Romeyn opened his argument, claiming the boy for her on the ground that he had been illegally sold out of the state, and he spoke of the penalties annexed to said crime, and of the money the defendant would have to pay the mother if she chose to prosecute. Isabella sat in a corner, scarcely daring to breathe. She heard Mr. Frederick Waring, of New Paltz, argue for the defense; this formidable gentleman, who was Solomon Gedney's uncle and a neighbor of the Dumonts, stressed the black boy's obvious fear of his alleged mother—it would be sheer cruelty to hand the child to a woman whose only aim was to make mischief and to slander honorable men. "She's the worst of devils," Mr. Waring said scornfully, and Isabella trembled at the thought of the powerful enemies she had made.

The pleadings ended. The judge sat looking at Peter, who was on his knees again: "Please don't take me away from my master—my good master—please don't—"

God, Isabella thought wildly, how did they beat those lies into him? Help me, God!

The judge was speaking quickly, monotonously, in language she was hard put to understand: ". . . the sentence of this court that the boy be delivered into the hands of the mother, having no other master, no other controller, no other conductor but his mother. . . ."

What did that mean? Did it mean he was hers? Had God helped? Isabella saw Mr. Waring shrug and turn to go. She saw Mr. Gedney angrily drop Peter's hand. But the boy slid after him on his knees, crying pitifully, "No—she isn't my mother! Please—please—"

Lawyer Romeyn held him back, and he knelt forlornly on the floor, sobbing into his arms. The Gedneys had left, so had the judge. The clerks stood around the boy, trying to calm him. "Take him home," Romeyn told his client.

When she touched him, Peter broke loose and ran into a corner. One of the clerks drew some sweets from a pocket and offered them to the child. Peter took one and munched it without looking up. Isabella went to him. "Don't you remember me, Pete?"

He cringed and whimpered, "When will they take me back South?"

"Is that what they told you?" She grabbed his arms. "Listen, child, you'll never go back there—never! Never!"

The child regarded her with disdain. "My master says Fowler can take me away from you any time. He says you can't protect me. But he would have."

Isabella seized the thin shoulders and shook them hard. "Nobody's going to take you away, you hear? It's the law brought you back, and the law protects you, and nothing else will." She knelt beside him, folding her hands. "Our Father which art in heaven," she began, and after the "Amen" she took him into her arms. "Now do you know me, Peter?"

Suddenly she felt the stubborn body slacken. "Well, you do look like my mother used to. . . ."

She half-carried him to her room. The little back felt strange under the clothes in which Mr. Gedney had decked him for the trial; the first thing she did when they were alone was to undress him. "Heavens, what's all this?" she cried as the clothes fell away.

From his neck to his heels, Peter's body was a mass of scars. His back looked like her own fingers, laid side by side. "It's where Fowler whipped and kicked me," the boy answered dully.

"O Lord, look at my poor child!" Her hands shook, tracing the scars. "Pete, how did you bear it?"

The small face twisted into a grin. "That's nothing, Mammy. If you'd see Phyllis, I guess you'd scare! She had a little baby and Fowler cut her till the blood and the milk both was running down her body. You'd scare to see Phyllis, Mammy."

She stood as if turned to stone. "God," she whispered, "render unto them double!"

Her days were spent working for Mr. Rutzer, and her evenings listening to her boy.

"Sometimes I crawled under the stoop, Mammy, with the blood running all about me, and my back would stick to the boards. And sometimes Miss Eliza would come down and grease my sores, when all were abed and asleep."

"What did Miss Eliza say, Pete?"

"Oh, Mammy, she said she wished I was with Bell!"

She wished, thought the mother, she wished—but what did see do? Isabella remembered Eliza Gedney as a young girl in New Paltz, gay and giddy, thrilled by the prospect of lording it over the Fowler plantation, over a thousand acres and two thousand slaves. She remembered the taunts of Eliza's mother: "Is your child better than my child?" the old lady's laughter echoed in her ears. And the thought recurred: God, render unto them double. . . .

As soon as she could in fairness quit Mr. Rutzer's employ, she left Kingston with Peter to return to the Van Wageners and to her baby girl. The news of the reunion had preceded them to Wagondale; everyone wanted to see the boy and wish him luck. Without difficulty Isabella found him a job tending the Rondout Creek locks near Greenkills, built only that year for the Delaware-Hudson Canal.

With Peter provided for and little Sophia in the Van Wageners' care, she became restless again. For the second time she took leave from her benefactors and wandered back to New Paltz. There, her last clash with her former mistress still vivid in her mind, she avoided Dumont's place; calling first on another family she knew, she was relieved to find them well-disposed and willing to give her work and news of what had happened in her absence. She heard that Tom had been freed on the Fourth of July with the rest of the adult slaves in the state, that he was working somewhere as a handyman, and that her older girls were doing well at Dumont's, getting almost better treatment than his white help.

Isabella waited for word that Mrs. Dumont had left town for a few days before she went to see her old master. He called her children, and when the oldest came in from her chores his eyes moved from her to her mother. "She looks like you did once upon a time," said John Dumont.

Diana had grown in the past year. She was almost six

feet tall, a dark young giantess with deep-set eyes; but her face was narrower, lighter than her mother's, and the nose longer, slightly aquiline. Isabella shook her head: no, the girl did not look like her.

Someone knocked. It gave her a start; the caller looking through the top of the Dutch door was Mr. Waring, who had described her in court as "the worst of devils." He greeted Dumont and told Isabella quite pleasantly that it was good to see her—what was she doing nowadays?

Nothing particular, she answered.

There was sickness in his family, he told her, and an extra hand was badly needed. Would she go over to his place and help out?

She said she would, gladly.

"Why should you?" Dumont asked her later. "You're a fool to help them out. I wouldn't."

"Oh, I don't mind," she answered. "I like them to forget they're angry with me."

At the Warings' she went to work with a will and was scrubbing the floor in the parlor when one of their young daughters burst in, chalk-white, her hands shaking. "Heavens and earth, Isabella," she gasped and stammered something about a letter and about Cousin Eliza's husband, Fowler. He seemed to have killed someone.

Isabella remembered Peter's tale of the girl Phyllis. "Ho," she said without rising from her knees, "it's no wonder. He like to have killed my child. Nothing saved him but God."

Miss Waring ran to answer the doorbell. From the parlor one could see Solomon Gedney and his mother rush through the hall and upstairs. After a while the sound of Mr. Waring's voice came down the stairwell.

"Go up and hear," another voice told Isabella.

She looked around; there was no one in sight. She hesitated. Slaves did not go unbidden to their masters' rooms, and besides, she disliked spying.

The command was repeated. "Go up and hear!"

She climbed the stairs. The door to Mrs. Waring's room stood open. Inside, in a state of patent shock and despair, the entire family was gathered; on the sofa, Mrs. Gedney seemed ready to faint but for the smelling salts the girls held under her nose. Isabella walked in, shut the door behind her, and listened.

Mr. Waring was reading from a letter. "He knocked her down with his fist, jumped on her with his knees, broke her collarbone, and tore out her windpipe. He then attempted his escape, but was pursued and arrested and put in an iron bank for safe-keeping . . ."

"My child!" cried the old lady. "My Eliza!"

The name fell on Isabella like a blow. The other women sobbed; no one noticed her as she walked out and went back to her work in a daze, scrubbing as if to wipe out the horror. This, then, was what she had been meant to hear—why else would she have been brought now into this very house, where she had not set foot before? God had wrought this, she thought; God had made her dreadful plea come true. . . . "Oh, God," she moaned, kneeling and straining to rub out the truth of it, "that's too much! I didn't mean quite so much, God!"

The truth remained.

"Eliza!" she heard tne old lady shrieking upstairs, "Eliza!"

Isabella ran out of the house. She ran out of New Paltz, faster than she had ever run, as though fleeing from close pursuit. The pursuit was in her. "Forgive me, God," she prayed all the way to Wagondale.

Once more the Van Wageners received her kindly. Little Sophia was thriving and so was Peter, yet she could not be glad. She felt dead inside. Mechanically she said the Lord's Prayer. "Forgive us our debts, as we forgive our debtors. . . ." But instead of God's voice she kept hearing her own: "Render unto them double!"

She was full of fear. What would happen to her? Always there had been God or the master to tell her what to do. Now she had no master any more, and if God had forsaken her also, where could she turn? One morning she said to Maria Van Wagener, "Today my master is coming to take me home."

"Who told you?" asked Mrs. Van Wagener, surprised.

No one had told Isabella. She simply knew that Dumont would be with her that day, and indeed, before nightfall she looked out the window and saw his open dearborn wagon pull up to the house. The Van Wageners were out, so she dropped her work and went to greet the man she had served most of her life. The news he brought was not cheerful: Mrs. Gedney had lost her mind over her daughter's death, and the murdered Eliza's children were in New Paltz now, brought up there from Alabama. Then Dumont talked of the coming Whitsuntide which Isabella had always enjoyed so much with her children.

"You want me to come home with you," she said.

He smiled. "You ran away from me. I'll not take you back."

It did not sound as if he meant it. Isabella's heart warmed to the memory of the years when he had seemed godlike, when she had lived in the safety of his rule and care, serving him, bearing her children—and she went into the house to get herself and Sophia ready. When she came out, Dumont was waiting for her in the dearborn. The horses stood impatiently pawing the ground. With the child in her arm she went to take her seat in the rear.

Suddenly, almost in reach of the carriage, she stopped as if struck by lightning. Pressing the child against her, she stood motionless, staring out of unseeing eyes, deaf to Dumont's puzzled questions. At last he drove off.

Thus the Van Wageners found her. "What happened?"

She could not utter a word. With difficulty they got her into the house; Mrs. Van Wagener had to put Sophia back into her cradle. They asked again what had happened.

Isabella shuddered. "God," it came from her bloodless lips, "God gave me a look—"

"You saw God?" they asked, uncomprehending.

"He gave me a look," she repeated, shaking in every limb. Mrs. Van Wagener took her to her room and lighted her candle. Isabella looked about as if there were someone else in the room. "I didn't know God was so big," she whispered. "He's all over!"

He was indeed, Maria Van Wagener agreed, and bade Isabella a good night. Isabella felt like calling her back, but fear and shame sealed her lips. Another such look, she felt, and one must be forever extinguished, as a lamp is blown out so that no spark remains. The candle flickered. Isabella shivered but could feel no breeze. What made the candle flicker? She wanted to say Mau-Mau's prayer, but the familiar words had fled from her poor brain.

A strange shadow seemed to have fallen upon her, moving with the restless candlelight. Was it her own? She stepped back, but the shadow kept advancing. It was like a dusky apparition, like King, perhaps, the colored man who had married her and Tom and so many other slave couples. But King's word was not God's, and the knot he tied bound only at the master's pleasure. The master was gone, she remembered, and anyway, he was not the true master. God was the true master. He was all over. . . .

Rays of light seeped through the shadow; Isabella could not tell whether from without or from within. She could not say whether she saw or felt the rays. She did feel them, warmly and deeply in her heart that only God could see— and her heart beat faster, and the warmth seemed to overflow and envelop her like a mantle and to radiate from her on all sides. It was as if ice and snow were melting around her, as on the day when she had knelt on the islet by the waterfall, crying, "I love—I can love even the white folks!"

The light stood still and ceased flickering. It took shape. "I know you," Isabella marveled, reaching for the light but unable to grasp it. "I don't know you—"

The light wavered back and forth restlessly, like rippling water. "I know you!" cried Isabella, trying with all her strength to hold the light—and the light filled the room until, dazzled, she shut her eyes. Then the light was in her. It became music; it rang like the organ at the first church service she had ever attended, and the sound soared in her and around her: "When He rose—when He rose . . ."

When she opened her eyes, only her little candle was lighting the room with a steady flame. The shadows had left. Isabella felt aglow. She could pray; she could sleep. God had forgiven.

In Search of the Kingdom

"WHEN I FOUND JESUS," Isabella later called this turning point in her life. She had first heard the name of Jesus when Bob groaned it in agony, but her questions about him had not been directly answered while she was a slave, not even by God. She had come to think that no one really knew much about "the Lord Jesus" and that he was like other great white men you heard about, like Washington or Lafayette. Now she knew better. When the awful "look" had shown her the truth and kept her from going back to the wrong master, it was Jesus' love, she felt, that had saved her from extinction. And she began to look out for his bodily appearance, feeling that she would know him if she saw him, and that when he came, she would go and dwell with him as with a dear friend.

She carefully guarded her secret. It was too precious for sharing; if people knew about Jesus, she was afraid, they might take him away from her. "I'll keep this close," she resolved. "I won't let anyone know." She did not tell the Van Wageners, in whose Dutch church she heard Jesus named in hymns and from the pulpit, but too distantly to make him seem approachable for her kind. Nor did she tell Miss Gear, the lady who had brought the news of Peter and was now acting more and more like his godmother.

Miss Gear was an ardent Methodist, and one day she took Isabella to a class meeting in Kingston. The members gave their testimony of spiritual experiences, and when the first to get up mentioned Jesus, Isabella gave a start. The man had found him, too!

Another rose to testify. "He's found him, too!" she marveled, and finally, uncertain whether to be glad or jealous, "Why, they all know him!"

She came back for other meetings. Obviously these people knew more about Jesus than she did, and she was eager to learn. They read aloud from the Bible, not at random like the Van Wageners but methodically and with interpretations, and Isabella learned that Jesus Christ had been born of a virgin, had died on the Cross for our sins, and had risen on the third day. She understood that the song she loved, "When He rose," referred to this resurrection. One day she misunderstood some remark to mean that Jesus was married. "Does he have a wife?" she asked hastily.

A chorus of gasps. "God have a wife?"

"Is Jesus God?" Isabella wondered.

"Certainly," was the answer.

It startled her. And when she heard of the disputes on the subject—that while most Christians believed in Christ as one with God, others viewed Him as God's only begotten son, and some as a mere man—she shook her head. "Of that I know only as I saw. I didn't see him to be God, or else how could he stand between me and God? I saw him as a friend."

A great change in her outward life was also wrought by Miss Gear. About to return to New York, where she was engaged in teaching, the lady had a proposition for Isabella. Domestic servants were in demand in the city and paid for more than upstate; besides, boys like Peter could learn better trades there than tending canal locks on Rondout Creek. Miss Gear never visited in Ulster without looking up her protégé and complimenting him on his wit, his ingenuity, and the frank confessions he would make when caught in mischief. "He's so smart he ought to have an education if anyone ought," said the teacher. Eventually Isabella and Peter accompanied her to New York.

The year was 1829. One could make the trip by stage then, via the Walkill and Goshen, but this was expensive; most people traveled by boat. Those in a hurry took the steamer—for things had changed on the Hudson since Martin Schryver's slave girl had heard a small boy come whooping up from the Stand: "Ma, Ma, come and see the wagon go through the river without horses!" The paddle wheelers

were a familiar sight now. They churned up to Albany
daily, fuming and spitting sparks, and on the downward
voyage they reached Kingston in the afternoon and New
York at dawn of the next day. These speed demons
landed only at their destinations; to catch them at Kingston,
you had to use a dory that was towed back to the moving
steamer by a windlass attached to the machinery. The
boarding in midstream was a difficult and not quite riskless
venture. Ladies such as Miss Gear, who desired to travel
with dignity, preferred the sailing packets that had been
plying the river for a hundred years.

There were four of them on the New York run, long-
tillered sloops with striped hulls and white sails, the mast
well forward and plenty of space in the cabin for the
comfort of passengers. They were easy to board, coming
right into the creek to tie up by the storehouses at Kingston Landing, and they made the voyage to the city in two
or three days, depending on winds and tide. Isabella, who
had been in nothing bigger than a rowboat in her life,
hesitated at first to follow Miss Gear aboard so fine a
vessel, but Peter only laughed. "That's nothing, Mammy"
she should have seen the ship Mr. Gedney had brought
him back North in.

The sloop had no staterooms, but Miss Gear had a berth
in the cabin and offered to have Isabella and her son provided with cots. Peter would not have that, either. He drew
Isabella forward where one could watch the crew, and as
the packet drifted sedately down-river, between the High-
lands and through the wide Tappen Zee, the boy told his
mother about the voyage from the Gulf port of Mobile,
round the Florida Keys and over the vast Atlantic—how
the great clipper flew before the wind, and how the sailors
went up, catlike, into the rigging, and about the chanteys
they would sing at work. And on the last stretch of the
North River, as the teeming harbor opened up ahead, Peter's eyes gleamed with the excitement of pointing out the
full-rigged vessels, their masts spread-eagled with the rolled
canvas that would soon be set to sweep them over the
seas.

"Would you like to go to sea, Peter?" Miss Gear asked.

"Would I!" said the boy.

She would see what might be done about it, said the lady.

Isabella remembered the glowing tales Tom had told of New York, but now, as the sloop docked at the end of the Battery, she felt bewildered. The houses here were jam-packed as far as the eye could see; the church spires were twice as high as in Kingston and ten times as many, and there were so many more people and vehicles in the street that she would not have dared to leave the dock without Peter, who had been there before. Nor would she have known how to find lodging or work if Miss Gear had not had a job waiting for her. A Mrs. Gatfield in Nassau Street, just a short walk from the boat, gave her bed, board, and wages sufficient to board Peter in the navigation school where Miss Gear paid his tuition. Most months, in fact, she would have something left over, and on her employer's advice she always carried the surplus to the Bank for Savings.

The Kingston Methodists had given her a letter to their church on John Street. There, around the corner from her place of employment, she found a plain, white frame building set behind a small cottage that housed the preacher and, in the lower part, the colored sexton and his wife; she found a kind welcome and was invited to join the colored class. It was a new experience to pray with brothers and sisters of her kind, but she made no friends among them.

One day she knelt at the altar rail beside a woman as dark as herself, whose head was bowed and whose hands were folded like hers, and she felt a sudden urge to reach out for the hand of this dark sister. It was the bony, work-hardened hand of a former slave; the upturned face seemed strange, yet oddly familiar. After a moment the woman withdrew her hand to resume her prayers. Isabella did the same. When she looked up again, the other had left. Her image remained. Where had they met before?

The question haunted Isabella. She told Miss Gear of the strange sister, and the lady, with an understanding nod, asked her to come along to a prayer meeting uptown. "It concerns our sisters—our fallen sisters," Miss Gear explained on the way to the Bowery, in the city's fashionable section. They went to the home of a fur merchant, James Latourette, a Methodist who had outgrown the church. Miss Gear was a friend of his family's, and any God-loving friend of hers was welcome at the prayer meetings he held, like Paul at Rome, "in his own hired house." His flock, chiefly female and largely in his employ, met in an upstairs room that was fitted up as a chapel. No dominie preached high-toned sermons, no organ solemnly accompanied the choir as in the Dutch church of Wagondale, but everyone sang and talked freely to God, as Isabella had done all her life. The service suited her better than any she had yet attended, though she wondered what work she was asking divine help for.

After the meeting of the ladies, led by Mrs. Latourette, donned capes and bonnets and went out. One of them had a colored maid along, and with a sense of relief Isabella attached herself to the maid, whose name was Katy. Katy came from Virginia, having run away from there after her children were sold. Her mistress here was Mrs. Sarah Pierson, an all but transparent-looking woman whose frailty Katy laid to too much fasting; she and her husband Elijah were a saintly couple, both deeply involved in such missionary ventures as tonight's.

About the venture Katy giggled, saying only that it would take them to "the Five Points"—which left Isabella no wiser.

The ladies turned off the Bowery, turned their backs upon its comfortable residences and ornamental foregardens, and entered another world. A block or two to the west, ramshackle houses lined squalid alleys teeming with black and white humanity; the whites looked vicious, and the colored, one said, "crawled over each other like flies on a dungpile." Ahead, a crossing of three streets formed five pointed corners, and roundabout it red lights shone from doors, and sound of revelry and music rang through curtained windows. It was not the kind of music heard in church.

The ladies halted to pray, ignoring a ring of male scof-

fers. Few women stopped; the ones who did moved their
lips silently and then walked away fast, as though afraid to
be seen praying. Katy's mistress asked one who lingered a
moment why she was living in sin. The girl shrugged, and
the lady gently pressed her: what had she been getting out
of sin? To what end would it bring her, here and in the
hereafter? Mrs. Pierson's eyes were so luminous that her
pale face seemed to consist of nothing else. She took the
girl's hand. "Why don't you come to Bowery Hill? It is
under my husband's protection. God has called my husband
to save you; he is praying for you day and night. Come,
repent, and God will help you!"

The girl glanced back to make sure she was not seen
by anyone she knew. Then she fell in with the ladies and
was triumphantly led out of her environment, to the hill
at the end of the Bowery where a few elegant homes
stood in a grove of old trees and well-kept shrubs. "A
sweet sylvan retreat from the city," people called the spot
where the repentant sinner was delivered to a stout blonde
woman at the gate of a large house—the Magdalene
Asylum which Mr. Pierson had founded right on Bowery
Hill, where he, too, lived with his disciples.

Isabella had heard about sin, but she still wondered what
it meant to "live in sin." Miss Gear told her it meant
"playing the harlot." When she did not understand this,
either, the lady explained with some embarrassment that it
meant to sell yourself, to take money for letting men take
their sinful pleasure of you—was that clear?

It was. Isabella grew thoughtful. Being sold had been a
matter of course to a slave girl, and if her master felt
like taking his pleasure of her, that also had been a matter
of course. But she remembered the "look" God had given
her at the thought of going back to Dumont as a free
woman. To be free and yet sell yourself to be used like a
slave—this must be sinful indeed.

She lost sight of the woman with the shining eyes, who
had brought the sinner to repentance, until one day she
met Katy and heard Mrs. Pierson was ill. It saddened her.
Could the doctors not help? "Oh, the master wouldn't let
none of *them* in the house," said the shocked maid, ex-

plaining that Mr. Pierson was in direct communication
with God. He had been favored with signs indicating that
he was Elijah the Tishbite and should gather in all the
members of Israel at the foot of Mount Carmel. Mount
Carmel was Bowery Hill, said Katy who prided herself on
being one of the members of Israel in the new kingdom.

Isabella, to whom God talked constantly, saw little wonder in the tale. She learned that Elijah the Tishbite was the
prophet who had foretold the coming of Jesus, and she
longed to meet the man honored with such a mission. She
heard more about Elijah Pierson: he was in the habit of
fasting two nights and three days at a time, refusing himself even a cup of water until the third sunset. This, Katy
quoted him, gave him "great light in the things of God."

"Well," said Isabella, "if fasting will give light, I need it
as much as anybody. If Mr. Pierson needs to fast two
nights and three days, I should fast more. I'll fast three
nights and three days."

On the morning of the fourth day she was too feeble to
stand. Her legs buckled under her as she got out of bed;
she was barely able to crawl to the pantry and felt raven-
ous enough to eat all there was in it. Afraid of offending
God by such gluttony, she forced herself to breakfast on
water and dry bread, finishing a six-penny loaf before the
pangs in her stomach went away.

Her testimony about the experience was that she did get
light from fasting, but it was all in her body, not in her
mind; and the bodily lightness would last a long time. "Oh,"
she said, "I was so light, I could skim around like a sea-
gull!"

At Mr. Latourette's meetings she began to talk to God
in the presence of others. It made no difference to her,
but it awed others. She could not read the Bible but was
soon quoting it fluently, and when her friends took her to
camp meetings, she amazed them by the power of her
speech. They took her to hear the great John Maffitt, an
Irish-born Wesleyan preacher of wide renown, and saw the
audience drift away in the midst of his sermon, to the far
end of the meeting grounds. They went to see who might
be speaking there—it was Isabella. "Even learned and re-

spectable people were running after her," James Latourette reported.

He made her quit her job in Nassau Street and move to his house, to work for his family and accompany them to the "wretched abodes of vice and misery." To Isabella, raised in the cellar of Stone Ridge, these abodes seemed not so wretched. The parlors looked luxurious, and all the inmates had rooms of their own with comfortable beds upstairs. Their clothes were scantier but prettier than hers, or Miss Gear's, or Mrs. Latourette's; their faces were painted as gaily as the river boats, and when they laughed, the walls shook. And yet Isabella felt sorry for these women, whom God had made free to withhold what they were now obliged to sell, and she shouldered her way past madams and bouncers to sing and talk so fervently of God that the ladies seldom left a house of ill fame without a Magdalene or two for the Asylum.

She also had a personal reason. Peter, dropping in from navigation school to see her and to get some pocket money, used to sing chanteys he had picked up from the sailors in port, and one in particular set his mother to thinking. It went thus:

> "Oh, Sally Brown of New York City,
> Way-ay, roll and down!
> Oh, Sally Brown you're very pretty,
> And I'll spend my money on Sally Brown. . . ."

In a foray to one of the most notorious houses, the reformers were joined again by Mrs. Pierson. Grown even thinner since Isabella had last seen her, she seemed no more than a starry-eyed wraith now, but her zeal was undiminished. "Elijah," she told the party, "prayed God to give us all the ground trod by the soles of our feet, and all the souls alive who have heard our voices in the neighborhood. And the Lord said to Elijah, You must go and fetch them out!"

As they went, she led them in her husband's favorite hymn.

"I bless the Lord, I've got my seal
    Today and today—
To slay Goliath in the field
    Today and today!
The good old way is the righteous way,
    I mean to take the kingdom in the good old way!"

Singing, they entered the establishment. It was the gau-
diest and rowdiest in town, gilt-laden, reeking of rum and
bare flesh, with a hint of bilge water. The customers were
either seamen or they wore gold watch chains. Down the
stairs, flanked by two burly bosun's mates, came a beautiful
woman, raven-haired and coffee-colored. Her jaws moved,
reminding Isabella of the chantey:

"Oh, Sally Brown's a bright mulatter,
    Way-ay, roll and down!
She drinks rum and chews tobaccer,
    And I'll spend my money on Sally Brown. . . ."

The madam looked at the intruders, ignored the ladies,
turned to Isabella. "You a churchgoing woman?" she asked
politely.

Isabella said she was.

"I go to Zion African Church sometimes," said the madam. "But I haven't seen you yet."

Isabella said she went to John Street Methodist.

The other spat her tobacco plug into a corner, hitting the
spittoon. "White folks' nigger." She smiled. Then she surprised everyone by announcing that the house would now
close for business, so the girls might have their chance at
this prayer meeting.

The ladies exulted. The girls ran to make themselves
decent and summon those who were busy, and when the
last grumbling customer had been routed out and the staff
reassembled, demure in attire, devout in attitude, the penitent glow on each face warmed the reformers' hearts. This
would be a glorious meeting! At the very first prayer, a
blowzy blonde burst into tears of contrition.

"Hallelujah," breathed Mrs. Latourette. "Hallelujah,"

shrilled the girls, a ragged chorus, and chimed in with
Mrs. Pierson: "I mean to take the kingdom in the good old
way . . ."

Isabella kept quiet. She was finding it hard to pray as
the meeting grew ever noisier. Girl after girl leaped up to
confess and testify, ranting and tearing her hair, while the
rest clapped hands and worked themselves into a frenzy.
It affected the ladies as well; Mrs. Pierson's delicate features
twitched, and Miss Gear's hallelujahs rang hoarse. The madam rushed in, wild-eyed, with flying hair, her beautiful
mulatto face ecstatically twisted. "Lord, we're sinners
—show us that we can be saved! Give us a sign!"

Her foot caught in Isabella's cloak; she stumbled but
regained her balance. Only Isabella was dragged to the
floor and could not move for a moment, and this sufficed
for Miss Gear to cry, "She's in a trance! She's in a spiritual
trance!"

"It's a sign," shrieked the madam. "Glory hallelujah!"

The whole crowd of women became delirious. They ran
wild all over Isabella, who was unable to rise and afraid
of being trampled to death if she stayed down; she cried
out, but no one listened. She buried her head in her arms
and heard them shout hallelujahs all about her, stomping
and jumping and praising the Lord for His sign—jumping
on her, too, bruising her body as they rejoiced over her
spirit.

Suddenly the din ceased. Looking up, Isabella saw the
girls walk upstairs, panting. Only the madam looked cool
despite the beads of sweat glistening on her high yellow
skin, and a smile curled about her lips as she left after
her women.

The parlor was empty, except for the ladies of the moral
reform movement and the bouncer who offered, grinning,
to straighten their clothes. They were too dazed to realize
that they would leave without a convert. This had been a
great experience, sighed Miss Gear.

"The voice of God," Mrs. Latourette murmured in awe.

Isabella hobbled home in silence. To her, this time, God
had not spoken.

It was her last visit to the Five Points. Her friends, dismayed by her refusal to go again, reminded her of all the sinners she had converted; they begged her not to abandon the good work—in vain. She kept attending Mr. Latourette's meetings but left his house to take a job in Duane Street, and she quietly withdrew from the John Street Methodist Church to the one established by and for her own people.

At the African Methodist Episcopal Zion Church, at the corner of Church and Leonard Streets on the west side of the city, she found a sense of fellowship she had missed in the mixed congregation. It was less a matter of common color than of common experience, or the likelihood of common experience. Zion had freeborn members, but everyone there might have been a slave. And while few of the white Methodists in John Street had ever held slaves, they all might have. It did make a difference.

On one of her first Sundays at Zion, Isabella thought she was again seeing the strange yet familiar sister who had knelt beside her at the John Street altar rail. This time she did not lose her. The woman was tall, handsomely dressed, and a good deal older than Isabella, who accosted her after the service. Had they not met before? In the John Street church?

The older woman shook her head; she had only just moved to the city, from Newburgh. Her hair was gray, and Isabella thought the other's had been black. The woman mentioned that her sister Nancy had been attending the colored class in John Street for a while.

Isabella also had once had a sister Nancy—one of the lost ones her mother had talked about in the dank cellar of her childhood, of the half dozen or so who had vanished without a trace. About Nancy there had not even been such rumors as about Sophia, said to have been freed in Newburgh. . . . Isabella stared at the gray-haired woman. "Who are you?"

The woman said, "Sophia," and a meaningless last name. "I was born on the Hardenbergh place at Hurley."

"So was I—I'm Bell! Mau-Mau's youngest."

The sisters embraced one another.

Later, the older asked Isabella to come along to meet their brother Michael; he was in New York, too.

Isabella's mind whirled. She saw a boy run toward an old-fashioned sleigh—and turn back, terrified, trying to hide in the cellar, only to be dragged out with his own parents' help. . . . "Obey!" she heard Mau-Mau's voice. And: "When you're sold away from me, child, and you don't know where I am and I don't know where you are. . . ." And the word that among the oldsters freed in Newburgh was Sophia, a daughter of Hardenbergh's Baumfree and Bett—and now a Sophia she had not recognized was taking her to meet Michael. . . .

The dark man was strong-looking, tall, and straight—straight as a tree, it flashed through Isabella's mind. She had remembered her father as she had last seen him, white-haired and bent, but a look at his son revived more distant memories: of a Baumfree resembling the Michael of today, playing with a little boy named Michael. . . . He could not believe it was she. Where did she come from? How had she met Sophia?

"It was Nancy," Isabella told her sister. "I thought you were Nancy." Nancy and she had knelt side by side last year, touching hands, but not speaking to each other. Where was Nancy?

Nancy was dead, they told her.

"Dead? Here she was; we met—and wasn't I struck with the peculiar feeling of her hand, so bony and hard like mine? I couldn't tell she was my sister, and now I see she looked so like my mother!"

Tears ran down her cheeks. Sophia wept. Michael wiped his eyes. Nancy's shadow stood between them.

Michael said she had died months ago, after lingering for years with a slow consumption. "She got it working for a hard master."

Isabella's heart went out to her dead sister. She thought of Neely, and of God's quick answer to her plea for another master—why had God not helped Nancy? Had she not asked?

Michael knew a story about that master. One of the black children on his place had been born an imbecile. At five, it could not walk or talk or cry like others; the only sound it made was a constant piteous moan. The expense of feeding it angered the master so he would play football with the useless creature, dragging it out from under chairs and tables and kicking it across the room and down the front steps. The mother wished it would die. "But it seemed as tough as a moccasin," said Michael.

Isabella thought of the scars on Peter's back—she, at least, had not been forced to watch him suffer. She saw Sophia listen raptly and wondered why; her sister must have heard the grisly tale before, and yet it seemed she could not get enough of it.

Michael went on. The child had died at last, but the master's contentment was short-lived. He fell ill himself and became as weak-minded as the dead child had been. Its mother was given the task of supporting him with her still powerful arms as he sat up in bed, and when her mistress was not looking she would squeeze the breath out of him, shake him, lift him, and set him down as hard as possible. If he gasped audibly and her mistress said, "Be careful, don't hurt him!" she would answer, "Oh, no, Missus, no," in her most pleasant voice—and when Missus' back was turned, he would get another bear hug, another shake, another bounce.

The ghost of a smile played about Michael's lips. Sophia drank in his words. Isabella shut her eyes; the words "render unto them double" came to mind and made her shudder.

She heard that Nancy's master had died just before Freedom Day, that Nancy then had found Michael in New York and told him everything. "I asked her," Michael said, "if she wasn't afraid of his spirit haunting her. And she said, 'Oh, no; he was so wicked the devil won't even let him out of hell long enough.'"

Isabella stared at her brother. Had Nancy done that?

He grinned.

"God have mercy on her soul," she whispered.

For a while no one spoke.

"Oh, Lord," Isabella burst out suddenly, "what is this

slavery that it can do such dreadful things? What evil can't it do?" She fell on her knees.

Sophia touched her. "Let's pray." And the three said the prayer they had learned as children, Mau-Mau's prayer— for Nancy, and for the brothers and sisters who were still living, and for those who were still slaves.

Katy came one day, in great excitement, to report that Mr. Pierson had bought her freedom from her old master, the one she had run away from in Virginia—she would get papers to prove it, and then she could go South openly to see her children! "He says his praying and fasting made him do it," said Katy, "but I think it was God." Isabella thought so, too, and was thrilled to be invited to one of Mr. Pierson's prayer meetings at the Magdalene Asylum.

At last, she would meet the holy man. At the Asylum, she was greeted by the matron she had seen before; the girls were already lined up in a bare room that served as a chapel. Before Isabella could look for her own converts, a pale, fortyish, intense-looking gentleman came in with two ladies. His jet-black hair was parted in the middle, the bristling black beard an inch long. "Bless the voice that crieth in the wilderness," intoned the matron, bowing to kiss Elijah Pierson's hand.

He humbly withdrew it. "Bless the Lord, sister," he said and went to greet the Magdalenes. The two ladies followed him. Their poised gentility reminded Isabella of his wife; in reply to her whispered question, Katy identified them as the ailing Mrs. Pierson's friends, Frances and Ann Folger, cousins married to two rich merchants by that name. Both were ardent disciples of the Prophet Elijah.

Mr. Pierson preached a sermon and led the meeting in prayer, hymn-singing, and testimony. At the close, the ladies Folger spoke to Katy and to Isabella, of whom they had heard from Mr. Latourette. "You must follow Elijah," said Frances, eyes sparkling.

Ann led Isabella to the black-haired man. "This is she whom Brother Latourette calls a child of God," she told him. Her voice was like velvet.

Elijah Pierson turned his sunken gaze on Isabella. "Have you been baptized?"

"By the Holy Ghost," she answered readily.

The reply seemed satisfactory. Yet Isabella heard no more of Mr. Pierson until Mr. Latourette bade her join him on a religious mission to Bowery Hill. It seemed that a day or two earlier—on the twentieth of June, 1830, to be exact—Mr. Pierson, in an omnibus going down Wall Street, had heard a voice saying, "Thou art Elijah the Tishbite, and thou shalt go before me in the spirit and power of Elias. . . ."

Mr. Latourette rang the bell at the Pierson home, and a worried-looking maid led the way to a bedroom where a score of people knelt in prayer. In the bed lay Mrs. Pierson, white as wax. Her husband held an open Bible; next to him, the ladies Folger sought to calm a weeping child. Isabella stayed in the background as Mr. Latourette went to the patient's side. Mr. Pierson read from the Bible.

"James five, fourteen and fifteen: Is any sick among you? Let him call for the elders of the church, and let them pray over him, anointing him with oil in the name of the Lord; and the prayer of faith shall save the sick, and the Lord shall raise him up, and if he have committed sins, they shall be forgiven." He shut the book and turned to Mr. Latourette. "James, I have called the elders of the church together. Let us fulfill the Word. Let us anoint Sarah, so my beloved wife will be raised up and recover."

"Let us pray," said Mr. Latourette, who held a flask of oil.

Pity gripped Isabella. The dying woman's skeletal face haunted her—and yet, somehow she was unable to ask God to raise up Sarah Pierson. The men at the bedside were praying in loud voices, but she did not hear them. "Thy will be done—thy will be done," she repeated, over and over.

Silence filled the room, for time without end. A child sobbed.

At last Isabella heard a thud. Looking up, she saw Mr. Pierson prostrate at his wife's bedside, his head buried in the pillows. Mr. Latourette's hand lay on his friend's shoulder. "She will be raised on the Latter Day, Elijah," he said and walked out swiftly, beckoning to Isabella.

In the street he enjoined her to mention this meeting to no one, to tell no one that he or she had been there. Isabella promised. She heard rumors of an attempted resurrection at the funeral but kept silent. At one of Mr. Latourette's meetings she met Ann Folger again—closely veiled, but there was no mistaking the voice—and after the meeting the lady approached with Mr. Latourette and raised her veil. Her amber eyes rested on Isabella. "You are truly a child of God," she said softly.

"Eminently gifted and favored by God," Latourette agreed.

Isabella did not know what to say.

Elijah Pierson was asking for her, said Mrs. Folger. He needed help. The sit of Sarah's passing had become unbearable to him, and he had moved to Fourth Street, next to Mrs. Frances Folger. "Cousin kept house for him, but she can no longer, and Katy has gone to her children. He has fasted and prayed God to send someone in her place."

"You are the answer to his prayer," Latourette said. Isabella sensed the hand of God.

The Mr. Pierson she found in the house on Fourth Street was a shadow of his former self. Up to the end of the funeral he had been hoping for Sarah to be raised, as Scripture promised—but the resurrection of the flesh might indeed await the Latter Day. "And her spirit," said Elijah Pierson, "lives now in the body of another, who is my wife as surely as the kingdom will come."

His faith in the coming kingdom of God on earth was unshaken. He spoke of it so convincingly that his little flock felt ashamed of monopolizing the great hope. The matron of the Magdalenes went about town urging people to hear the Prophet Elijah, and Ann Folger brought her husband Benjamin, a handsome young man with a courteous, fixed smile; his eyes never left his wife, as though in fear of missing a chance to serve her. Her cousin's husband never came—he just was not spiritually-minded; Ann often pitied poor Frances on this account—and Frances came less and less.

Isabella regretted this, for Mr. Pierson seemed revitalized when Frances Folger was present; he would look at her almost as Ben Folger looked at his Ann. Once, Isabella heard the cousins talk in the hall. Ann, gently but urgently, spoke of a dream about Frances and Elijah. It made Frances laugh aloud. "Well, Cousin, a dream is but a dream," she said and walked out of the house.

Mr. Pierson became despondent. He began having fits. The first time, Isabella wanted to run for a doctor, but he cried out against it, praying until the convulsions passed. Afterward he was exhausted, and Isabella had to fetch his diary. "Can you read?" he asked feebly.

She could not.

He would read to her, said Mr. Pierson, shakily turning the pages on which he noted each day's spiritual and temporal events. "Prayed for the harlots at Five Points . . . Anointed Sarah with oil . . ." He thumbed furiously, until he found what he was looking for. It was a letter he had received after Sarah's passing.

"A few days ago I saw a vision," he read. "I beheld my cousin walking into your back door. She went into the parlor, and I thought in the vision that she was at home in your house. I knew not the meaning of it but was constrained to send it to you; perhaps the Lord will show you the interpretation."

Glancing heavenward, Elijah Pierson put Ann Folger's letter back and read another one that she had sent him a week later.

"I thought, sir, that an apology was due to you for the abrupt note I handed you. I have felt quite uneasy about it and wished to say to you that after I had the vision I thought I must write it and thought I had better tell it to you than cousin, as I know she has a remarkably pure mind —and I judged that if she suspected that I let you know it would make her feel very unpleasant. I have taken up a cross in letting you know; if I have done wrong, be kind enough to forgive me."

Blotches of excitement showed on Mr. Pierson's hollow cheeks. Forgive? Ann had his undying gratitude! Thanks to her, he could be sure now that his wife's beloved soul was near him, living in Frances Folger. But she must not be told that he knew, he warned Isabella.

Isabella promised not to tell. Nor did she tell him that Ann's dream had made her cousin laugh. She had learned to hold her tongue.

Since Frances Folger's withdrawal, the only person who seemed capable of rousing Mr. Pierson from his melancholia was the matron of the Magdalenes. "Fat, fair, and forty," and a past sinner herself, she did not confess at meetings only but came alone to seek spiritual solace from the prophet. He often heard her private confessions in the presence of Isabella—who was reminded of her slavery days, when a slave in the room had been noticed no more than the house cat—and the sessions usually closed with the matron on her knees before Elijah who would place his hand on the fair head in his lap and quote from Scripture: "Her sins, which are many, are forgiven, for she loved much. . . ."

Isabella, listening quietly, could not but wonder if the woman who had seduced so many others might now be seducing Mr. Pierson. When she expressed these doubts to him, she was rebuked. "It is written that harlots shall enter the kingdom of heaven before others," Mr. Pierson was fond of saying.

Gradually he resumed preaching the good news of the kingdom, and his band of disciples grew without distinction of class, color, or creed. The matron bowed her fair head beside Isabella's dark one; Ben Folger, the merchant, bared his soul as frankly as his groom, and the velvety voice of Knickerbocker-bred Ann Folger accorded with the guttural tones of Mrs. Drach, a poor old Jewish woman in quest of salvation. There was James Mills, another rich merchant who had just returned from London and Paris; the voyage had led him into so many temptations that he was now in great fear of hell-fire. He prayed fervently and loudly at all times and in his Pearl Street store would talk religion to his clerks and customers with such zeal that he had to ask his friends to stop him, lest he go too far.

Mr. Mills had only to hear of Elijah Pierson's calling to know in his heart that he must follow the Tishbite. He sought him out; they talked; they understood each other. With Pierson as his mentor, Mills came to be of good cheer, full of faith and hope, and when relatives warned him that Pierson was not considered quite right in his mind, he replied, "Oh, he is now."

He joined the little flock that had gathered at the foot of Mount Carmel to await the kingdom. At his first meeting, Mr. Pierson happened to preach on humility. The subject was threshed out mainly by the matron and the Jewish woman, both of whom were rather talkative, but also by the rest; the only ones with nothing to say about this cardinal virtue were Isabella and the new initiate, Mr. Mills.

His eyes ranged over the females in the group, down to his groom's wife, a little kitchen drudge, and Mr. Pierson's daughter Elizabeth, eight years of age. Finally they came to rest on Isabella, standing in a corner. Mr. Mills kept watching her as the discussion of humility droned on.

"I am for doing, not for talking," he spoke up at last. "There is too much talking and too little doing." He went to Isabella, got down on his knees, and kissed her bare brown feet.

One could hear a pin drop. Isabella, too surprised to move, saw Mrs. Folger's lips curl, saw the groom's wife fight the giggles, saw the Jewish woman stare in ecstasy. Then she heard tre jubilant voice of Elijah Pierson:

> "The good old way is the righteous way—
> I mean to take the kingdom in the good old way!"

Spring came to Manhattan, the spring of 1832. When Elijah Pierson's psalm-singing disciples left the windows open, the passers-by would listen and sometimes chime in, carrying his prayers with them out of Fourth Street, through the city and to the river fronts and the ships in port, and across the waters into the world.

In the spring Isabella always felt a kind of wanderlust. The city seemed confining. She thought of the time when she had roamed in the fields with the sheep of John Dumont. It was so long since she had seen him. At first glance,

walking into Schryver's tavern, he had impressed her as
godlike. The idea made her smile.

She thought of her year with the Schryvers, that year
of untamed freedom in slavery, of "browsing around" in
the woods and along the Strand and in the tavern, of
handling drunks and fetching liquor and fishing and boating
in the wide river—her boy would soon be sailing the ocean
now, as soon as he finished school. How quickly time had
passed since Fowler had whipped him! Isabella thought of
her own whippings at Neely's hand, and of the one at
Dumont's when she had fled to her islet and snow and ice
had melted roundabout.

It was the same longing that gripped her now, alone in
the house of Mr. Pierson who had gone to conduct a meeting at the Magdalene Asylum. I love, I love—I can love
even the white folks . . . She had not known, then, that
this boundless love came from the Son of God.

Dusk fell, but it was light in Isabella's heart. She started
humming the song that was her favorite, not Elijah Pierson's:

"When He rose . . . when He rose . . ."

Had someone pulled the door knocker? It rang again.
She went to open—and congealed on the threshold.

The man outside was bareheaded, tall and slender, his
dark, graying hair parted in the middle and falling down
on his shoulders. A wavy beard framed his face, and his
eyes were searching, threatening and forgiving at once.
Isabella rubbed hers, but the apparition did not vanish.

Had God answered Mr. Pierson's prayer? Isabella drew
back. The tall figure followed her into the parlor and asked
for Elijah the Tishbite. The voice sounded human.

Isabella stammered that Mr. Pierson was at a prayer
meeting. The stranger nodded, asked a few questions about
the meetings, and seemed pleased with her answers. "Who
are you?" she dared to ask.

"I am Matthias, the spirit of Truth."

She remembered: I am the Way, the Truth, and the
Life . . .

"From time to time," he went on, "the heavenly Father has sent his spirit down to earth. The spirit of Truth disappeared at the death of Matthew in the New Testament and entered into Matthias."

Isabella was uncertain whether to stand or kneel. She wanted to pray but did not know to whom, until Matthias folded his hands. "Do you not know how Jesus prayed?" he asked her.

On her knees she repeated after him: "Our Father which art in heaven—hallowed be thy name—thy kingdom come—"

He broke off. Isabella trembled as he raised his voice: "It is the Father's kingdom which is to come, not the Son's!" Slowly he turned to the door. "Tell John the Baptist that I will be back on Saturday," he said and vanished.

Isabella remained on her knees. How could she tell John the Baptist? She did not know; she would have to ask Elijah, since Matthias was gone. Unsteadily she rose and went to the bookcase. She knew where to find Mr. Pierson's Bible with the frontispiece of Christ. Had she seen Jesus in the flesh?

It surely seemed so.

The Kingdom

ON SATURDAY the man who called himself Mathias came again. Isabella heard him answer Mr. Pierson's questions. He had been Robert Matthews of Albany, a carpenter with a wife and five children, but one day, about to shave with the Bible before him, he had found proof that no beardless one could be among the chosen. "Adam never shaved, nor are there razors in Israel," he said, adding that Matthews had been a Scotsman but Matthias was Jew.

Elijah Pierson fondled his own beard. Isabella recalled that Jesus had been a Jew. But Jesus had not been married.

"The wife of Matthews would have no truck with a Jew," said Matthias. She had refused to fly with him from the destruction that would be visited on Albany for its wickedness, and so he had laid down his tools and left house, wife, and children for the kingdom of God's sake—Luke 18, 29. And the light of Truth had shown him the meaning of Scripture and taught him to tell the spirits in men. For the spirits of the dead were not in heaven; they were in the bodies of the living.

Mr. Pierson nodded happily.

The light in Matthews, the carpenter, had increased until the Holy Ghost had come over him and turned him into Matthias. This, he stressed, had happened on the twentieth of June, 1830.

Mr. Pierson gasped. That date—?

Yes, he was solemnly told, on the very date when he himself had heard the Father's voice in an omnibus, naming him Elijah the Tishbite.

Mr. Pierson stammered incoherently.

"I possess the Spirit of the Father," said Matthias, draw-

72

ing himself up to his full height. "Your mission is like that of John the Baptist, who was Elias."

Mr. Pierson knelt humbly. So did Isabella until she was sent for a wash basin, so the two prophets might wash each other's feet.

Matthias stayed overnight, and on Sunday he preached to Pierson's congregation. "Ours is the mustard-seed kingdom which is to spread all over the earth. Our creed is truth, and no man can find truth unless he obeys John the Baptist who has the spirit of Elias. John the Baptist, read the tenth chapter of Revelation."

Mr. Pierson read of the angel who came down from heaven clothed with a cloud and said, "Rise, and measure the temple of God, and the altar, and them that worship therein."

Matthias's eyes passed searchingly over the little flock. "Well, let's measure the temple and them that worship therein." He chuckled. "The Christians nowadays are for setting up the Son's kingdom. It isn't his; it is the Father's kingdom. Puts me in mind of the man who took his son into the business and had a sign made, 'Hitchcock & Son'— but the son wanted 'Hitchcock & Father.' That's how it is with your Christians."

His tone changed abruptly. "The spirit that built the Tower of Babel is abroad; it is the spirit of the devil! The spirit of men never goes up in the clouds; all who think so are Ninevites! Abraham, Isaac and Jacob are now in this world; they didn't go up in the clouds, as some think— why should they? They don't want to box the compass from one place to another. God don't speak through preachers. He speaks through me, his prophet!"

With outflung arms Matthias stood by the window, a tall shadow in the shape of a cross. The sunlight wove a halo round the hair that fell upon his shoulders. "In a short time the world will take fire and dissolve—it is combustible already. There is no resurrection of the body, but the spirits of the saints will enter the bodies of this generation, and the sons of truth will enjoy all good things in this world and must use their means to bring it about! The only heaven is on earth," he proclaimed, with a gesture embracing mankind.

A tidal wave of joy engulfed the meeting.

Soon, Matthias explained, there would be twelve apostles again and twelve patriarchs, but for the present he and John the Baptist had to run the kingdom. John the Baptist would be treasurer. Building the New Jerusalem cost money; the first step was to have the faithful hold their worldly goods in common. "All who admit members into their church and suffer them to hold their lands and houses," Matthias preached, "their sentence is, 'Depart, ye wicked, I know you not.' "

Everything must go into a common fund, which all could draw on. Isabella happily went to the Savings Bank, asked for the money she had carried there every pay day, and gave it to Mr. Pierson, the new John the Baptist. It was so simple, she never knew the sum. The rich, as the Bible says, found the kingdom harder to enter. The fortune of Mr. Mills, who had shown his humility by kissing Isabella's feet, was estimated in six figures but owned jointly with relatives; he needed time to sell out. Mr. Folger, about to move to the country for the summer, could not liquidate his assets so quickly, either. Jerusalem would have to wait.

The kingdom came in other ways. Matthias made Elijah Pierson's house his own and changed the regime to accord with his revelation that the sons of truth should enjoy all good things in this world. The little flock had been known as the "Retrenchment Society" when the Piersons had fasted and the ladies Folger had shed all idle adornment, when pictures, mirrors, carpets, curtains, and sofas had been discarded for the austere life. Those days were gone. Isabella bustled in the kitchen as the fasts turned into feasts. Pierson—John the Baptist, rather—thrived so his cheeks filled out visibly. Both he and Mills introduced Matthias to their drapers and tailors, asking that the bills be sent to them.

Some curbs remained. There was no drinking in the kingdom, and pork was taboo: "All who eat swine's flesh," Matthias taught, "are of the devil. Just as certain as one

eats it he will tell a lie in half an hour." The disciples
learned of other anathemas: "All who say the Jews crucified
Jesus; all who say that the first day of the week is the
Sabbath; all females who lecture their husbands; all who
preach to women without their husbands . . ."

The kingdom would not know death. Death was a devil
appointed to punish sin, and the righteous lived forever.

One day a young Methodist woman came and tried to
testify, but she had only to utter the word "heaven" to be
cut short. "The only heaven is on earth," Matthias thundered, "and in the Father's kingdom women hold their
tongues!" He grabbed a rattan cane and cracked it over her
back. "Go to your father, that he teach you to obey!"

The girl left without a word. "Obey!" a voice rang in
Isabella's ear, distant, admonishing—Mau-Mau's voice.
Surely the obstinate girl had received her just deserts.

Matthias decided to move to the Mills home in Franklin
Street, taking Isabella with him. There the kingdom at-
tained its full glory. The relatives who had kept house for
the widowed Mills moved out rather than become disciples,
and a servant couple, John and Catherine Galloway, took
over, leaving Isabella to minister to Matthias. The prophet
had a new frock coat for every day of the week now, and a
ceremonial costume with twelve silk tassels representing the
twelve tribes of Israel. He wore lace-fringed wristbands, silk
stockings, merino morning gowns. His two nightcaps of
linen cambric, folded like mitres, were embroidered with
the names of the Apostles and the words "Jesus Matthias."
He carried the sword of Gideon which had been miracu-
lously handed down to him, and the gold key in his pocket
fitted the gates of Eden. Strolling on the Battery, he wore
an olive cloak lined with velvet, a gold-mounted cocked hat,
and kid gloves, and he rolled down Broadway in Mr. Pierson's landau or in a superb carriage which Mr. Mills had
placed at his disposal. "The time of abundance has come,"
he preached. "In the midst of the New Jerusalem will rise
a temple grander than Solomon's, and there I will sit with
John the Baptist on my right, Mills on my left . . ."

Isabella and John Galloway carried the large silver tea

service in the house to a fancy store on Broadway; Matthias and Mills came along to order every piece of the set engraved with a lion and the words "The kingdom of God is at hand."

"The British lion?" asked the storekeeper.

"The lion of Judah," said Matthias. "The British lion is a devil. And you, sir, had better dispose of your stock in trade and commence manufacturing articles of this pattern, for soon none other will be in demand." He placed an order for similarly lion-crested plate and for a silver chalice with the legend: "Presented to Matthias the Prophet by James Sylvester Mills and his family."

Next morning, Mr. Mills's brother Andrew arrived at the house with two family friends and two constables.

Matthias saw them from a window and shouted orders against their admission, but before Isabella could reach the door, John Galloway had opened. Gently but firmly, the family friends took Mr. Mills to a waiting carriage. The policemen found Isabella at Matthia's door; Andrew Mills bade her step aside, and when she did not move, he slapped her and motioned to the constables; a moment later she sat on the cobblestones of Franklin Street.

She picked herself up, found the door bolted, ran to the servants' entrance, and got back just in time to see Matthias dragged from his room in his underwear. One constable held him while the other gleefully fished money out of his pockets. Isabella rushed in, but two men jumped on her, pinning her arms.

She struggled in silence as Andrew Mills lectured her on religion and denounced the impostor. Matthias was led out. Iron fetters cut into his wrists; the constables cuffed and mocked him, pulling his beard. He went humbly, offering no resistance. Only in passing Galloway he muttered, "Be accursed, Judas." The door fell shut.

Isabella went limp. They released her, and Andrew Mills said not unkindly that she could keep her job; Catherine Galloway came from the kitchen and asked her to stay. Through her tears Isabella stared at the door that had closed behind Matthias.

"They'll crucify him," she sobbed.

God must help, she thought. The law must help.

Elijah Pierson sent her to his attorney, who explained that no one would be crucified: the two men had been arrested on a lunacy charge and would be confined as harmless fools, Mills in the Bloomingdale Asylum and the insolvent Matthias in the apartment for the insane poor at Bellevue. It was all according to law.

It could not be, said Isabella; it was unjust. Matthias, she told Mr. Pierson's lawyer, was no more crazy than Pierson himself: they had both heard God's voice. God had talked to her as a child—why not to them? They did not believe in going to the sky—was that crazy? "Paradise used to be on the earth," she pointed out, "and it would be now, if the wicked weren't here. When they are driven from the earth, it will be a paradise again."

The lawyer looked amused but promised to do his best.

She went to visit Mr. Mills in Bloomingdale, taking the stage that ran up Broadway, past Greenwich and on, where Broadway veered toward the river and became Bloomingdale Road. It was a long trip, and throughout it she felt curiously watched by other passengers—the story had made all the papers. At the asylum, which was five miles out of town in a beautifully wooded section at the foot of Morningside Heights, she was refused admission, but Mr. Mills saw her from his window and came to the gate, looking well and relaxed. "I like it here," he said, inhaling the cool air under the trees.

Isabella prayed for him on her return to the city.

The freeing of Matthias took time, but finally he arrived at Mr. Pierson's, beardless and full of sad tales. He had been forcibly shorn and penned together with as wicked a pack of rogues as ever cheated hell; when he could give them no money, the sons of Belial had tossed him on a blanket till the very breath had left his body. He described his patience under the ordeal as a miracle of God.

"Verily, you have drunk the cup of affliction," Pierson sighed, and Isabella thanked God for the restoration of the kingdom.

But the kingdom shrank. The Ben Folgers were in the country; the publicity scared off the Jewish woman; the matron of the Magdalenes unluckily ran into Mr. Pierson's married sister, who forbade her the house as an improper person to associate with her brother. He went to ask Frances Folger to come to the meetings again, but she and her husband had just moved to Long Island because the cholera was raging in the city, that summer of 1832. Mr. Mills stayed in Bloomingdale, and Galloway, his servant, succumbed to the cholera.

"The word is choler, meaning God's wrath," declared Matthias.

With a shudder, Isabella recalled his curse upon the traitor. There was no doubt in her mind about the source of the pestilence. God's wrath was driving the wicked from the earth . . . "John the Baptist" changed, too, and was suddenly seeing much of people who were not disciples. One dealt in inventions, another in real estate. Isabella wondered what they had to do with the kingdom.

The men were present, one day, when Matthias preached vigorously against the purchase of land. "He who buys land buys his mother," he shouted. "Why buy land, Elijah? The whole earth is ours; when the kingdom is complete, we shall possess it."

In that case, said Pierson's new friends, it could do no harm to acquire some of it now that opportunity offered. Pierson agreed; the Spirit, he told Matthias, would show them what to do about Mr. Hunt's globe stove and other inventions, and about Mr. Parker's lots on Third Avenue. Matthias beckoned to Isabella and walked out.

In the fall, Pierson proposed to pay Matthias a monthly sum to live elsewhere, with Isabella as housekeeper. He knew a house for rent in Clarkson Street across town, near St. John's burial ground.

The house was unfurnished; Isabella drew her savings from the common fund to buy furniture. Soon after moving in, they heard a familiar voice in the street: "Come and hear the Prophet Elijah!" The matron of the Magdalenes was back soliciting. Isabella felt outraged, but Matthias bowed his head. "Pierson has taken my place. He is wrong, but he has the power. I must submit for a time."

In the spring, Pierson stopped the allowance. Isabella

went to call and found him with Messrs. Folger and Hunt, inspecting the Ne-Plus-Ultra Kingdom Stove that would sell for seventy dollars and finance the building of a temple to outshine Solomon's. Regarding Matthias, Mr. Pierson opened his diary and read to her from the instructions of the Spirit: "Mr. Matthias shall go from you, and you shall go on with your work and be prospered and have every needful gift and wisdom. Give him no more money." He closed the diary.

She brought the bad news to Matthias, who took it calmly. The Lord, he said, would bring him through this trial, and Elijah to repentance. They vacated the house. A friendly storekeeper took in Matthias and the furniture while Isabella went to look for work. At a Mr. Whiting's in Canal Street she got room and board, wages—which she gave to Matthias—and permission to do his washing.

Matthias moved to a cheap hotel downtown, at the corner of West and Marketfield Streets, near the Battery where he had gone riding behind four black horses not long since. Now one saw him walking on the esplanade, pacing along the iron fences like a caged lion. He ignored the curious, but every day a crowd trailed him to the hotel and to the barroom where he would sit in the evenings—not to drink, but to look at the harbor and at Castle Garden, the round-walled old fort where fashionable New Yorkers met nightly at concerts and balls. The barflies found the lonely figure fair game, joshing him until he poured out a torrent of curses. Then the tavern keeper would say, "Mr. Matthias, it is time for you to go to bed," and the prophet would obey like a child.

Isabella saw him only to bring money and his laundry. His beard, full-grown again, covered hollow cheeks; his clothes, the ones he had come to New York in, hung loosely on his shrunken frame, for Isabella's wages paid his room rent but left little for food. Mr. Hunt, the inventor, brought a few supplies to the hotel now and then, and one day she met him there and heard him tell Matthias that Mr. Pierson was sick and asking for him.

Matthias seemed to grow taller. "There's no need for my coming," he said, the old fire in his sunken eyes. "If Elijah has faith in me he will get better; if not, he will die."

The next time Isabella found him triumphant. "The Lord," he said, "has passed judgment upon Elijah. He's repenting. I shall return to the kingdom." He refused her money. "Well done, thou good and faithful servant," he said, handing her the dirty laundry.

Some days later, while Isabella was at work, Mrs. Ann Folger appeared at her place of employment with little Elizabeth Pierson, asking for Matthias's laundry. He was staying at the Folger home in Sing Sing, the lady explained; Mr. Pierson and his daughter were there, too, and all would be happy to have Isabella come and help. The laundry could be forwarded by the Union boat to Tarrytown—or, better sill, Isabella could bring it herself.

It was on a bright midsummer afternoon that she walked down the post road from Tarrytown to Sing Sing. The sun approached the hills across the Tappan Zee, leaving a trail of glittering scales on the water; the villages on the far side lay in the shadow of the cliffs. The road was stony and dusty. A high hedge ran alongside, screening a large estate between river and road. Then a narrow lane, bordered by shrubs red with berries, led up to a small mansion adjoining a fruit-laden orchard. A line from the Bible ran through Isabella's mind: "Every tree that is pleasant to the sight . . ."

On the front lawn, Elijah Pierson's daughter played with two other children, smilingly watched by her father and Benjamin and Ann Folger and Matthias, and on the kitchen stairs stood Catherine Galloway, beaming all over her plain face. Isabella walked up the lane, feeling that this was truly another Eden, a paradise before the Fall. "Here at Zion Hill," Mrs. Folger told her, "we have one Father. We have all things in common. We are one family."

The family spent little time in prayer and psalm-singing. All were employed in accord with their capacities. Isabella and Catherine did the common work; Mrs. Folger helped with the light work; Mr. Folger, when he did not have to go to town on business, kept busy on the farm; Mr. Pierson puttered around house and garden; Matthias did what he pleased. Some chamber chores and garden duties fell to the ten-year-olds, Elizabeth Pierson and Edward Folger—the Folger girl was only six. Lastly, a young Englishman named Henry, a tailor described as "a little bit of a fellow" by Catherine, with whom he would sit in the kitchen below stairs, was man of all work, tended to horses and carriage, and made clothes for the children.

With all things in common, no one, of course, received wages.

Members who had achieved a higher degree of perfection devoted their free time to spiritual pursuits. Elijah and Father discoursed about Scripture; Ann Folger and Father made music on the piano in her room and rode out with the children to enjoy the beauties of nature. They also discussed religion, much to the surprise of Isabella who recalled Matthias's past views on teaching women.

Soon after her arrival Mr. Folger went to New York, and his wife, rather than sleep alone, made her bed in the wing with Isabella and the children and spent the night asking the woman who had known Matthias so much more intimately how he might think and feel about this or that. Until dawn Isabella had to repeat his sayings. Mrs. Folger then went to her room and came back before breakfast, dressed and scented, to prepare Matthias's place, air his napkin, and shake out his pillow. When he came, she inquired after his wishes in her velvety voice: "Father, will you have a glass of milk? Father, would you like your bread warmed? Father, shall we close the window?" And as conversation became general, Isabella heard Father's pet notions—all the ones she had recalled last night—humbly put forth as the lady's own.

Isabella listened speechlessly. It was quite an experience.

At dinnertime Matthias preached against baptism. Man's need, he said, was purification; sprinkling wouldn't do it, nor would dunking with clothes on. Purity required washing the whole body—one's own, where possible, and each other's, where necessary—without allowing feelings of shame to interfere. All shame was sinful; it was consciousness of want of purity. The pure had no shame.

A closet in the wing, off the children's bedroom, was outfitted with a tub and designated as the bathing-room. The family gathered for purification, disrobed outside the closet, which the tub almost filled, and went to bathe in pairs, one helping the other. Father and "John the Baptist" set the example; the last to prove her purity was Ann Folger whose delicate face paled and reddened in turn as she curbed her sinful shame before following Catherine into the closet.

Next day, at dinner, she told of a recent vision in which she had seen two smoke pillars rise and unite, and had felt that one was she, the other Matthias. When he did not answer, she cast down her eyes. "If I have done wrong, be kind enough to forgive me."

"I'll think of it," said Matthias and preached on marriage. The wicked, he said, had never been commanded to increase and multiply; preachers who pronounced them man and wife and said God had joined them together were of the devil. "Be ye not unequally yoked," it said in Holy Writ. God alone had power to tell men's and women's true mates, their "match spirits."

The word drew a sigh from Mr. Pierson and made Isabella think of his futile dreams of Frances Folger and his penitential exercises with the matron of the Magdalenes. Ann Folger stared at Matthias. That evening, and the next, they both stayed up long after Mr. Pierson had retired. Isabella, going into the parlor to take coals for the morning, found them deep in conversation by the fireplace felt unwanted, and withdrew in haste.

"Follow the dictates of the spirit," Matthias suddenly declared on the third day and told Isabella to warm a bath. Instead of sending for Mr. Pierson to assist him, he simply stripped and went into the bathroom, but after a moment's hesitation Ann Folger opened the door a bit to ask, "Father, shall I wash you?" and followed him. In the children's room, little Elizabeth was diligently making beds.

Isabella sent her out to play with the Folger children. They came back, for some toys, when the bathroom door was still closed and one heard only occasional splashes of water. "Father will be clean enough this time," Elizabeth whispered to Isabella . . .

Ann Folger went to join her husband in New York. She

stayed away for a week, and when the carriage brought her back at last, she flew into Matthias's arms, shut herself up in the wing with him for an hour, and then issued directives to put the house in order, notably the master bedroom. To Isabella she gave three new chemises to wash, also a new man's shirt and nightcap that she herself had made, the wristband of the shirt carefully set with edging. Matthias took the carriage to Tarrytown to meet Mr. Folger's boat, and Isabella, while helping Mrs. Folger dress, was given great news: the Spirit had told Ann that Father and she were match spirits. He, too, had seen her in a vision, as Mother. This was why she had gone to New York, to bring the revelation to Benjamin, her husband in the world, and to make him bow to God's will.

Later, Isabella saw Ben Folger take his wife's hand to lead her to Matthias like a best man. His voice shook as he solemnly gave his wife into Matthias's hand in her maiden name of Ann Disbrow, to be Matthias's wife in future, renouncing her as his own. Elijah blessed the union, and Matthias kissed his bride and declared that her name henceforth would no longer be Ann, but Mother.

As the wedding day drew to a close, Isabella saw Ben follow his ex-wife about the hall and the parlor, plaintively calling, "Ann! Ann!" and being rebuffed at every turn. He sought her hand; she withdrew it, scolding, "Benjamin, behave yourself!" He tried to hold her and was pushed away. At last she escaped upstairs, where Matthias was waiting, and Ben collapsed on a chair.

"My God," Isabella told Catherine in the kitchen, "when I saw him lying there I thought he looked like a dog with his tail singed, or one dragged through the gutter. I couldn't help pitying him."

Catherine had tears in her eyes as they went to bed.

In the morning, a curious Isabella watched Ann— Mother, rather—at her routine of preparing Father's breakfast seat. Her innocence seemed natural as ever. She was not properly beautiful but most attractive, with delicate skin and finely chiseled features, a slim figure, a charming smile, and a disarming gentleness in her soft voice and manner. One could understand Father's infatuation if one saw her bowed over his chair, whispering tenderly, "I have taken up a cross . . . If I did wrong, please forgive me . . ."

Isabella looked around; no one else was present. Curiosity got the better of her. "Did you sleep with him?" she asked.

"Certainly," said the new Mother. "I have never known a man but Father," she confided; he was more than a man, just as Benjamin was less than a man.

For days, the couple hardly left their room. The deserted husband paced about the house or roamed aimlessly in the bare autumnal fields. Sometimes Elijah went with him, trying to buttress Ben's faith in the doctrine of match spirits. The children, kept busy by Isabella, saw nothing amiss. Only Catherine reacted oddly to the revelation, beginning to have dreams and visions of her own; so powerfully did the spirit work in her that she would roll around the kitchen floor, crying that she "burned." The next time Father, Mother, and Ben left for New York, they took Catherine along to keep house for them at 8 Third Street, which was Elijah Pierson's new address in town.

Elijah stayed at Sing Sing, and Isabella took the occasion to ask his opinion about recent events. It turned out that he considered them highly spiritual, as the work of God.

There was fresh snow on the ground when the others returned from the city. The strains had eased. Father and Mother were visibly, deeply in love; their bliss was a constant topic of conversation. Another was Mr. Folger's property. "Well," Isabella heard him twit his ex-wife, "you're been doing all right, Ann, getting everything made over to Father and then taking him yourself!" He laughed at his own joke and seemed quite cheered up, and the Mother smilingly confided to Isabella that Father had found Benjamin's match spirit, a beautiful virgin to whom he would soon be betrothed.

There was now a good deal of talk about the children Father had left in Albany at the commencement of his mission. Their mother, he said, was a wicked, lying devil; he wanted the children delivered from her and brought into the kingdom. The oldest, a girl, would be as useful in the house as the boys would be on the farm.

In January, Ben Folger drove to Albany, returning in high spirits. In the carriage with him he had Matthias's daughter who was eighteen and very pretty, and one boy, a nosy eleven-year-old named Johnny; two older brothers were following on the stage. The trip had been smooth, the roadside inns comfortable, and at Albany things had gone well. Finding Mrs. Matthews in reduced circumstances, Ben had given her money and impressed her with her wayward husband's good fortune. She had kept her youngest, but readily entrusted the four older ones to Mr. Folger, whom many in Albany knew as a merchant of repute.

Matthias made his daughter acquainted with the family. "This, my child, is the Mother—"

"She isn't my mother," the girl said.

"She's the Mother of the kingdom of God. You will address her as Mother."

"I won't," she said stubbornly. The veins on Father's temples rose, but the Mother interceded, asking that Miss Matthews be given time to adjust herself.

And Matthias's daughter, in the same ladylike manner, replied, "Mrs. Folger, why don't you call me Mrs. Laisdell?"

"You married?" bellowed Matthias. "Without my permission?"

Isabella stood dumbfounded, the only one present to be struck by the evident flaw in Father's omniscience.

"We thought you were dead." The young woman shrugged.

"Insolent, disobedient devil!" Matthias seized his daughter with one hand and reached for a cowhide whip with the other.

Isabella hurried Johnny off to the kitchen, fed him, and put him to bed. He knew something, he whispered between worried glances in the direction of the parlor, but he wasn't supposed to tell.

"Well," she said, "don't tell."

The small face looked mischievous in the candlelight. It had happened last night, at the inn. He had been in bed with his sister, and Mr. Folger had come and talked about a spirit, and then—

"Hush your mouth, child, and go to sleep," said Isabella and went back to the kitchen, where Catherine was ready to burst with details of the whipping that Father had given the insolent "Mrs. Laisdell." It had served her right, Catherine thought, for being so uppity.

The shouts and screams upstairs had long faded away when Mother came into the kitchen, smiling and lively, to ask the two if they would come to a wedding. Isabella was ready; Catnerine drawled a faint "Ye-es," and her feet seemed leaden as she dragged herself to the parlor, where the festive party sat round the fire. Mrs. Laisdell looked happy, showing no marks of her beating. Isabella remained standing by the door; Catherine huddled under the mantel.

An act on the road, Matthias began, had annulled his daughter's marriage to Mr. Laisdell, whoever that might be. As she and Benjamin loved each other, he thought it best for them to be espoused. Were they willing?

Both said they were. Elijah, Mother, Henry, and Isabella also expressed their consent to the union. Only Catherine had to be asked twice before a doleful, long-drawn "Ye-es sir" came out from under the mantel and Matthias went on to pronounce the pair man and wife.

Good God, Isabella asked herself, did Catherine have ideas about Ben? It seemed impossible. A refined, handsome gentleman and the homely, uneducated widow of Mr. Mills's servant? As Isabella saw it, Catherine Galloway was only fit to be in the kitchen with her.

But when they were back in the kitchen and could not help talking of what had occurred, Catherine said she had a better right to Ben than Mrs. Laisdell. In New York, in Third Street, he had slept with her many times since giving up his wife to Father—and Father and Mother had helped, Father saying that Catherine must be Ben's match spirit, and Mother lending her some of her dresses, to please Ben. And now, six weeks later, they gave him another match spirit!

Catherine wiped tears off her dumpy cheeks. "Ben loved

me all right," she sobbed. "Just ask him which of us here he likes best in the dark . . ."

Isabella thanked God that she was near forty, not handsome, and colored, so no match spirit was apt to be found for her. Her faith was shaken by a revelation that let the Mother live under one roof with two successive husbands, and Ben with three successive wives; it was harder and harder to think of Father's and Mother's relations as quite spiritual as he would call her by pet names and she would spend her time hanging on his neck. She no longer helped with the light work. She no longer was the first for breakfast. Each morning, when she went into their room to light the fire, Isabella would see Mother and Father in bed together, her head resting on his beard. "You see, Isabella, this is my pillow," she would say, laughing.

When Isabella remarked that the late breakfasts threw her back in her work, Matthias sat up, his beard aquiver. "My spirit shall be with you," he proclaimed, "and so shall Mother's, and you shall be able to do twice the work in half the time."

At first Isabella took it for a joke and laughed, but when the point was repeated in all seriousness, she started wondering what kind of spirit would simply double their pleasures and her labors. She saw Elijah, too, grow obsessed with the new doctrine, all wrought up before his trips to Long Island, to see Mother's Cousin Frances, and all upset when he returned alone. It was on Elijah's say-so that Isabella had come to believe in Matthias. If Elijah's godliness could no longer be relied on, should she remain?

The question troubled her heart. Here she was doing God's work; should she work once more for other people? Here she was a member of God's family that did not distinguish white from black and had all things in common; should she go back to a world where whites had everything, blacks nothing? Doubts kept her awake at night. She felt that Matthias was not speaking with God's voice, but the voice that had spoken to her in the past was silent.

Feeling tired and unwell, she had a talk with Mother. She said she was sick and wanted to go away. "Oh, you mustn't," gasped the Mother, her amber eyes wide with alarm, and hurried to ask Father to let Isabella take it easy.

Matthias growled that there was no such thing as sickness; there were only sick devils in people. Awaiting his decision, Isabella huddled in the kitchen when a new crisis arose: a bowl of cherries had vanished. The entire kingdom was summoned to testify. "I can trace the devil from one of you to the other," Matthias thundered, brandishing his whip over the frightened children. "All are part of the conspiracy of sin!"

Isabella stood protectively before the children. Were not all things common in the kingdom? "Don't whip them," she said.

"Shall a sick devil dictate to me?" thundered Matthias.

He brought down the cowhide, and she took three lashes without flinching. "I'm not sick," she said then, testifying in the presence of all that the sick devil had departed. In her heart she knew that for the children's sake she must stay.

Loss of faith is a slow process—a drifting in doubts, a clutching at straws, a tortuous floundering. Time had been when Isabella believed in Matthias; a time would come when she no longer believed in him. Few were the days between when she could have honestly said whether or not she believed.

The kingdom's fortunes fluctuated in the early months of 1834. Ben Folger had just begun to enjoy his new bliss when it was threatened by Mr. Laisdell's arrival. English-born, a combmaker by trade, and definitely not a gentleman, Laisdell cast admiring eyes on the opulent setup, cocked a respectful ear toward the preaching Matthias, and readily took the money Pierson offered him to go away. Then, instead of taking the stage back to Albany, he made the round of the village taverns and told his tale to all and sundry. Next morning, the hillsides swarmed with watchers as a deputy approached the house with a writ requiring the lawful wedded wife of Charles Laisdell of Albany to be brought before the magistrate at Crosby's tavern on the hilltop. She was quite reluctant to exchange her rich, handsome second spouse for her first, poor, uncouth one, but the judge, in awarding Laisdell custody of her person, gave short shrift to the claims of her match spirit.

The Laisdells' departure did not still the clamor at Sing Sing. New crowds gathered; neighbors called, urging the dismissal of Matthias; Isabella was hard put to stall them until Mother could get out of Father's bed and join Ben downstairs to ask them to mind their own business. The postman delivered anonymous threatening letters which Matthias furiously burned, cursing their writers, the pens they had used, and the geese that had supplied the quills.

And then, suddenly, there was ground for rejoicing. A while new family, Thompson by name, came to Zion Hill, and a fatted calf was killed to celebrate the arrival of the first of the chosen.

Mr. Thompson was a combmaker like Laisdell, from whom he had heard of the kingdom and its idea of communual country living. He liked the work in the fields, the food, the company, even "the old man," as he called Matthias. The sermons were over his head, but he saw no harm in the match-spirit doctrine as long as he had to do no more than listen. Only the bathing ceremonies and the prophet's anger at Mrs. Thompson's refusal to undress in front of him—"You have a little devil about you, which I will see some time despite your pride," he chided her— gave the new members pause.

One night, awakened by a shouting match between Matthias and Ben Folger, they peeked from upstairs and saw how peace was restored: Isabella brought the bathtub, and the penitent Benjamin was jointly, lovingly purified by Matthias and their common spouse. When Mrs. Thompson heard Matthias and Elijah Pierson arguing whether she was Elijah's match spirit or Ben's, Mr. Thompson had enough. "I've a nice little woman and shouldn't much like to lose her," he told Isabella.

The Mother handled the farewells. "So you're going to leave us; now what can you say you have seen here? You can't say you've seen me sleeping with Father Matthias, can you?"

"No, ma'am," replied Mrs. Thompson. "I can't say I ever

saw you sleeping together. I've only seen you in his room in your nightclothes, with your shoes and stockings off."

Without the Thompsons, both Ben Folger and Elijah Pierson grew more restless. They accused Matthias of mismatching the spirits; Elijah even went so far as to suggest that he might make a better Father than Matthias. The uprising was quelled, but Elijah developed fits of staring at the Mother, during which his eyes bulged, his tongue thickened, and his hands fumbled oddly until he would writhe on the floor. "You have a devil that likes the floor," diagnosed Matthias. Recovered, Pierson would be much concerned about what he had said or done while the fit was on him, and he begged Isabella, if she saw another coming on, to strike his hands and neck and to restrain him from improper acts and gestures.

Ben Folger had fallen back on Catherine Galloway— Isabella heard it from little Elizabeth Pierson, who shared Catherine's bed in the pantry and was glad to have it to herself now that Catherine would "sneak up to Ben"—but his discontent was plain and understandable. Isabella agreed that if Ben had a match spirit, it could not be that kitchen drudge. He seemed to have other cares as well, notably when Mr. Hunt, the inventor, came to press for what he called "a settlement." There was a good deal of talk about Ben's "bankruptcy." Isabella did not know the word; she thought it meant money in the bank.

During Mr. Hunt's last visit she heard Elijah inform him that at last the temple would be built. It would consist of twelve temples, each grander than Solomon's, forming a harmonious whole on the bank of the Hudson river. "The city of God will rise here on my property," said Mr. Pierson, pointing through the windows.

Isabella was stunned. Ben Folger had owned Zion Hill and given it to Father as the common property of all; what did Elijah mean by calling it his? The Mother whispered an explanation: the property had been turned over to Elijah for safekeeping. From Ben or Father it might be taken away, like Mr. Mills's.

Ben went to New York with Mr. Hunt and came back a changed man. Isabella smelled liquor on his breath as he made a grab for Mother; she was his wife, he yelled when she told him to behave; he was going to take her and his children away from Matthias; he would kill that imposter and wife-stealer . . . The turmoil brought Mr. Pierson and little Edward Folger from the garden, and Ben lunged for the pruning knife in his son's hand. The boy threw it away. Ben dashed for the poker; Pierson headed him off. The whole kingdom was rushing about, Ben in search of weapons, the others throwing knives, forks, fire tongs out of windows or down the cellar steps. Isabella wrested a broom away from Ben and pinned him against the wall. "I've never done you any mischief," she said, holding fast.

At a safe distance, Matthias drew the sword of Gideon. "Let that spirit be destroyed," he intoned. Isabella let go of Ben. In vain, mild-mannered Elijah Pierson sought to mediate; it was not till the Mother asked Ben to talk to her privately that things quieted down. For half an hour Matthias paced outside the closed doors of the wing, and then the two Folgers reappeared, she looking radiant, he following her like a tamed lion and sheepishly confessing his wrong.

Later, when some villagers came to eject Matthias with or without Mr. Folger's consent, Ben begged them as friends and neighbors to desist; he had no complaint, he assured them. Night had fallen when he got them out. And at the break of dawn Isabella saw the Mother in her night-gown, walking from Matthias's room to Ben's.

The sun rose on a Zion Hill ringed by a thin line of local bullies and half-grown boys gesturing and yelling ominous-ly. Ben set out for the village, to appease the people. While he was gone, the mob grew. The grounds were invaded. Teen-agers climbed the trees, hanging from the boughs like bad fruit. About noon, Ben returned in a carriage—not for his family but for Matthias, whom he implored to fly from the gathering storm. On his heels, a young man drove up, saying he was Constable Elephant Taylor and had to bring in Matthias.

Mother wrung her hands. Outside, the mob howled. Ele-phant had an idea: if he were allowed to cut off the prophet's whiskers, he'd guarantee to see him safely to Sing Sing. Isabella watched breathlessly, recalling that no beardless one could be among the chosen.

Elijah engaged Elephant in conversation while Matthias made the supreme sacrifice. The weeping Mother wielded the shears, Catherine stood by to receive the sacred relic in her apron, and Isabella hid it under the rug. A changed Matthias left between Folger and Pierson, with half the crowd hurling threats at the still bearded Pierson and the rest cheering the departure which Elephant supervised.

In the village, Ben and Elijah learned that Elephant was not a constable at all; he was a local wag who had wagered that he would bring the prophet's beard to the tavern. He might have won his bet if someone besides Isabella had known where the prize was hidden—but Isabella did not tell.

Father did not return from the village. Mother shed bitter tears on his bed and had all windows shut as if the house were in mourning. It did not seem so to Ben, nor to Elijah who took Matthias's seat at table, aped his manner, and laid events to God's will. Mother frowned upon this interpretation; Ben ignored it. "Let's go to bed, Ann, I've had enough trouble getting you," he said and led the heartbroken one upstairs.

The next day saw him contented, solicitous, and eager to divine her slightest wish. She had but to say, "I wonder where Father is, Benjamin?" and a trip was made to New York. Isabella came along; en route, Mrs. Folger confided to her that in some months she would give birth to Father's son, a holy child who would be borne without sickness and delivered without pain.

"Does Ben know?" Isabella asked, but got no answer.

She stayed with the Folgers in Third Street, at the New York headquarters of the kingdom. Ben was downtown about his bankruptcy when Matthias came and the Mother flew into his arms, insisting that he move at once from his hotel. When Ben came home, however, he would not cede the marital bed as at Sing Sing. Isabella had to make three beds, in separate rooms—an arrangement that annoyed the threesome as well as her, for besides the housework she now had sentry duty whenever Ben went out, lest his return embarrass Matthias and Mother.

In June there was considerable to and fro between New York and Sing Sing. First, Mother took the boat up; then Matthias followed in a coach-and-four with two servants, to fulfill a prophecy made in his hour of persecution. The village was still so excited that he returned on the same day, with his sons and Catherine, in whose place Isabella was sent up to cope with a new trying situation. Elijah seemed obsessed with the Mother. He devoured her with his eyes; his head bobbed as though drawn to her by a string; the lips mumbled, "Ann, Ann," until he would end up on the floor. Ann Folger found him revolting.

Isabella, obeying instructions, would slap his hands and neck and put him to bed. Mother tried a different cure: she persuaded him to go to Long Island again, for an outright annunciation—he should now really reveal to Cousin Frances that she was his match spirit and true wife. He should bring her with him; then his poor soul could rest and there would be peace in the kingdom.

Having sent him on his way, the Mother left for New York.

Mr. Pierson came back after a week, alone, oddly quiet, preaching hardly at all. He still could not understand what had happened. Had Sarah's spirit left Frances Folger's body? In Oyster Bay he had found her outside the cottage she shared with her so-called husband, "feeding their chickens and looking after their pigs," as the boorish fellow put it. To Elijah's revelation they had reacted half in anger, half in pity—and she, the spirit of Sarah, had told him to get out! "They thought me mad," sighed Mr. Pierson. In vain he had assured them that this widespread delusion was God's work. "They wanted faith," he muttered.

His fits now recurred almost daily. He would roll on the floor of his room, hugging his bedsheets like a human body; Isabella had a hard time keeping the children out of sight. In between he seemed in good health, well enough to take walks and help in the garden.

The family—except for Ben, who was upstate on busi-

ness—came back late in July. The weather was fine, and
Matthias took Johnny for a stroll, from which they brought
back a basketful of blackberries. As long as she lived,
Isabella would not forget those blackberries.

Little Elizabeth Pierson sugared them, and Matthias
passed them out after supper, though he himself had only
his usual dry toast and coffee. Mother said they seemed
not quite ripe, but ate some anyway. Catherine emptied a
plate, and Elijah, in good appetite, helped himself to a
second. He liked the taste of the fruit so well that when he
was out haying the next day he picked and ate a few
handfuls.

That afternoon he was in the barn with the Folger boy,
salting the hay, when he had one of his fits. The boy ran
for Matthias, who came and helped Pierson to the house
and up the kitchen steps, where another, stronger fit left
him unconscious. He was carried to his room, and there, as
Mother doused his head with cold water, he had a third
attack, retched and vomited violently, and involuntarily
moved his bowels. He was utterly helpless, unable to stop
the fits or to control his bodily discharges. He smelled hor-
ribly. His beard was full of vomit. He looked pitiable and
disgusting.

Catherine ran off, nauseated. Matthias led the Mother
from the room, lest she get sick, and remarked that he, too,
would get sick if he stayed. Isabella stayed. No one else
was willing and able to help Elijah now that he needed
help. The seizures continued all night; she and his daughter
sat up with him until morning, when the Mother came to
ask if he would have some toast-water. Mr. Pierson wished
no medicine or anything used on sick people. He drank
some coffee instead, but threw it up at once.

Matthias came and cursed any nursing activities as "har-
boring the sick devil in the house of God." He called Pierson's fits "fifty devils" and said they must be mortified until
they came out of him. Both men had frequently preached
against physicians; Matthias had banished their medicines as
well as the pills of the quacks, to which Mr. Folger had in
the past been addicted. Now he said a doctor might be

called in case Elijah should lose faith and request it, though he, Matthias, would not send for one.

Elijah did not request it. All week he grew feebler, but his fits declined, so he was thought to be improving. He lay on the floor; his linen was seldom changed. Isabella, who spent her nights dozing on a chair in the sickroom, was scolded for neglecting the housework if she looked after Elijah in the daytime. "Always in his room, running in as soon as my back is turned," complained the Mother. "Go and help poor Father gather up his hay!"

On Saturday night Isabella was baking in the kitchen and Mother was bathing her children when Elizabeth came, asking Isabella to go up and wash her father's feet. Isabella felt Mother's eyes on her. "I'm busy," she said.

"Can't you wash his feet if Isabella takes up the water?" Mrs. Folger asked Elizabeth.

"Yes, but he wants to speak to her," the child answered.

Mr. Pierson was too weak to say more than a few words. Coming out of his room, Isabella found Mother waiting for her in the hall. What had Elijah wished to see her about?"

"He wanted me to forgive him," said Isabella.

"You forgive him!" cried the Mother of the kingdom. "What has he ever done to you?"

Isabella did not know. It was not Elijah's fault that his ailment made him repulsive. Did he want forgiveness for being rich when she was poor? For being white when she was black? Or for bringing her into the kingdom? She did not know.

On Sunday Pierson had fit after fit while Matthias, in the next room, preached against the sick devil for hours on end. On Monday he was still worse; from time to time Isabella sneaked in to drive the flies away from him. On Tuesday a visitor came from New York: it was Mrs. Drach, the old Jewish woman who had joined the kingdom in the city and received help from Elijah in the past. Evidently, she hoped for more. Matthias tried to talk her out of seeing the patient; when she insisted, he agreed to take her in after Elijah had been given a bath.

Isabella heated the water and lifted Mr. Pierson into

the tub. He promptly had a fit. Matthias commanded Isabella to bring him out of his "hellish sleep"; when she slapped Pierson's neck and jaw, he relaxed but remained in a stupor. Matthias rejoined Mrs. Drach on the porch, promised to let her see Elijah in the morning, and stayed with her until she went to bed.

He retired to the master bedroom, where Ann Folger joined him at midnight. From the hall, Isabella saw her pull off her stockings. "Mother," she called in, "do I stay up with Elijah or go to bed?"

Mrs. Folger threw herself into bed. "Father, should Isabella stay up or go to bed?"

Matthias turned around. "How is Elijah?"

"Well, he's somewhat better."

Isabella had better go to bed, Matthias decided.

She obeyed. Wearied by the long night watches, she sank into a restless sleep. At dawn she was called by Matthias, who stood at the foot of the stairs, his sunken eyes burning in the dim light of a candle. "Elijah is dead," he said.

She gaped. Father said dead? Impossible. Had he not banished the devil Death from Zion Hill? Had he not taught that the great enemy would be forbidden to touch anyone in the kingdom?

Somewhere a child whimpered.

Isabella left Matthias to follow the sound. Had she heard it before? Time and space faded out. Once more, little Elizabeth seemed to be sobbing at the bedside of a luminous-eyed woman, and Mr. Latourette's voice said, "She will rise on the Latter Day, Elijah . . ." Isabella had all but forgotten the Latter Day.

In the twilight of the sickroom she could make out two prone figures: the sob-racked child, and next to her the Mother of the kingdom, staring vacuously. Mrs. Folger was dressed; apparently she had been up before.

Isabella rocked the child in her arms.

The dead body of Elijah Pierson—once John the Baptist—lay on a board in his room. A sheet covered it to the neck; the mouth and eyes stood open. No one dared to touch it, to close the eyes.

Matthias lectured in the parlor. "Elijah wanted faith; he died of a palsy from loss of spirit. He had to go down as John the Baptist because of a sin unto death that would not suffer his body in the kingdom of heaven. But his good spirit lives on . . ." He was addressing Mrs. Drach, who gazed upon the corpse with shocked incredulity, as if its lifelessness might be a trick. She seemed too heartsick to speak, but her eyes shifted from Mother to Isabella and from Catherine to the corpse, and what Isabella read in those darting eyes was not grief but fear and suspicion.

Matthias gave the poor widow the money she had come to ask from Mr. Pierson, and Mrs. Folger asked her to be kind enough to look up Mr. Folger in New York and let him know what had happened. The old woman promised. She said not to bother calling the carriage for her—she could walk to the village. The afternoon boat was not due for hours, but she seemed eager to leave. Matthias saw her off and then went to discuss burial arrangements with a friendly neighbor.

In the afternoon it appeared that Mrs. Drach had set people talking in Sing Sing. A group of men drove up, identified themselves as a coroner's jury, and proceeded to hold an inquest into Mr. Pierson's sudden death, questioning everyone but Matthias. It troubled Isabella to find them less interested in the fatality than in the ways of the kingdom—its bathing habits, sleeping arrangements, and religious beliefs. When a juror asked what had become of Pierson's devil, she replied tartly, "Maybe it's gone into one of you."

That would do from her, they said and called Mrs. Folger.

The mistress of the house regretted her husband's absence and her own ignorance of legal matters; the coroner had to assure her that the proceedings were according to law before she would describe Mr. Pierson's sickness and death, pointing out that she did not regard them as Providential visitations. "The devil Death has robbed us of his body, but his spirit is as much with us as ever," Ann Folger explained.

She was calm, cooperative, and so ladylike that no juror

dared to put the questions that intrigued them all. When
the record was published later, everyone wondered why
Mrs. Folger had been confronted with none of the rumors
then flying wildly in Sing Sing. Asked if the deceased had
been given medicine, she answered, "No. Mr. Pierson
would not have taken any while he had his senses, and we
respected his feelings about it after he had lost his senses."

Would she not call a physician if she were sick? She
answered, "No. I've already passed through the hands of
so many that I fear my body may yet be denied admission
to the kingdom of heaven."

Asked about Pierson's property deals with Mr. Folger,
she disclaimed knowledge of details. One should ask her
husband, who was a correct businessman and would render
a true statement; she knew only that he and Pierson had
trusted each other and been partners in some kind of business. "If you're not satisfied," Mrs. Folger concluded, "or
if you find any marks of violence on the body, you'd
oblige me by letting me know it."

Isabella showed the jury to the room where Elijah
Pierson lay untouched. The coroner lifted the sheet, found
no marks of violence, and closed the inquest. Meanwhile,
the neighbor had bought a coffin and had a grave dug in
the local cemetery; burial was to be at noon of the next
day, Thursday, August 7.

On Thursday morning Ben Folger came from New York,
in a coach with Mr. Pierson's married sister and a cousin.
They were going to take Elijah's boy to his brother's home
in Morristown, New Jersey, for burial in the family plot.
A hearse, with a sealed coffin ordered by Ben in view of
the warm weather, was on its way from the city.

The funeral at Sing Sing was called off. The remains of
Mr. Pierson left the kingdom with the relatives he had
shunned all his life; Mr. Folger traveled with them as far
as New York, the coach leading the way, the hearse following. In the coach, looking very small between the black-
clad ladies, sat a pale child.

As the cortège disappeared, Isabella thought of her last
glimpse of Elijah, before they had sealed the coffin—lying
still, eyes and mouth open as if once more to sing his song

of righteousness: "I mean to take the kingdom in the good old way . . ."

Much had happened since . . . The past year seemed a lifetime. Last summer Isabella had come into Paradise, into the true kingdom ruled by the Spirit of Truth, with plenty for all and neither sin nor sickness or death. There had been sickness and death now, and sin, and the Spirit of Truth had fallen. There was an exodus from Zion Hill, with Matthias taking the carriage to town and the Mother following by boat, with Isabella. Looking back at sundown, Isabella could imagine Cherubim in the Westchester hills, and a flaming sword.

The Fall

THE KINGDOM had been too busy with its own affairs to notice what went on around it. On the Fourth of July, the family had left Isabella at Zion Hill to await Mr. Pierson's return from Long Island; the others had spent the day in New York, and New York had spent it on its worst rampage in living memory—with homes plundered, shops gutted, people fleeing for their lives and barricading their doors with planks an inch thick. Around the Five Points, mobs had been burning and looting night and day.

Most of the victims were colored, though the violence began with the breaking up of a white Independence Day celebration, and the house it was held in, the first to be sacked, belonged to a leading white merchant whose brother was president of the new American Anti-Slavery Society. The cause of abolishing property rights in human beings throughout the land was unpopular, to put it mildly. "Abolitionist" was a dirty word not merely in the South. Out West, anti-slavery men were tarred and feathered; in sedate Boston, their leader Garrison was dragged through the streets by a rope. In New York, the press all but unanimously sided with the mobs of July 1834, urging strong action against the obnoxious "radicals." The reign of terror lasted a week, and the hatreds it kindled kept smoldering for a long time.

The news never reached Isabella. Elijah Pierson came back to Sing Sing obsessed with his failure to regain his reincarnated wife; the others' return was followed by "the sick devil," the "devil Death," and the expulsion from Eden. Third Street offered no respite. Almost on the heels of the family, Catherine Galloway arrived with the children and a tale of woe. They had simply been run off

Zion Hill, by deputies from White Plains, the county seat,
who were taking over for the heirs of the late Mr. Pierson.
All personal property on the place would be auctioned; not
even Mother's clothes could be removed from Father's
room, where the men had found them and snickered. The
Folgers rushed back to Sing Sing, to sort out what was
theirs, but the furniture which Isabella had brought into
the kingdom was forgotten in the excitement—she never
saw it again. A Cedar Street merchant named Burnham,
acting for the heirs, went through every drawer in the
Sing Sing house and pocketed all papers. After the sale he
came to New York with the lawyer for the estate, to demand the deeds to Pierson's real property, which Matthias
had in his possession.

Matthias seated himself in a rocking chair and com-
menced preaching. "There are three kinds of black-coats
and devils: the priests, the doctors, and the lawyers. The
priest's business is to make men willing to die; then the
doctor steps in to help them out of the world, whereupon
the lawyer helps himself to their estate . . . I shall test the
strength of the Gentile law," he told the gentlemen. After
they left, he said the Spirit had warned him not to give
God's property to the devil.

For some days Mr. Folger examined papers in the Third
Street house, and Isabella collected the Pierson linen for a
second sale. The search took her to a chest in an upstairs
room, and when she touched the top drawer, thinking there
might be sheets inside, it fell out and spilled many neatly
bundled papers. She could not read, so she put the bundles
back. Something else in the drawer intrigued her: a shav-
ing mirror. She had never seen one. Amazed at the way it
magnified her face, she took it down to show Catherine.

Catherine took it to the Mother, who promptly casti-
gated Isabella for forcing the drawer. Her excuse that it
had come out at a touch was brushed aside; Mrs. Folger
insisted that she must have broken the lock—by accident,
perhaps, because she was so strong.

Isabella shook her head. "It wasn't locked now."

Mrs. Folger lowered her voice. Ben, she said, would be
ruined if it got out that the drawer had been opened.

"Now if Mr. Burnham had come again, he'd have put in
the key and opened it and wouldn't ever have known that
it was opened . . ."

Mr. Burnham came again, about the deeds. Suit had
been filed for their recovery; unless Matthias gave them
up, the law would make him post bond for ten thousand
dollars. Matthias decided to give them up. The transaction
took time; Isabella, busy in the house, heard only scraps of
talk from the parlor. She heard Ben's excited query:
"Elijah exhumed? Why?" and Mr. Burnham's cool answer
that the body had been taken from the grave and the
stomach removed and examined by four learned physicians.
Agreeing that Mr. Pierson had not died from natural
causes, they had sent the stomach to a professor of chemistry in New York, to see whether a white powder in it
was poison.

A hush fell in the parlor. Puzzled, Isabella went on with
her work. Poison? Who should have poisoned Elijah?
Later, the Mother explained that it was a mistake; the
professor had found no poison.

City life complicated the kingdom's marital problems.
Ben, whether from new love or fear of gossip, kept his
wife from Matthias's bed. She would not share Ben's, and
with Catherine and five children in the house there was no
space for the old three-room arrangement. Mrs. Folger
slept with Isabella in the garret, and in these nights Isabella was shown exactly how Matthias kissed and made
love. She also heard of new plans: enough had been saved
from Ben's bankruptcy to let Father go west with Isabella,
leaving Mother with Benjamin, who would speculate and
soon make enough money for them to rejoin the kingdom.
After all, said Mrs. Folger, she was still carrying the holy
child and must be with Father when her time came.

Ben kept urging Matthias to leave. At last Matthias did,
without baggage, giving no destination and no time of return. All he would say was that his flight was like David's,
whose son Absalom warred upon his father. His departure
plunged Mother into gloom; before nightfall Ben was muttering, "I wish he was back." When Matthias reappeared
next morning—the trip had not taken him beyond Newark

—Ben solemnly reiterated his decision to give up Mother forever and to take Catherine instead, also forever.

Yet a few Sundays later, Catherine burst into the kitchen: "Lord God, Isabella, Father has catched Ben and Mother together! I never seen such a woman—she wants Father all night, and Ben all day!"

Isabella had never seen such a woman, either. That night, the lady crept into her bed: "I've come to you for protection," she panted, clinging. "Father's gone and left me alone in bed, and Pierson's devilish spirit haunts me so I don't know where to go."

"I wish to God he would appear to me," Isabella said serenely. "I'd ask him what he wants."

The door flew open—but it was only Matthias looking for Mother. "Have I had that devil in my bosom! Get up," he barked at Isabella. "Leave the harlot! God will curse you if you lie in bed with her!"

"Well, where can I go?" wailed Ann Folger. "I must go somewhere, and if you don't hold your hand over my eyes, I keep seeing Elijah's spirit. Where shall I go, Father?"

"Go to the pit from whence you came!" He slammed the door.

In the morning, Mrs. Folger went to Mr. Folger's room as soon as Catherine left it. Later, Ben again told Matthias to depart. "Ann prefers me," he taunted. "She never enjoyed you much, anyway."

"She told me differently." Quoting a candid comparison of their powers, Matthias challenged the lady to deny that it was hers. She blushed and sent Isabella to the kitchen.

On the next day, Thursday, September 19, there was no family breakfast; no one had an appetite. Ben came down to the kitchen where Matthias raged, Catherine moped, and Isabella cleaned up; he offered Matthias money to go, any amount, anything. "If you feel you have money that belongs to God you may give it to me," Matthias said at last. Ben got a moneybag and called Isabella and Catherine to witness that he was giving Matthias five hundred dollars in silver and gold; he also insisted on paying Isabella wages, though she wanted none. Her one year's services were worth twenty-five dollars, said Mr. Folger, and while counting out the sum, he solicitously inquired where, when, and how Isabella and Matthias would be going.

He had made no arrangements yet, said Matthias. His sons stood stock-still in a corner. Suddenly Ben remembered promising their mother to bring them back when he could no longer keep them; they would be in Albany Saturday, he said. He also advised Matthias to carry only the silver he had and let Isabella take the gold; it was safer to split up so large a sum, if they traveled together.

Isabella never touched the gold. She gave Matthias her twenty-five dollars, helped him pack, and found a cartman for his baggage. When they were alone, he gave her back the twenty-five to travel to Albany, and made her promise to meet his sons there Saturday and to explain to his wife. About himself he would leave word in a nearby store, he said on his way out of the last seat of the kingdom.

Isabella saw Catherine look after him. She had no high opinion of the widow Galloway, but they had worked together off and on from the time at Mr. Mills's, and in a way they were friends. Catherine took her aside now, to warn her against going with Matthias. "He'll be picked up," Catherine whispered.

Isabella shrugged it off. Why should Matthias be picked up? He had done nothing. Was Catherine going to stay at the house?

Catherine raised her bovine eyes; she would stay where Ben was.

"The curse of God is on that house," Isabella said, going away.

The storekeeper knew only that Matthias had left town without a forwarding address. She reached Albany by steamer Saturday morning and had no trouble finding Mrs. Matthews—and there, surprise! was Matthias. He had taken a fast boat and had already given his wife the five hundred, because, as he put it, "the kingdom must go into the wilderness for a time." The boys had not yet arrived.

They came that night, not with Mr. Folger, but with a man from a towboat he had sent them on. They looked uneasy, waiting for the sailor to take his leave. "Mother,"

Johnny blurted out then, "Mr. Folger has got the law after Father for stealing things."

Isabella was more stunned than Mrs. Matthews, who questioned her husband in tones suggesting that she not think the charge incredible; but he simply told the facts that Isabella knew. Folger had all but forced the money on him: "He was with me as Pharaoh with the children of Israel," said Matthias. "Anything to get rid of them, and then to pursue them." He made no plans to escape. Nor did he seem worried.

Isabella was worried. The law had helped a poor black woman to her child; it had freed Matthias after the trouble with Mr. Mills; the law, she felt, was God's arm on earth. Had it turned against Matthias? And against her? She had ceased believing in Matthias as the Spirit of Truth. He might be a false prophet or a madman. But he was no thief. Would God now brand him a thief? And her? God never talked to her any more. Matthias had banned prayers, and when she tried to pray again, there was no answer.

On Monday she took the boat down to New Platz Landing, to the place where she had spent most of her life, to the children she had not seen since the coming of the kingdom, to John Dumont. He looked aged; his hair was flecked with white. Her older daughters had grown handsome. She asked about Tom and heard he had died in the county poorhouse. Dumont had no advice to give for Matthias, being no expert on prophets, but if ever she needed a witness to her own character, she should come to him.

She stayed overnight, and when the next day's boat from Albany arrived there was excitement aboard: passengers and crew talked of nothing but the impostor who styled himself Matthias the Prophet and had just been seized at his wife's home. Back in Albany, Isabella heard that he had been taken to New York in handcuffs, along with two trunks and a carpetbag containing his wardrobe, the sword of Gideon, the measuring-rod for the New Jerusalem, and the key to the Pearly Gates. The measuring-rod was found to be inscribed, "Kutz, maker, 164 Water Street, New York," and the blade of Gideon's sword bore the U. S. Army device "E pluribus unum." To New York, too, went the five hundred dollars that Mrs. Matthews had turned over at once. One of the constables had wished he could let her keep the money to divorce the rogue—but maybe he'd hang, anyway. Had he done things he should hang for? the rogue's wife asked Isabella.

No, said Isabella. Had he been crooked before?

No, said Mrs. Matthews. Crackbrained, but not crooked. And she agreed to come along to New York, so they might help him together.

New York was seething. The newspapers were brimful of Matthias and his dupes. "No more horrifying tale is to be found in all the annals of fanaticism," said one. "This knavish lunatic must feel the implacable revenge of outraged society," said another. He had been arrested in Albany on no more than Mr. Folger's published offer of a reward, but the capture obliged Mr. Folger to make a deposition before a magistrate; once that got into print, few readers doubted that Matthias had not only stolen, defrauded, and blasphemed, but committed worse crimes. For, though the deposition did not claim to be sure, it strongly suggested that Matthias and Isabella had killed Mr. Pierson and tried to kill all the Folgers.

The papers felt sure. Pierson's death had been laid to poison by four doctors who had seen his stomach; that case was open and shut. The attempt on the Folgers had happened on the day when the impostor was finally forced to depart—when the Folger parents and children were reported to have become violently sick. "Mr. Folger did not suspect the cause of the sickness until after the villain had left the city, when he learned that the black woman, who did the cooking for the family, had also abstained from the use of any coffee upon that morning, and from other circumstances he became confirmed that the woman was bribed by Matthias to poison the family . . ."

Isabella could not read. No one told her what was in the papers. She had to sense it from the tone of those she knew, from the chill voices and set faces. Mrs. Matthews dissociated herself as soon as they reached New York; she was going to consult with friends, she said, and to call on Mr. and Mrs. Folger.

"The black woman," Isabella heard people whisper as she passed. She saw them point at her and shudder. Inwardly she shuddered too. She did not know what the mob had lately done to black people, nor how much venom it had left behind, but she saw reminders around the Five Points, and Negroes still cowed, staring at her like the whites, as at a murderess . . . This must be what the Albany constable had said Matthias might hang for—murder. But whose? The Folgers were alive. Only Elijah was dead. Did they think she had killed Elijah?

"The black woman," she heard the whispers in the street. "She's the black woman . . ."

One thing that never occurred to her was to run away. She knew she was innocent; she believed in the law; she felt in no danger. But lies were being told and believed, about things known only to those who told the lies, and to Matthias who was in prison, and to her. No one else knew the truth. "Don't lie," Mau-Mau had taught her, "and don't be scared."

She went to Morristown, New Jersey, to tell the truth to Mr. Pierson's family and friends. They received her, listened, and remained suspicious. Suspicion plagued the people who had known her in New York. They found it hard to believe what they heard; they did not think they could have been so greatly mistaken; they thought, too, that by now she would surely have been arrested if there were anything to the gossip. And yet, and yet—where there was so much smoke, must there not be some fire? For the first time Isabella heard a word that would confront her again and again: "white evidence." Was there white evidence, her friends asked, to back up her story? If not, who would take her word against that of the Folgers?

She traveled back to New Paltz. Dumont had promised to bear witness for her, if need be. Surely, his was "white evidence."

"This is to certify," he wrote on October 13, 1834, "that

Isabella, this coloured woman, lived with me since the year 1810, and that she has always been a good and faithful servant, and the eighteen years that she was with me, I always found her to be perfectly honest; at the time she came here she was between 12 and 14 years of age, and we have never heard anything disparaging against her since she left here, until I heard this; on the contrary, I have always heard her well spoken of by everyone that has employed her."

On the same date, Isaac Van Wagener gave her as good a character for her one year in his service as Dumont for his eighteen. So, the next day, did A. Bruyn Hasbrouck and John H. Rutzer of Kingston.

She got back to New York just in time for Matthias's arraignment in criminal court. The indictment was read, charging that "the said Robert Matthias . . . did falsely pretend that he was God the Father . . . and that the said Benjamin H. Folger, believing those representations, gave the said Matthias five hundred pieces of gold coin." Isabella waited for the poisoned coffee. It was not mentioned.

The defense counsel retained by Mrs. Matthews did not appear, and a young lawyer who volunteered to substitute said he knew only what he had read in the papers; he did not mean to excuse the impostor, but any man was entitled to a fair trial, so he would enter a plea of not guilty and ask for a postponement. Matthias was led back to jail, and his wife groaned about having to find other counsel.

Rumors swept the city—about a threat to deliver Matthias from jail, about the black woman's imminent arrest for murder, about the secrets of the kingdom. Newspaper reporters had been to Sing Sing and found it agog at the disclosures and bursting with tales. The villagers had known all along what a Gomorrha had risen in their midst. They had been the first to see through the new Mahomet with his harem of seven concubines, one for each day of the week and the black one for Sunday—the black witch, the sorceress from the West Indies who could brew poisons and cast spells . . .

The last family she had worked for before going to Zion Hill was the first to give her a reference in the city.

"I do state unequivocally," wrote Mr. Whiting of Canal Street, "that we never have had a servant that did all her work so faithfully, and one in whom we could place such implicit confidence. In fact, we did, and do still, believe her to be a woman of extraordinary moral purity."

She was taken to see a prospective lawyer for Matthias —one who claimed he was going to "act like a Christian" although he considered Matthias "a beast." Isabella suggested trying somebody else. How about the young man who had spoken up in court for a fair trail? His name was Western; she went to his office with a gentlemen friend of Matthias's wife. The lawyer heard her story and said the first step in his defense of Matthias would be to make Isabella an effective witness of unimpugnable credibility.

What did he propose to do, the friend asked—bleach her skin?

"I propose to establish her character," said Mr. Western. The way to do this was to have her prosecute Mr. Ben Folger for slander.

The notion shocked Isabella. Prosecute Ben Folger? She had not even dared to prosecute Solomon Gedney, who had sold her child.

"Are you afraid?" Western asked her. "You know the truth."

And the truth, she knew, shall make you free . . .

Her suit was filed quietly. It did not get into the papers which were still full of Matthias. Pictures, by an artist who had attended him daily in his cell, showed the prophet in his star-studded coat, a silver sun on his chest, the sword of Gideon by his side, a richly ornamented cocked hat on his head. The artist had wanted to draw his face only, but Matthias had insisted on a full-length portrait in his pontificals, according to a story much chuckled over on Canal Street.

Isabela was back with the Whitings, in full charge of their house and property, and their confidence seemed contagious. "Isabella Van Wagenen, a coloured woman," wrote Mrs. Gatfield of 73 Nassau Street, "lived in my family as a domestic above a year, 1829, and we never had a

servant that we could place such implicit confidence in."
Mr. Downing, 177 Duane Street, called her "worthy of
any trust," adding, "I believe her to be a strictly honest,
moral woman, and her equal I have not found since she
left me." And Daniel Smith, a grocer of 44 Hudson Street,
wrote, "I have known her many years, and she has ever
borne a character superior to her colour." Isabella could
not read these papers, but she faithfully collected them for
Mr. Western, who said they were good to have.

The only one of her former employers to refuse her a
reference was Mr. Latourette. "My church was yours; my
house was yours; your family was mine—and you deserted
them all," he said, shutting the door in Isabella's face.

On the other hand, soon after the filing of the slander
suit, Mr. Folger called on Mr. Whiting, contradicted all he
had been saying about Isabella, and offered to give her a
good reference of his own. She did not see him, and her
lawyer, told of the surprising turn, professed disinterest in
Mr. Folger. He had already heard by the courthouse grape-
vine that Folger was begging his own lawyer to have the
matter dropped; this silly hue and cry about fraud and
imposture would soon end. The real threat, in Western's
opinion, lay elsewhere.

On Friday, November 7, the Court of Sessions was
thronged long before half past eleven, when the Recorder
and two aldermen took their seats on the bench. The defendant sat in the grand jury box, calmly reading letters.
His wife was in court with two other ladies; the reporter
for the *Transcript* saw him chat with them "with apparent
hilarity." His attire was properly noted: "a brown-cloth
cloak lined with pink satin, on the collar of which were
two elegant silver and gold clasps, beautifully embossed
and ornamented; a green frock-coat lined with pink silk,
having gold stars on the right side and silver stars on the
left side of the bosom; a yellow damasked vest, and dark
brown pantaloons; he had worked ruffles to his wrists, and
wore round his waist a crimson-colored silk sash." The
newspaperman found him "quite a grotesque looking object."

Isabella sat back in the courtroom, waiting to tell the

truth and listening to talk of which she understood little. The district attorney voiced doubts about the indictment; though the absurdity of the claim must be apparent to all, he was at a loss to know how to present legal evidence that the prisoner was not God the Father. The grand jury had felt in duty bound to find a bill, but as the complainant's counsel had since urged a dismissal of the case, the district attorney, believing that further inquiry would only tend to make Mr. Folger and family more unhappy, asked the court to enter a *nolle prosequi*.

Mr. Western moved for a trial. In pleading not guilty, he said, he had waived any and all objections to the indictment. A trial on the issues was vital to his client, since the evidence would tend to extenuate a capital complaint apparently lodged against the defendant in a sister county.

The audience craned its necks, whispering, and the court decided to study the indictment over the weekend. On Monday Matthias appeared in a claret-colored frock coat, decorated with seven silver stars on each side, and green pantaloons. When he stood before the bar, the Recorder announced that a warrant had just been received from the county of Westchester, founded on an affidavit made by a Mrs. Drach, who on such and such day in August last had come from New York to Sing Sing . . .

Isabella heard the droning voice of the judge and remembered how the old woman had asked for Elijah, how she had been put off, and how frightened she had seemed on learning that he was dead.

". . . and she has the impression on her mind that Matthias has, by some means, been instrumental in his death. And having seen the certificate of four respectable physicians that some unwholesome or deadly substance was found in the stomach of Pierson, she founds her belief thereon that he has been poisoned, and therefore . . ."

Mr. Western argued briefly. Then the court gave its decision: the prisoner should be surrendered forthwith to Westchester County, there to be tried for murder. Matthias was led out. The courtroom emptied.

Isabella sat thunderstruck: murder? Had that ghost not been laid? Ben Folger had admitted that the charge was false—how could it be raised again? Straightaway she went to Mr. Western, to swear that Matthias was innocent.

The lawyer thought so, too. But the feeling against Matthias ran high; he was in great danger. Juries would want to convict. Judges might not dare acquit him. Still, things might have gone worse—at least, no charge had been brought against Isabella. She should prepare herself to go to Bedford, Westchester, in two weeks.

On November 25, she was waiting in the Bedford courthouse when Matthias was brought in, followed by a hooting crowd. The deputies joked about his latest prophecy: on the way from prison, a rock had fallen near the carriage, and Matthias, allowed to get out and look at it, had rammed his stick into the ground with an air of mystery and proclaimed, "By my order the judge will not attend!"

Everyone was still laughing when a bailiff came out to announce that the judge had been taken sick; the trial would be held later, at White Plains. Isabella walked out through a sudden silence.

Her first chance to tell her story came before the grand jury in White Plains. At first glance, it looked like the one in Kingston, which she had begged for her child without even knowing how to swear. But the mood here was different. The Westchester jurors were not so much after the truth as after Matthias. They joked about him, but they wanted him hung. Isabella told the truth, but they wanted to hear about the seven concubines. Had Matthias ever kissed her?

"Yes," she said.

"Now, didn't he kiss sweet?"

"No sweeter than Ben Folger," she replied, thinking of Ben's wedding to Mrs. Laisdell, when he had kissed everyone in sight.

The jurors excused her. The trial was put off once more, and before Christmas Mr. Whiting got a letter from Ben Folger that blamed Catherine Galloway for all the accusations against Isabella. It was Catherine, it seemed, who on that famous morning had said that the coffee was bad and had something white in it—and Catherine, Ben wrote, was "an infernal liar."

After Christmas, a shabby-looking Catherine came to the Whiting house with another sady story to tell. Mrs. Folger had been jealous of her ever since the breakup of the kingdom, more so as the "holy son's" birth drew near. Now the child was born—a daughter, delivered with as much sickness and pain as any child—and the mother no sooner could go to bed with Ben again than Catherine was fired. She had found no other job and was ill and in want.

Isabella shared what little money she had saved in her few months of working for wages again, and the greateful Catherine told her what had gone on in the family. The reward for Matthias had been offered because of the trouble over Mr. Pierson's money, but the Folgers had really not expected him to be taken. They had told the coffee-poisoning story only so people would not believe Isabella, and her slander suit had set off a big scare about having to go to court and be cross-examined. Also, both of them had gone to Mr. Latourette to confess their sins—though Mrs. Folger had laid most of hers to others. "You know how she can smooth it so," Catherine told Isabella.

The penitents had sworn their confessor to secrecy, but he had talked to his wife, and she to a friend, and the friend to Frances Folger, who had been Pierson's match spirit. By now, everyone was talking, said Catherine.

Isabella took her to Mr. Western, to whom she repeated her story, holding nothing back, not even her relations with Ben Folger. The lawyer, in turn, promised to do his best not to expose her, if she remained faithful and told nothing but the truth. This bargain was stuck in Isabella's absence, or she would have cautioned Western not to rely on Catherine—and indeed, right after the New Year of 1835 Catherine was back with the Folgers.

Mr. Folger wrote once more to Mr. Whiting. "The public is beginning to believe what Isabella says," he admitted ruefully. Could he not see her and talk things over? Isabella declined.

Catherine brought a message from Mrs. Folger: she was most anxious to see Isabella and to have her join them against Matthias.

Thou shalt not bear false witness . . . Isabella would join

nobody against Matthias and was not anxious to see Mrs. Folger.

Catherine sighed. "All this blessed winter she's been writing against you and Matthias. You'll see—she'll overcome you, and Matthias will be hung."

Isabella towered over the widow Galloway. "I've got the truth, and I'll crush them with the truth," she said vigorously.

They did not meet again until Catherine walked arm in arm with Mrs. Folger into the Court of Oyer and Terminer in White Plains. At long last, on Friday, April 17, 1835, Matthias was to be tried. The witnesses were there to damn him; a panel of jurors looked forward to sending him to the gallows; the audience waited eagerly for titillating disclosures and wriggled for "a peep at the old devil." On Thursday, after a last postponement for conferences in chambers, reporters had heard him say, "I feel that the Lord is my stay; like gold seven times refined will I come out of this fiery furnace. But as I have lost my dinner, I am weak and should like a bite of something . . ." He had recovered from that weakness. A man offering to shake his hand was rebuffed: "Know ye not that it is written, 'Touch not the prophet of the Lord'?"

When the court entered, Isabella was startled. The presiding judge was Mr. Ruggles—Mr. Hasbrouck's law partner from Kingston, who had so often seen her at the Hasbrouck home! He looked at her but gave no sign of recognition.

The clerk was calling the jury. Matthias rose. "I protest—"

Judge Ruggles told him to be quite; counsel would speak for hom.

Matthias raised his voice. "I speak concerning the grand jury—it is a secret institution, and I here proclaim all secret societies dissolved, for they are cursed of God!" He ignored another warning. "They have the curse of Almighty God upon them and are dissolved!"

Bailiffs stepped in to remove him. He went quietly, turning only in the door to cry at the top of his lungs, "Dissolved! Dissolved!"

He was carried out. Mr. Western suggested that there might be a question of sanity, and a jury was sworn in to try it. The defense called four witnesses—three New York doctors and a brother-in-law of Matthias, who had known him for twenty years and had observed the development of his wild notions. All considered him of unsound mind. The prosecution countered with five witnesses, none medically trained, but four from Sing Sing. One found the prisoner "sane and a rogue," another "perfectly sane, except on the subject of religion," a third "an impostor, but not insane," a fourth "sharp at a bargain and like anyone else when he chose to behave rationally." The last, a pastor from upstate, had seen Matthias show fear in moments of danger, which he regarded as strong evidence of sanity.

Two of the doctors were recalled to state that usually the insane are more fearful than the sane. Then the jury withdrew and returned in a matter of minutes, finding the prisoner sane.

Mr. Western looked unworried. Matthias was brought back, held responsible for his previous outburst, and sentenced to thirty days for contempt. His counsel had no objection. The parade of prosecution witnesses began. One told of seeing Matthias order Mr. Pierson about like a hired man; asked by Mr. Western if he had ever noticed signs of ill will between the two, he said he had not. The sexton of Morristown testified to the disinterment of Pierson's body, and two Morristown doctors to the examination of his stomach, gullet, and intestines, which had led them to believe that death had been unnatural and to suspect poison as the cause.

The doctors gave Mr. Western a chance to show his skill at cross-examination. He all but tied them in knots with sarcastic sallies that had the audience tittering; only the jury remained stone-faced and grim, especially when the second doctor stammered an admission that he would think one might have to find poison before convicting a man of its use. "Thank you," said the defense counsel— and the relieved witness no sooner left the stand than the district attorney admitted a deposition from the professor of chemistry in New York, that no poison had been detected. Mr. Western smiled.

"Mrs. Ann Folger," the clerk called into the tens eroom.

Calm and poised, the well-dressed figure walked to the stand and swore to tell the whole truth, nothing but the truth. "I had heard of Matthews and received his doctrines through Mr. Pierson, before I knew him personally . . ." The velvety voice slid back into the past, tracing the course of the kingdom—a kingdom as pure as Isabella had once imagined, though perhaps a little harshly run. "When displeased, he was exceedingly violent, of which his conduct in court today was but a faint specimen," the lady said with a forgiving smile.

Spectators began to cough—this was not what they had come for. Mrs. Folger took up Mr. Pierson's death. The coughing ceased.

"The blackberries had been prepared, we supposed, by Isabella, the colored woman . . ."

Isabella listened intently. What would come now? She knew, without supposing, that little Elizabeth Pierson had prepared the berries. But the subject was dropped. The witness explained why nothing had been done for Elijah: "We thought the evil spirit must be mortified. I did not think Mr. Pierson's life was in danger; I thought he would live forever. I believed that death was the last enemy to be destroyed, and that Matthews had come to destroy it."

Mr. Western politely declined to cross-examine Mrs. Folger. Catherine Galloway followed her on the stand, her testimony a brief, awkward repetition. Western had no questions for her, either. Instead, he moved the prisoner's discharge for lack of evidence.

Isabella gasped. So did the whole audience. All but the court's and prosecutor's faces registered surprise and shock; balefully the jurors eyed their elusive prey. What of the rumors, the orgies, the seven concubines? Would none of that come out? Isabella, too, felt disappointed and at the same time ashamed of her diappointment.

"It's a lie," Matthias shouted. "All a lie!"

He could not mean the fine points of law which prosecutor and defense counsel were now so amiably arguing. A big lie was being spun here to conceal the truth; the district attorney seemed to wink at Western as he said he had no further evidence to offer. Muttering was hard as the judge slammed his gavel. He told the jury that no evidence had been presented to connect Pierson's death with poison; if it had been hastened by culpable neglect on the prisoner's part, he would be guilty of fourth-degree manslaughter, but in the court's opinion this had not been proved, either. They would advise an acquittal, Judge Ruggles instructed the jury.

The jurors did not even leave the room. They merely nodded.

The muttering spread—but suddenly the district attorney was on his feet again, reading another charge: of assault, committed on the prisoner's daughter, Mrs. Charles Laisdell.

"This is another branch of my persecution," Matthais exclaimed.

Mr. Western read a note from Mrs. Laisdell, acknowledging satisfaction in this case and asking the court to dismiss it.

The prosecutor called for Mrs. Laisdell—and Isabella, who had believed her in Albany, was surprised to see the daughter of Matthias come into court with her husband, to confirm that she had nothing against her father. But Mr. Laisdell did not concur, so the trial proceeded. Both Laisdells testified, and again the truth remained unmentioned; the net result of it all was a bruise that Laisdell claimed to have seen on his wife's arm, weeks after the whipping.

The case went to the jury, and one could not really say that it withdrew to consider it; it filed out of the room and back in, with a verdict of guilty.

Judge Ruggles addressed the prisoner. If he had anything to say, he would be heard now—provided he behave himself, the judge said, reminding Matthias that he was already under a thirty-day sentence.

To some, Matthias rang subdued. "I have been confined near seven months now, and nothing has been made out against me until this last; it has been a great affliction, though I've been sustained under it, knowing that I was innocent. They misrepresented my doctrines—"

"We don't want to hear about them," said Judge Ruggles.

"I was going to say that as I felt innocent, I think this outcome most extraordinary and unjust, and if it's in the power of the court to make an offset in my favor in the latter case, I hope it will."

"The prisoner was not confined on account of the present offense," the judge pronounced with formality, "but the court have taken it into consideration in determining on the sentence. He stands convicted of an assault under peculiar circumstances; under other circumstances, if punished at all, it would be very lightly. But we find that in the very first interview with his daughter he told her that marriages were void, and endeavored to inculcate in her the same immoralities he had already inculcated upon the inmates of the house."

The judge knew! it flashed through Isabella's mind. But the subject was dropped as quickly as it had been mentioned.

"The chastisement was also inflicted without her deserving it, or allowing her to be heard. The court sentences the prisoner to be confined three months in the county jail, from the termination of his first sentence." Judge Ruggles turned to Matthias. "We now tell you that the times for practicing those foolish impositions are past. The court is satisfied that you are an impostor and do not believe your own doctrines. We advise you therefor, when you come out of jail, to shave off your beard, lay aside your peculiar dress, and go to work like an honest man."

Court, prosecutor, and defense counsel seemed equally content as Matthias was hustled out. He could only turn his bearded head and shout at the legal trinity, "It is not true!" before he vanished.

What is truth? shrugged the servants of justice.

A bewildered Isabella saw the doors of the law close behind the "Spirit of Truth." For the first time she felt pangs of doubt about the law. It seemed not always true, not always one with God. This time lies had prevailed and remained at large. She had hoped to "crush them with the truth," but the truth seemed as safely locked up as Matthias.

The newspapers reported the trial in full, with little comment on its conduct. Judge Ruggles was a man they did not care to tangle with. None mentioned the obvious: that court, prosecutor, and defense counsel had been aware of the facts and worked hand in glove to keep them out of the record—to avoid a scandal and to spare the reputations of some fools, to save a man's neck, perhaps, and yet to give the rogue about what he deserved, if not just why he deserved it. Above all, by keeping Isabella off the stand, they had averted a real threat of new mob violence. A colored woman testifying for Matthias might easily have set it off.

Court, prosecutor, and defense counsel might well feel that they had ennobled the law, making it serve not only justice, but charity, morality, and peace. The public, though deprived of a sensation, did not grumble for long. Life went on, and other things made news. The impostor sat behind bars, and the spicy rumors remained sewing circle gossip. Honest people could not claim to know the facts.

Life went on for Isabella. Her life was work—for the Whitings and such other New York families as would hire a domestic touched by scandal. She did not rue the passing of the kingdom or pity Matthias who had not been hung or crucified; she only wondered at times about the crime that had now cost him his freedom. He had left a bruise on his daughter's arm, had he? What of the scars that Neely had left on her back, and Fowler on her child's?

Peter was fourteen now, growing up to be a handsome, gay, quick-witted lad; whenever she saw him, which was not often, Isabella felt proud of his looks but anxious otherwise. He was no longer in navigation school. There he had fallen into fast company and succumbed to many temptations, and though the school, appreciating the regular tuition payments made for him by Miss Gear, had carried him on the rolls long after he had ceased attending classes, he had at last been expelled. However, this seemed to have shocked him as much as his mother, and he had sworn to her, by all that was holy, to better himself in the coachman's job she found him with the aid of friends.

In time her notoriety wore off. People ceased staring, and she ceased listening when they discussed the kingdom. She shrugged off questions about her law suit; Mr. Western had made no mention of it any more. When her employers and their friends began to pass some little books around, glancing at her as they thumbed the pages, she paid no attention. Books were for those who could read.

Eventually she understood that this one was about her.

It was the book Catherine had mentioned, the one Mrs. Folger had been writing all last winter, against Isabella and Matthias. The Mother's story was not the half of it; the bulk was the work of Col. William L. Stone, the well-known editor of the *Commercial Advertiser*. Stone's paper, by the way, had been the most vociferous in fanning last year's mob violence. His book was published by the respected house of Harper and Brothers in Cliff Street, under the title *Matthias and His Impostures*.

People read things from the book to Isabella, asking if they were true, until she knew it as well as if she had read it. It was like Mrs. Folger's testimony in court: Mr. Stone, too, skirted the facts while spreading one big falsehood. He, too, left out whatever did not fit in with a chaste, pure kingdom. He, too, accused Matthias only of imposture, dropping the charges that had put him on trial—yet hinting that no one in the Folgers' place could have doubted his guilt. No wrongdoing at all was laid to Isabella, yet she was termed "the most wicked of the wicked" and always referred to as "the colored woman," never by name. Her white friends found this most offensive.

Isabella did not. The colored woman? It seemed the one word of truth in that book.

One day, word came that a gentleman wished to see her. She was given his card to show if she needed directions; it said:

G. VALE, 84 ROOSEVELT STREET,
Teacher of the Arts depending on Mathematics,
and Editor of the Citizen of the World.

Isabella never bothered about her employers' occupations. Having found G. Vale, she asked what he wanted
done.

"I want the truth," Mr. Vale said.

She had never known such a man. Isabella had experience with old and young, rich and poor, good and bad,
wise and silly; with masters, mistresses, lawyers, judges,
preachers and their flocks, whores and their customers,
people interested in her labor or in her faith, in money or
the law or the lusts of the flesh or the rewards of heaven.
She had never met one who wanted nothing but the truth.

To Gilbert Vale, truth was not revealed but established.
It was tracked down, questioned, checked and re-checked
until logic would bear it out; what did not result from
this elaborate process did not interest Vale. He taught "the
arts depending on mathematics"—that is to say, on logical-
ly demonstrable truth—and for years he had been pursuing
truth as a journalist with various publications. On the *Sunday Reporter* he had first heard of Matthias, after the Mills
raid which the rest of the press hailed with glee. Mr. Vale,
though considering the man a fanatic or impostor, had
been obliged at the time to blame the police; paid to preserve the peace, they had broken it at the behest of private
parties. "It is precisely this spirit," he had written then,
"which is ruining the country and blasting its fair fame in
the eyes of Europe."

The *Citizen of the World*, which he now edited, was a
small paper fired with his passion for truth, justice, and
humanity. A review copy of Mr. Stone's book had come to
his desk and shocked him with its veiled appeal to the race
hatred that had led to last summer's outrages. A detail
that was false on its face prompted him to make per-
functory inquiries, which disclosed other falsehoods, but
the truth remained a mystery until he heard that Isabella
wished to tell all.

His informant said that different members of his family

had heard her story at different times, and in parts, without discrepancy; her words had the ring of truth.

Vale sent for her at once.

"She has African features," he recorded his first impression, "and no apparent mixture of blood; she is not exactly bad looking, but there is nothing prepossessing or very observant or intelligent in her looks; yet throughout we find her reflecting . . ."

He asked first about her life before she had known Pierson, Matthias, or Folger. Isabella thrust a sheaf of papers into his hand: in the belief that he wished to hire a servant, she had brought her references all the way back to Dumont, who had owned her as a slave. But it was not Vale's way to take such statements at face value. He called on the signers, starting with those in New York, to learn if they stood by their views before he had another talk with Isabella.

What had made her believe in Matthias at first sight?

"I felt as if God had sent him to set up the kingdom," she said simply.

Might the Folgers not have felt the same way?

"I've had my own thoughts about that," Isabella answered. It was all she would say then, so Vale took another tack. He was going to read her letter to Mr. Pierson, about some dream and some cousin—a letter which Mr. Stone made quite a mystery of, hinting at a "Mrs. M." who had allegedly prepared the way for Matthias.

He read two lines, and Isabella broke in to tell him what was in the rest. Mr. Pierson had read this letter to her; Ann Folger had written it; "Mrs. M." must be her Cousin Frances, whom she had kept throwing at Elijah. Isabella tried to imitate the "Mother's" manner of speaking, her graceful gestures and gentle inflections, but gave up in disgust. "Oh, I can't do it," she said. Vale was amused.

He noted, "This colored female is, like Mrs. Folger, not exactly what she seems." Her appearance was deceptive, her simplicity misleading. "She has shrewd, common sense, energetic manners, and apparently despises artifice." Her private thoughts were strikingly astute, but she was tight-lipped: "If circumstances did not prompt her to tell all she knows, it would be difficult to get at it."

After a few talks with her, Vale felt as sure of her honesty as of the trouble he would have in convincing others. "White evidence" was needed for a story that he already believed in his heart. Mr. Western furnished some corroboration, chiefly based on his interviews with Catherine Galloway; the slander suit against the Folgers was also still pending and would some day be tried. When? There was no telling. Were "the law's delays" not proverbial?

The investigator called on James Latourette, the only one of Isabella's employers to refuse her a reference, and was surprised to find the fur merchant still under her spell. He came to the conclusion that jealousy of Pierson or Matthias must have cost her a character from this man, who now praised her morals, veracity, industry, and intelligence—though not, Vale observed, "when it would have been of use to her."

Mr. Vale went traveling. At Oyster Bay, Long Island, still in the same pleasant cottage where Elijah Pierson had come to propose, he found Frances Folger and her hospitable, social, jovial husband. The lady seemed "equally hospitable, of easy manners and pleasing appearance, literary and pious, but without prudery or fanaticism, at least in her appearance and conversation." She denied holding the views of Stone's "Mrs. M." She had not even shaken hands with Pierson after the first signs of his delusion. Her cousin's role had not occurred to her till Vale suggested it; then she said, "Now I see!"

In New Jersey, Vale asked the Pierson family to shed some light on the finances of the kingdom. He saw the inventor, Hunt, the realty agent employed by Pierson and Folger, the former owner of the Third Street house. He went to Westchester to talk to trial witnesses and jurors; one said frankly he had "wished to find Matthias guilty." An innkeeper of Sing Sing thought that no illiterate like Isabella could tell so consistent and detailed a story unless it was true.

Vale traveled to Albany, saw Mrs. Matthews, and found her, too, writing a book about her wayward husband. They exchanged notes; he heard details about the Laisdell epi-

sode which even Isabella had not known. Mr. Vale felt
amply repaid for his three-hundred-mile journey.

He called his book:

FANATICISM;
Its Source and Influence,

illustrated by the simple narrative of Isabella, in the case
of Matthias, Mr. and Mrs. B. Folger, Mr. Pierson, Mr.
Mills, Catherine, Isabella, &c &c. A reply to W.L. Stone
—with descriptive portraits of all the parties, while at
Sing-Sing and at Third Street—containing the whole truth
—and nothing but the truth. By G. Vale.

Vale's style was not as plain and to the point as Isabella's. Only the truth told in his book was hers, bolstered
at very turn by additional "white evidence." Vale did not
venture to say that all men were equal, or equally credible;
he did say that in the singular case of a poor, unlettered
colored woman being more honest than some rich, well-
educated whites, it was singularly wrong to slander her.

Mr. W.L. Stone of the Commercial has written a book,
and like charity has covered a multitude of sins: for this we
might give him credit for benevolence, if not honesty, were
it not that he meanly attempts to transfer the sins of those
he has taken under his protection to others, not guilty of
crimes, but unfortunately poor, uneducated, and
colored . . .

Isabella's references were reprinted in full, the originals
available for inspection at Vale's office. He had opened
Stone's book in good faith, had read of the colored woman
as "the MOST WICKED of the wicked," and had waited
in vain for proof, finding instead only suppositions "as un-
scientific as they were ungenerous." For instance, Stone
kept hinting that Pierson had been poisoned—that for all
the insufficiency of evidence his death was probably due to
poison in the blackberries he had consumed a day before
the outbreak of his fatal illness. But "the next afternoon,"
Vale pointed out,

as related in the book, p. 134, he was hay making, and
picking and *eating* blackberries; that is, just previous to
his fit and to his purging and puking, in which he brought
up blackberries (the mysterious circumstance!). What
blackberries, we ask? Those supposed to be poisoned,
which had lain in his stomach without inconvenience 24
hours? Or those he had so recently been picking and eating, as stated by W.L. Stone himself?

"How Col. W. L. Stone of the Commercial could thus
commit himself, we cannot conceive," Mr. Vale wrote.
For his part, he took care not to commit himself to more
than he could prove without Isabella. He chose to publish
now only part of the truth, reserving the kingdom's decline
and fall, the money matters, and Pierson's illness and death
for a sequel. To back up Part I, he had Isabella's references for her background, the word of Mrs. Matthews for
the prophet's and for the Laisdell episode, Frances Folger's word for Pierson's background, and Catherine Galloway's statements to Western for the early days of Zion
Hill and the relations between Matthias and "Mother."

Part I went no farther. It gave facts, gave sources, and
missed no chance to confute Col. Stone and to refer in
terms of withering scorn to him and his informants, notably
Ben Folger, who had once said in a public statement, "I have
no objection that Matthias, or any one else, should state
the whole truth in reference to any transaction of mine."

"We have endeavored, and shall endeavor, to oblige
him," Vale replied.

His little volume was rushed into print, and a copy forwarded to every paper in New York. Several reviewed it;
none found errors of fact. Nor did the bitingly abusive
language draw a reaction from the Folgers or Stone—
and yet it was soon clear that Vale had failed in his purpose. There were too many like the bookseller who chided
him for ever so faintly suggesting a not altogether spiritual
interest of Mrs. Folger in Matthias. "We will accept other
facts, for which you have given other evidence, but you've
rested this point on the credit of a colored woman. We can
never believe it," said the bookseller.

Vale had the whole truth, but he might never have published it if Isabella's word had not suddenly become as good as gold—or as good, at least, as U. S. currency.

One day, Mr. Western sent word that her slander suit was coming up. She followed the summons, unaware of the entirely novel furor she was causing. The courtroom was thronged, though the case had not been mentioned in the press, had not been argued in the streets like the Matthias trail. No mob was inflamed by an ordinary civil law suit. Nor, indeed, did it interest the Negro population of New York, or the abolitionists who cared so passionately whether or not human beings of color might be bought and sold and bred and whipped and worked like animals. To them, it seemed a matter of small concern whether or not Negroes might be slandered.

But it was a matter that touched the foundations, if not the emotions, of a white society. The difference showed in the courtroom. In Kingston, struggling to recover her child, Isabella had drawn smiles of pity; vindictive glares had focused on her at the Matthias hearings; now black-robed lawyers and well-dressed substantial citizens stared at her as at a freak of nature. After all, the bankrupt Folger was still a white businessman. If his wife had acted scandalously, she was still a lady of breeding. Were they really on trial for damage to the reputation of a recent chattel? Was the world upside down?

Mr. Western called witnesses. The Whitings and others testified to Mr. Folger's attempts to withdraw the slander. The Folgers did not take the stand; their counsel merely argued points of law and remarked for the jury's benefit how absurd it was to imagine that the plaintiff in this case could be defamed.

The jury found for the former slave, awarding her damages in the amount of 125 dollars. The audience gasped.

To Isabella, the verdict rang with an odd echo. "Sold—to John Neely, for a hundred dollars . . ." Her good name was now worth more than all of her had once fetched on the auction block. "I felt so tall within as if the power of a nation was in me," she said later.

Sojourner in the Land

AT LAST, Vale was able to tell all. The seal of truthfulness had been placed on his main source, by judicial process; a white jury had found Mr. Stone's informants "capable of falsehood of a most atrocious nature." The editor of the *Citizen of the World* no longer needed to worry about being sued himself. Part Two of his book appeared with details of the Folgers' love life, with all the dialogues that Isabella remembered from the disintegration of the kingdom, with caustic footnotes to Mr. Stone's "tolerably minute" account, and with strong hints that money might have been the root of the evil. If anyone knew what had happened to the Pierson fortune, must it not be Ben Folger, the undischarged bankrupt who was now living comfortably with his wife in a fine house at Sing Sing, while Matthias, penniless after his jail term, had gone west to preach, Isabella was "getting an honest living by work," and Mr. Stone was "repenting his late publication"?

The truth was out. Its circulation remained limited; not many readers had the fortitude to wade through Vale's jumbled prose. Besides, the Folgers were not such colorful culprits as Matthias or Isabella. Their amorous and financial peccadilloes could not hold a candle to a "new Mahomet" or a poison-mongering witch. The black woman was not a sorceress from the West Indies? She was an ordinary servant from upstate, well spoken of by her employers? Interest in her dwindled.

She did not long feel "so tall within." The money award paid her lawyer, but the surplus was soon needed for her son. Peter had not reformed in his coachman's job. In fact, one day his mother heard shocking news: as "Peter Williams"—a name he had lately assumed—he was in jail

on a charge of selling his livery and other things belonging
to his master.

Isabella found the employer kindly rather than vindictive; if restitution were made, he would not prosecute. She
drew her money out of the bank, handed it over, and went
to the Tombs to get her son. The fifteen-year-old who
emerged from the gloomy prison was as tall as she, with
his old ready smile, eager to bare his soul with perfect
frankness. He had so tried to be good! He never meant to
do wrong, and yet he kept finding himself in trouble. "I
don't know how it is," he said contritely.

The mother blamed only herself, though nobody else
did. What better care could a woman in her circumstances
give her son? Her only opportunity to make a living was
as a domestic, sleeping in; she could maintain no home,
could not keep the boy with her, and even among whites it
was usual in those days for the children of the poor to be
"bound out" for labor. But Isabella did not think in terms
of parental neglect. She thought of her own dreadful error,
of her own pursuit of a way that was not God's, and she
felt that this beam in her own eye would not permit her
to cast out the mote in Peter's. When he promised to be
faithful in another job, she gladly took his word and
looked for the rest of her family.

Her brother and sister no longer lived at the place of
their reunion. At the African Zion Church they were believed to have left town. The congregation faced Isabella
uneasily, wondering how to treat one of its own who had
been one of the whites, in a manner of speaking—written
up in white newspapers as one of a white kingdom, called
a murderess by whites, yet remaining their friend. What
sort of woman was this? Some brethren and sisters knew
her from upstate as a troublemaking "white folks' nigger"
whose quarrels about her boy had made things hard for
everybody else. She was not likely to arouse much sympathy among her kind.

Once again she went upstate, to see her daughters. The
visit lightened her heart. Diana had grown to womanhood;
in a few years she would be twenty-five, legally free of Dumont's service. Twelve-year-old Elizabeth looked rather

like the slave girl Dumont had bought, and Sophia, the baby who had left his house on her mother's arm, was ten, like the girl once owned by Neely or Schryver. All of them were well, and so was Dumont. Only Isaac Van Wagener, the man who had given Bell his name but would not be her master, lay in a fresh grave in the old Dutch churchyard of Esopus.

Isabella was hardly back in the city when a new call for help came from Peter. He had been arrested for another theft. Again she ransomed him, reasoned with him, heard vows of improvement; then the process began afresh. Besides her steady work, she took up scouring and polishing brass doorknobs around the neighborhood, toiling day and night to have money on hand at all times, if needed for Peter. In winter the Whitings used to give her a half dollar after each snowfall, to hire a poor man to clear their steps and sidewalks; she now got up early and shoveled the snow herself. The man protested when she sent him away: he was poor, he said, and needed the pay for his family. "I'm poor, too; I need it for mine," she replied, her mind on Peter.

The Latourettes, whose son Samuel was in the China trade, knew of other young scamps who had been straightened out at sea. Any strong lad, white or colored, could ship on a man-of-war, they told Isabella. She urged Peter to go to sea: had he not always been talking of ships and sailors? He promised to go, but it never seemed to work out, for a variety of reasons. Isabella feared he was simply too fond of his boon companions and of the girls at the Five Points.

His next arrest was for pandering. He sent for her, as usual, but she did not respond. The messenger painted the Tombs in the most awful colors; she remained firm. She would let the law take its course. The law had given him to her, and she would bow to it if it took him away again, though it be for months or years.

It took only days. He came back—freed, he said, by a man named Peter Williams who had chanced to hear of the bad luck of a boy using the same name. Peter said the man wished to see her; she understood he was a barber. She came along.

Mr. Williams was an elderly, very light colored man who received mother and son at his home, without coat or collar, but talking as refinedly as Mr. Vale. He liked to aid delinquents without family or friends, shipping them out of harm's way on whaling vessels; the *Zone,* out of Nantucket and bound for a voyage round the Horn, would be just the ship for Peter. "Your son stood in great need of sympathy and assistance," said Mr. Williams. "I could not think he had such a mother here, although he told me he had."

Isabella poured out her tale, mingling prayers of thanks with admissions of fear lest her son deceive his benefactor and miss the boat. Even after his tearful farewell she could not stop worrying whether he would keep his promise. She worked restlessly and slept fitfully until Mr. Williams himself came to the Whitings' house, one rainy day, to tell her that Peter had sailed.

She breathed easier. "I pray the Lord he'll be good," she said and went on working. The kindly "barber" went downtown, and on Vesey Street, shedding his muffler so that his clergyman's bands appeared, the Reverend Peter Williams, first Episcopal minister of his race and famed intercessor for colored boys in trouble, entered his church with the feeling of another job well done.

Isabella remained suspicious. The *Zone* had left port for the South Seas in August, 1839, yet throughout the fall, whenever she passed by one of Peter's old haunts, she would be afraid of seeing him step out of some alleyway. Months passed before her anxiety changed to that common to seafarers' kin in those days, when ever so often a ship would sail and be never heard of again.

The seasons made the round; another winter came and went without word of Peter. In the spring a letter for Isabella arrived in Canal Street. The Whitings read it to her; it was dated October 17, 1840.

My dear and beloved Mother,

I take this opportunity to write to you and inform you

that I am well, and in hopes for to find you the same. I am
got on board the same unlucky ship Zone, of Nantucket.
I am sorry for to say that I have been punished once
severely, by shoving my head in the fire for other folks.
We have had bad luck, but in hopes to have better. . . .

He asked about his sisters and other people. He seemed
to have forgotten one thing only: that his mother had not
learned to write.

I wish you would write me an answer as soon as possible.
I am your only son that is so far from home in the wide
briny ocean. I have seen more of the world than ever I
expected, and if I ever should return home safe, I will tell
you all my troubles and hardships. Mother, I hope you do
not forget me, your dear and only son. I should like to
[know] how Sophia and Betsey and Hannah come on. I
hope you will forgive me for all that I have done.

Your son, Peter Van Wagener.

Dazed, Isabella took in the words that had traveled so
far. She had seen whalers like the Zone in the harbor, the
deck hands climbing masts and yards high above the slim
hulls. Peter was doing that now, in all kinds of weather,
but she could not visualize him at his work. He was good
now, she assured herself. It had to be God's doing.

More and more often she came to think of God again,
who had been so close to her once. How sure she had been
as slave girl and as a young freedwoman—getting her child
back, testifying at meetings, obeying every command that
Elijah and others read to her from the Bible! "Beware of
avarice," they had read, and she had turned over her savings
"He that loveth son or daughter more than me is not
worthy of me," they had read, and she had forgotten her
children to follow Matthias, the self-styled Spirit of Truth,
until the falseness of his spirit was borne in upon her and
made her feel unworthy of lifting up her face to God
again. Not even the confessor of her "private thoughts"
got anywhere on that subject. "What her fixed religious
opinions now are," Vale had to admit, "we do not know."

A void took God's place in Isabella, after the kingdom fell. At first she tried vainly to fill it with work; then conscience stirred in it, and for a time the emptiness was covered up by the effort to reform Peter. That, too, was now a thing of the past. Her boy was gone. Her daughters had lives of their own. Two had husbands; only the oldest remained at Dumont's. The inner stirrings were rare and hard to make out. God did not speak, and Isabella dared not.

Around her—all over the country, in fact—a deep concern with salvation was spreading. People spoke of a religious revival, and Isabella's employers took her to the fields where the revivalists waged their thunderous battle for souls. The scenes were familiar, but she had learned that such preaching could lead astray. Warily she listened to William Miller, the Vermont Baptist who came to New York predicting the end of the world in 1843. Thousands shivered in anticipation, but Isabella glanced at the hall, at walls covered with symbolic pictures that she could not understand, and decided that Miller's faith was not for her. The void remained.

Another letter came, dated March 22, 1841. Peter expected to be "home in twenty-two months or thereabouts." He had seen Samuel Latourette, whom he spelled "Laterett," and wrote about another young ne'er-do-well who had gone to sea with him:

There has happened very bad news to tell you, that Peter Jackson is dead. He died within two days sail of Otaheite, one of the Society Islands. The Peter Jackson that used to live at Laterett's; he died on board the ship Zone, of Nantucket, Captain Hiller, in the latitude 15 53, and longitude 148 30 W. . . .

Isabella's friends searched the globe for the Society Islands but did not find Otaheite—also called Tahiti—only some nameless dots in the middle of the Pacific. The boy had gone far indeed. But the distance meant little to the woman who could think only of the other boy she had seen at the Latourette house, who would never return.

What had made them go wrong? Lust and sloth, she thought, the idle pleasures of the city. To be good in the city, one must keep too busy for sin. Isabella worked early and late, doing a lot for a little, turning her hand to anything that promised pay. And yet, somehow she could not manage to lay by a dollar.

A printed poem fell out of Peter's next letter. He must have cut it out of some book or magazine.

"Get me to my home that's in the far distant West,
To the scenes of my childhood that I like the best;
Where the tall cedars grow and the bright waters flow,
Where my parents will greet me, white man, let me go!"

The poem dealt with an Indian boy; Peter had never seen the West. He had written on September 19, 1841—"out from home twenty-three months. . . . Dear Mother," her friends read to Isabella,

this is the fifth letter that I have wrote to you, and have received no answer, and it makes me very uneasy. So pray write as quick as you can. . . . Tell me if you have been up home since I left or not. I want to know what sort of a time is at home . . .

What, wondered the friends, was "up home" to the boy who had been sold down South at six and from his eighth year on had lived in New York? Isabella understood him. When he thought of home now, halfway around the globe, her son was not thinking of the city that had led him into temptation.

"We had very bad luck when we first came out," he wrote, "but since we have had very good; so I am in hopes to do well yet; but if I don't do well, you need not expect me home these five years."

Why, wondered the mother, should he not do well? This time, others understood him. Youngsters who went to sea did not like to return with empty pockets. Sea pay was low, not worth saving, but whalemen hoped for a bounty from the catch, and there was always treasure to be gulled or bullied out of the natives, and gold to be won or lifted from unwary strangers in port. A lad with his wits about him had all sorts of ways to strike it rich at sea. This, evidently, was what Peter meant by "doing well" and gave himself five years to accomplish.

"He's good now," Isabella repeated incredulously. But then she thought of her own life in recent years, of her own scramble for money regardless of those who might need it more. The first thing she had learned in freedom was that henceforth no one would be responsible for her, that she must fend for herself, not merely earn her own living but hoard enough to keep her in her old age. So she had piled pennies upon pennies in the bank, until Elijah said she would be cared for by the kingdom. On the strength of his promise she had turned over her savings, and now they were gone—gone, Mr. Vale thought, into the pockets of the Folgers, along with Elijah's fortune—and she was scrambling once more, robbing others, not of the fruits of their labor but of their chance at it, taking their living away from people as poor as the snow-cleaner who needed a half dollar for his family.

"Yes," she said, "the rich rob the poor, and the poor rob each other." Everyone did it to everyone else. It was the way of the city. The city would not let you live by the Golden Rule; it would not permit you to love your neighbor. Many here would talk about the Lord, but none would follow Him.

Isabella waited for her son. His last letter said he was "in hopes to be home in fifteen months," and she heard this meant next December or January. As the months went by, she made inquiries. There were men on the water front who knew that Captain Hiller had brought his ship back to Nantucket in November, with three thousand tons of sperm. The voyage had been most successful, and the Zone had already put out to sea on her next.

No one knew of a crewman named Peter Van Wagener.

One night Isabella heard the voice again.

In the morning she put a change of clothes into a pillow-case, some food into a basket, and two York shillings—

twenty-five cents worth of Spanish coin, then still in use in the country—into her purse. Thus equipped, she went to tell Mrs. Whiting that the Lord had given her a new name. "I'm Sojourner, and I'm going away."

The lady was startled. Going away? Where?

"Going east," she said.

What was that supposed to mean?

"The Lord told me to leave the city and go east," said the woman who wished to be called Sojourner. "I'll find friends there."

It sounded crazy to her mistress. Where would she find friends?

"How should I know till I get there?" was the answer.

Mrs. Whiting called her husband. "Why, Bell's crazy!"

Thoughtfully, Pierce Whiting eyed the colored woman. "I guess not," he said and urged her to have breakfast first.

She would not hear of it. "I must be on my Father's business," she said and left with her bundle, heading east on Canal Street.

It was on the first of June, 1843, that Isabella walked out of the house that had sheltered her so long. The street ended at the East River, and she took the boat to Brooklyn, paying the fare out of her two York shillings, and continued eastward into Long Island. Mindful of Lot's wife, she did not look back till the city was out of sight. A pall of smoke hugged the western horizon, the only sign that tens of thousands were milling about there, grasping, battling, cheating each other in the pursuit of Mammon. Isabella thanked God for removing her from Sodom and walked on, guided by the rising sun.

After four or five miles she felt thirsty. A Quaker woman who was drawing water from a well gave her a drink and asked her name. "Sojourner," she answered.

The Quakeress looked puzzled. "Where does thee get such a name as that?"

"The Lord gave it to me," said Sojourner, " 'cause I'm to travel up and down the land."

The other was not satisfied. Had she had no name before?

"Yes. Bell."

"Bell what?"

"Well, whatever my master's name was."

"And now thee says thy name is Sojourner. Sojourner what?"

"Why," said Sojourner, crestfallen, "I hadn't thought of that." She felt wretched and sad of a sudden, trudging on alone—and just after her new name had made her so happy. "God," she called, "give me a name with a handle to it!"

"Sojourner Truth," her guiding voice answered.

She cried for joy. "Thank you, God—that's a good name!" Why had she not thought of it? It was clear as the light of day. "You are my master, and your name is Truth . . ."

Cheerfully she lugged her bundle over the sandy roads. Just as she began to wonder where to spend the night, a man accosted her. Was she looking for work?

She told him that she was not on the road for that reason, but if anyone wanted, she would gladly work a few days. When it turned out that a sick member of his family needed care, she came at once and no sooner entered the house than the patient felt better. The family called her a God-send and urged her to stay, but she declined. Offered money as a token of thanks, she took twenty-five cents worth and continued on her eastward journey.

One night, far out on the Island, she had trouble finding shelter. Turned down at door after door, she was familiarly approached by two Indians; by the dim light of stars and new moon they mistook the dark figure for one of their tribe. Sojourner set them right and asked to be shown to an inn.

The nearest was some miles off, the Indians told her. Then they inquired if she was alone.

"No," she said, "not exactly," and left in a hurry, trotting until she came to a building that served the region as an inn, a courthouse, and a jail. There she was told she could stay if she would not mind being locked in a cell until sunrise.

Locked in? The thought was unbearable. She walked away. Hearing a woman's voice from a shed by the roadside, she called into the darkness: could someone tell her a place where she might spend the night?

Eyes peered out at her. "Not less'n you come with us," the woman answered. A man hiccuped agreement; then the couple talked about "a ball" where they wished to drop in before going home.

Though caring little for balls, Sojourner had no choice. The ballroom was bare, low-ceilinged, jammed with revelers, reeking of whisky. She ducked into a corner while her hosts joined in the merriment. The woman soon lay snoring, fast asleep in the din.

Sojourner remembered such scenes from her missionary days around the Five Points. But there all men and most of the women were white, and the women sinned because it was their trade. She had also seen colored carousals, on the Dutch holidays in Ulster, when the slaves were plied with liquor and given free rein for a day, to keep them docile otherwise. But these people weren't slaves; freedom had come here on the same day as in Ulster. Was this what they did with it?

Eventually the drunken woman's husband shook her awake and they staggered off, trailed by Sojourner who kept looking forward to their hospitality until she saw the hovel they called home. Few slaves had been housed so wretchedly. The couple had no bed, just a pallet on the floor, which they offered to Sojourner. She declined. Squatting against a wall, she waited for dawn. Sunrise found her on her way.

At Huntington, a village nestling at the head of a deep harbor between wooded hills, the streets looked festive. Flags flew from every pole—it was the Fourth of July. Char-à-bancs and coaches carried neatly dressed and decorously mannered passengers through the village, for the citizenry, in that year of 1843, had resolved to celebrate the national holiday soberly, in keeping with the principles of temperance, at a convention in neighboring Cold Springs.

Sojourner, the past night's experience fresh in her mind, ardently joined in this laudable public endeavor. She walked the few miles to Cold Springs, a village where whaling ships like Peter's lay moored in the harbor, and when she saw a procession form before a church, she followed it to a grove and offered her services to those in charge of the meeting. Unaware of her preaching talents, they had her help with the dinner that was served on the grounds. The local ladies got new recipes as well as diary material from the dusky visitor who "whipped up dishes à la New York."

She spent three weeks at Cold Springs but refused to tarry longer. From Huntington she embarked for Connecticut, landed at Bridgeport, and kept "going east." She accepted free lodging, if offered; otherwise she worked—never taking more than two or three shillings wages "to pay tribute to Caesar," as she put it. In New Haven she went to many meetings and met many people who impressed her as "true friends of Jesus." She did not distinguish between sects as long as they let her speak, and she began to express thoughts she had been keeping to herself. One clergyman in Connecticut squirmed through a long session at which she bore strong witness against a paid ministry.

Her listeners begged her to discuss religion with their friends elsewhere. They gave her letters of introduction to take from town to town; she carried them in her hand, so passers-by had but to take a look to show her to her destination. The letter from Bristol to Hartford was returned to her by the recipient, and she would still have it thirty years later. "Sister Dean," wrote the brother in Bristol,

I send you this living messenger, as I believe her to be one that God loves. Ethiopia is stretching forth her hands unto God. You can see by this sister that God does, by his Spirit alone, teach his own children things to come. Please receive her, and she will tell you some new things. Let her tell her story without interruption, give close attention, and you will see that she has the leaven of truth, and that God helps her to see where but few can. She cannot read or write, but the law is in her heart. Send her to brother Rice's, brother Clapp's, and where she can do most good.

From your brother in looking for the speedy coming of Christ,

                              Henry L. Bradley.

A tall, gaunt, awkward woman with a sunbonnet on graying hair, lugging her bundle, traveling on and on, talking to all she met—this was Sojourner Truth. "Chillun," she would say whenever she found men gathered, "chillun, I talks to God, and God talks to me." On her lips, they said, the word God had a sound all its own.

She no longer needed to shout at the sky, as in her childhood. Her very thoughts were heard now, and she alone heard the answers. Day and night, awake and asleep, she resumed her dialogue with God. "Testifying of the hope that's in me," she called her mission.

She called people "chillun" but had left no word for her own as she walked out of the city, taking leave from no one but the Whitings. She felt if others, children or friends, had known her purpose, they would have raised such an ado as to spoil everything. To follow the call in peace, she must go in secret. When word reached her, somewhere in Connecticut, that her daughters had shed many tears at her loss, racking their brains where she could have gone and why, and whether she might have become a maniac or committed suicide, she shook her head in wonder. Was she not in God's hand? "Let the dead bury their dead," the Lord had told those who overdid filial piety. To put their minds at rest, though, she had someone in the town of Berlin write a letter to them in her name. She waited until an answer came; it told her that she would soon be a grandmother, and that Elizabeth had been allowed to leave Mr. Dumont's household at nineteen. Sojourner and her daughters never lost touch again.

She was in Berlin for a camp meeting of the Adventists. Most of the brothers and sisters in Hartford and vicinity had wanted to know if she believed in the "Second Coming," or "Second Advent." She did not know what they were talking about until they mentioned William Miller, who had calculated from the prophets that the Saviour's return in the flesh was imminent. Then she recalled Miller's meeting

which she had attended in New York, with the mysterious
pictures, and her own first glimpse of Matthias, when the
picture from Elijah Pierson's Bible seemed to have come
alive, misleading her as well as Elijah. She did not want to
fall for another "Second Advent."

"Oh, don't you believe the Lord is coming?" asked the
eager ones.

"I believe the Lord is as near as can be, and not be it,"
answered Sojourner.

Her praying, talking, and singing convinced the Adventists—or Millerites, as they were called—that even as an
unbeliever she deserved a hearing. Having won their confidence, she set out to calm these people whose delusion
was so much like hers had been. At Berlin, finding a wildly
excited group on the grounds, she mounted a stump and
cried, "Hear! Hear!"

They flocked around, ready to listen to anything.

"Children," she asked, "why do you make such a to-do?
Aren't you commanded to watch and pray? You're neither
watching nor praying." In motherly tones she bade them
go back to the tents without noise or tumult, for the Lord
would not come to a scene of such confusion. "In the state
you're in, the Lord might come and walk all through the
camp and go away again, and you'd never know it!"

At her next camp meeting, at Windsor Locks, the agita-
tion surpassed that of Berlin. Sojourner felt it was mainly
due to the preachers who seemed to be doing their utmost
to excite the crowd, overwrought as it was. For a while
she listened quietly to their haranguing; then the preachers
gaped as a dark figure rose before them, and by the time
they found their tongues again it was too late.

"Here you're talking about being changed in the twink-
ling of an eye. If the Lord should come, he'd change you to
nothing—'cause there's nothing to you! You sound like
you're expecting to go to some parlor away up somewhere,
and when the wicked have been burnt, you're coming back
to walk in triumph over their ashes—that's to be your New
Jerusalem!"

Smoldering in her own mind were the embers of the
New Jerusalem of Sing Sing.

"Now I can't see anything very nice in that, coming back to such a mess as that'll be, a world covered with the ashes of the wicked! Besides—if the Lord comes and burns, as you say he will, I'm not going away. I'm going to stay here and stand the fire, like Shadrach, Meshach, and Abednego!" From her full height she looked down on the ministers. "And Jesus will walk with me through the fire and keep me from harm. Do you tell me God's children can't stand fire?"

The crowd drank in her every word. Many burst into tears. They flocked about Sojourner, to thank her and to invite her to come and see them in their homes. After the close of the Windsor meeting she wandered on as before, "lecturing some and working some," receiving her wants as from the Lord, and telling people what she had often thought: "What a beautiful world this would be if we'd see things right side up! Now we see everything topsy-turvy, and all is confusion."

She wandered up the Connecticut valley to Cabotville— a factory town that later took the name of Chicopee— and visited with friends she had made at Windsor. There were now hundreds of places where she could expect a glad welcome. And she was beginning to tire, to hope for some quiet spot where a way-worn traveler might rest, at least for a season; but she had not found one yet. The thought of living long in a family not her own—half guest, half servant—displeased her. Unconciously she grew homesick for something like Zion Hill, where all worked for the Lord and were provided for as one family.

She left Cabotville for Enfield, across and down the Connecticut a way, where a group known as the "Shakers" had a village. She had met some at camp meetings and found them God-fearing; now she had a mind to look in on them and see whether they had an opening for her. But she never reached the Shaker village. Passing through Springfield, she knocked on a door to ask for bread, was invited in, and found the house belonging to Adventists who had seen her at Windsor. The man at once proposed a meeting and rounded up some friends and neighbors, whom Sojourner readily addressed. They responded so well that she stayed till far into the winter, working wherever her work was needed, and talking where work was not needed.

She listened, too, and heard much that was new and strange. The Springfield Adventists believed not only in the Second Coming but in free speech. Their meetings were not restricted to those in accord, and they acquainted Sojourner with a welter of humanitarian movements that had grown out of, or along with, the religious revival. To her, it was new and startling to see God worshipped less by faith than by works. She heard talk of "practical Christianity" and about words ending in "ism," which meant nothing to her. Others got learning from books, but Sojourner had to see in order to grasp.

Her new friends talked of settlements where people lived by the Gospel. Several such had lately come into existence, here in Massachusetts in particular. In these places there were neither rich nor poor; all worked for the community and were provided for by the community. They were in the world, yet out of it, the Adventists told Sojourner.

You were free in these islands of peace, but not all on your own. They had names such as "Hopedale," or "Fruitlands"—names that rang sweet with the promise of Canaan and stirred a longing in Sojourner to rest there after her wanderings. Her only fear was of being led astray again as in the kingdom, of losing her newly regained communication with God.

Her friends made light of the danger. They had circulars from a particular community they had in mind for her; listed foremost among its aims was "to promote . . . the practical responsibility of every individual to God alone in all his pursuits." There would be no interference with a person's faith. The circular lashed out at formal religion as "a device for tyrannizing over the minds of men by arraying them into hostile sects, by substituting audible and visible forms for the inward power of truth and goodness, and by rendering the superstitious fear and irresponsible dictation of men paramount to the veneration and authority that belong only to God . . ."

This was difficult language, but Sojourner got the drift. What was condemned here looked much like a portrait of

Matthias with his arrogant rule, his pomp, his curses. What would be pursued instead was "truth, justice, humanity, the equality of rights and rank for all. . . . The family relation, between husband and wife and between parents and children," said the circular, "is sacred and permanent, the root and fountain of all human excellence and happiness." Sojourner understood: there would be no "match spirits."

Where was this blessed spot?

At Northampton, her friends said, just a few hours from Springfield. They would take her there and introduce her themselves.

At first sight she was far from enchanted.

The trip had been pleasant—from Springfield along the banks of the broad river, flowing here between mountains that reminded Sojourner of her native Hudson Valley, to Northampton, a town of magnificent old trees, and on into farm land blanketed with snow and bounded by wooded hills. Then the coach turned off the highway toward a pine grove by a brook, and next to the grove rose the biggest, ugliest of brick buildings, unsightlier than any Sojourner had seen in New York, except for the Tombs prison.

It was the site of the Northampton Association of Education and Industry, the "factory boarding house" where its members lived and engaged in silk manufacture that was their principal business.

The place crawled with people. On the ground floor, whirling machines were operated by a score of women and girls; a back room, fitted up with bunks, served as dormitory for single men. One end of the second floor contained the kitchen and a long dining hall; next came the community store and a room where more women and girls skeined and packed the silk; at the other end several families lived behind crude partitions. The whole top floor was partitioned into a number of cubicles for families and single "boarders."

There was hardly more privacy than had prevailed in Ulster County slave quarters. Small children were under foot everywhere. In the dining room a lady taught a class of older children; others were at work in the "cocoonery," spreading mulberry leaves for the silkworms. The basement contained the community laundry—and there, though the membership was visibly outgrowing the available space, one noticed a definite shortage of hands to do the washing.

Sojourner felt a deep, encompassing disappointment. Why had she been told to leave the city? Surely not because it happened to reek with vice and greed, but because it had to—because people could not help turning greedy and vicious if they were jam-packed, made to work with machines rather than with the hands God gave them, made to live and labor as in stone prisons, more like ants than like creatures in God's image. And here, between grove and meadow and brook, in this lovely, wide, rolling country, you found all city horrors carefully transplanted by the Northampton Association of Education and Industry.

"I'll stay for one night," Sojourner promised herself.

Dinner was served to some seventy or eighty at the common table. It was plain, wholesome, and of sufficient variety to accommodate vegetarians of every degree. The manifold approaches represented in the community were explained to another visitor, a clergyman who wished to know what the members were doing on Sundays. "We rest," he was told, "sometimes do pressing work, read, think, hold meetings, and try to behave as well as we do Mondays."

"Have you no minister?"

"No. We all speak if we wish, men and women. You can come and say what you please; we will treat you well, but we may not agree with you and may ask questions."

"How do you get along when you don't agree?"

The answer came from a very young man, and Sojourner would never forget it. "Suppose you rap a stick on a fence rail," he told the minister. "When you rap on one spot, it sounds monotonous; when you move your stick, it varies. Don't you like the variations? You're not foolish enough to quarrel with the stick or the rail because the sounds differ. You like to hear them and make up your mind which is best."

The young man's name was Giles Stebbins; he called himself a Unitarian, a prospective clergyman, here to study with the community's leaders, ripe scholars and fine men.

Names swamped Sojourner on her first evening in Northampton, unknown names and puzzling backgrounds. The
majestic figure with flowing gray beard was David Mack, a
friend of Nathaniel Hawthorne's and a teacher in Cambridge
before coming here to direct educational activities. The
younger man with the chin-beard was Samuel Hill, a businessman who had quit the Baptist Church after an anti-
slavery lecture by Wendell Phillips was broken up by a mob
led by a brother deacon. The beardless, thin-faced, sharp-
nosed man at the head of the table was George Benson,
the community's guiding spirit, an abolitionist born and
bred whose father had already fought the abomination,
whose sister Helen was William Lloyd Garrison's wife,
whose interests ranged from religious reform and pacifism
to work for the *Liberator*, with Garrison and Samuel May.
An intriguing, perplexing new world opened before the
woman who had walked out of slavery at God's bidding
and still saw people in terms of their relations with God.

A gray-haired Negro was led into the dining hall by a
white child. Sojourner saw he was blind. Some members
affectionately called him "Doc." Others said, "Dr. Ruggles,"
and astounded Sojourner by their respectful treatment of
the disabled old colored man.

Strict rules governed the factory boardinghouse. All
boarders were "required to retire to their sleeping apart-
ments" at nine-thirty, and to turn lights out at ten. But
Sojourner wondered about the men and women around her
till far into the night.

"Well," she resolved at last, "if these can live here, I
can." In the morning she announced her decision to stay.
She could take over the washing, she said matter-of-factly.

It was long remembered in Northampton that the chief
silk dyer helped Sojourner Truth wring out clothes on Mondays, when work in his department was dull. No one pulled
rank at the community. The educational director's wife
scrubbed floors between classes, and a Harvard professor of
Oriental languages saw his wife and daughters "engaged in
occupations which once, while residing in India, were performed for them by eighteen servants."

Washing was included in the half dollar a week charged

for board and lodging, but the rules cautiously added: "Should any boarder appear at the end of the year to have occasioned disproportionate expense on this account he will be debited with the excess." The only recorded complaint came from George Benson, who questioned Sojourner about a farm worker's shirt that had not been washed clean. She said if the man would change his shirts more often, several of them would be easier to wash than one that had lasted a week. "Ah," smiled Mr. Benson, "he's so stuck up now, I don't know what I'd do with him with more than one clean shirt a week."

Sojourner quickly became a prized feature of the community. At the evening assemblies in the dining room she proved that she could spellbind a sophisticated audience. Her singing provoked literary allusions; her quaint sayings were told and retold. One day a boy fell off the mill dam into a deep pool a few feet wide, the one spot where he could escape serious injury. "If the devil made him fall, the Lord had fixed a place for him to light in," was Sojourner's oft-quoted comment.

The children loved her. They had a cherished privilege: to read to her from the Bible. Adults tried to teach Sojourner to read and write—in vain; the letters blurred before her eyes. And she was willing to depend on friends for her correspondence, but not for the Word of God. She had found that grown men and women, asked to read something over, invariably sought to explain what it meant, and explaining Scripture had been the curse of the kingdom. Only children would read you a verse as often as you pleased, without comment, until it was clear in your mind. "That's what I want," said Sojourner, "not what someone else thinks it means."

The community's children not only read better than others: their entire education was unusual. Instead of memorizing lessons, they studied botany wherever flowers grew, climbed Mt. Tom in search of minerals, and learned geography building miniature islands, capes, and isthmuses on the banks of the Mill River. The factory yard was their schoolroom, and when the cold forced them indoors, the girls would sew, braid straw, and knit silk purses while the teacher read them Shakespeare, Scott, or Prescott's *History of the Conquest of Mexico*. Boys and girls worked in the mulberry orchard and in the cocoonery and went in for swimming and athletics.

At the sight of old "Doc" they would run, elbows bent, and ask the blind colored man to feel their muscles. His touch was deemed infallible; people said that by feeling a body he could locate any disease. The community was enthusiastic about his plan to set up a "water cure" for the hydropathic treatments he had learned to give after the restoration of his own health by this modern therapeutic method.

What had ailed him in the first place was another story, which Sojourner had yet to hear.

Each new day brought strange new people. At one meeting a young guest said a prayer which she did not understand—it was the Lord's Prayer, recited in Latin by a student for the Catholic priesthood. Another visitor was introduced as a Mormon. When he quoted from the teachings of his prophet, Joseph Smith, Sojourner felt she was hearing Matthias again, and her reaction got into the next week's *Hampshire Gazette*: "We understand that one of Joe Smith's disciples held forth at the 'Community' in this town last Sabbath. After he had stated his belief, a member of the Community got up and exposed the fallacy of the Mormon system." The local paper refrained from identifying the member as a colored woman.

She never quite appreciated the tolerance of the community, the open-minded welcome it would extend to a diversity of creeds. "Three thirds of the people are wrong," she once said in speaking.

The audience tittered. "That takes them all, Sojourner," someone pointed out.

She looked around, unflustered. "I'm sorry; I had hoped there were a few left."

Soon after her arrival, a camp meeting was held at Northampton. The community member who ran the daily express to the town brought her to the meeting ground; it was near sundown. The tents were set up, the preachers waiting, but the crowd seemed out of hand. There was much hooting and yelling and scurrying about and brandishing of torches. It turned out that a band of young hoodlums, ejected for disturbing the morning service, had come back with their friends, a hundred or more of whom were now threatening to set the tents afire while those in charge of the meeting wrung their hands and sent for the constable.

Fear gripped Sojourner. As the only Negro in the place, would she not be the first target? The community's wagon was gone. If she tried to run across the fields, the whole mob would be after her. She ducked into a tent full of quaking believers.

There, huddled behind a trunk, she reasoned with herself. "Shall I hide from the devil—me, a servant of the living God? Have I not faith enough to go out and quell that mob, when it is written, 'One shall chase a thousand, and put ten thousand to flight'? I know there aren't a thousand here." And suddenly, as she put it later, she felt as if she had three hearts, not one.

She got up and asked the others to join her in trying to calm the crowd. They called her insane. Night had fallen, and a full moon shone as she walked out, alone. On a small mound some hundred paces away, she started singing at the top of her powerful voice.

> "It was early in the morning,
> It was early in the morning,
> Just at the break of day—
> When He rose . . ."

The mob surged forward. Hemmed in by torch-carrying, club-armed young roughnecks, she broke off.

"Why do you come about me with sticks? I'm doing no harm."

"We aren't a-going to hurt you, old woman; we want to hear you sing! Sing to us . . . Talk to us . . . Pray, old woman . . ."

She shook her head. "You stand and smoke so near me, I can't sing or talk."

"Stand back!" The ring widened. Silence fell upon the

moonlit field. Then the deep voice resumed where it had been interrupted.

> "When He rose—when He rose—when He rose—
>   And went to heaven on a cloud."

"Louder!" cried the ones in back, and the leaders beckoned for her to use a near-by wagon as a pulpit.

"They'll push it over," she protested.

"No, they won't! If anyone dares hurt you, we'll knock him down, damn him!"

Courteously, they helped her mount the wagon. She looked at the sea of curious faces. "Well . . . It is written that there'll be a separation, and the sheep shall be separated from the goats. The other preachers have the sheep, and I have the goats. I've got a few sheep among my goats, too —but they're very ragged!"

Laughter swept the crowd. Then she told them of God— and again the word, on her lips, had a sound all its own. She talked for an hour, and when she finally wearied and paused, a clamor rose: "More! Sing! Sing more!"

She motioned to them to be still. "Children, I've talked and sung, and now I've something to ask of you—will you do it?"

"Yes," they cried.

"If I sing another hymn for you, will you go away then and leave us in peace?"

A few said yes, feebly.

"I want to hear from you all," she said. "If I sing you another, you'll go away and leave us this night in peace?"

"Yes," called a good many.

"I want you *all* to answer."

"Yes," the mob thundered in unison.

"Amen! It is sealed," Sojourner responded in her deepest, most solemn voice and intoned the hymn that had been Elijah Pierson's and had ushered him out of the kingdom.

> "I bless the Lord I've got my seal, today and today,
>   To slay Goliath in the field, today and today . . ."

Singing, she heard some make ready to enforce their promise.

> "The good old way is the righteous way;
> I mean to take the kingdom in the good old way!"

The voice echoed from the hills and faded away in the moonlight. As it faded, the converted goats ran off the field behind their bellwethers as fast as their legs would carry them, swarming like bees past the stand where the other preachers still stood smitten with fear. Once Sojourner was out of sight, some of the hoodlums slowed down and proposed returning, but the bellwethers drove them on. "No— we've all promised to leave; we must all go—and you'll none of you go back!"

None did.

The Community

DOC RUGGLES, hearing that Sojourner Truth came from New York, inquired what her name had been in the city. Isabella, she said. The unseeing eyes fixed upon her. *The* Isabella?

Suddenly the past appeared. She did not deny it, nor did the blind man say more, though it seemed to puzzle him that any Negro from New York should fail to know his name.

David Ruggles was a New Yorker himself, born free, never a slave, yet the first Negro to edit an anti-slavery newspaper and a veteran of the informal, illegal, nation-wide conspiracy of compassion known as the Underground Railroad. For years, virtually no escaped slave had touched New York without Ruggles's knowledge. As secretary of the New York Vigilance Committee he had been the station master of the secret railroad's main Eastern yard—a keeper of names that must not be known, a director of traffic that must not be noticed, the liaison between the men and women who helped runaways up from the South and those who hid them in the New York area and those who sped them on, to safety in parts of New England where the conscience of local authorities forbade the enforcement of the Federal Fugitive Slave Act, or across the Canadian border, the magic line where human beings ceased to be any man's property under the law.

The conspirators were black and white, rich and poor, Methodists, Quakers, atheists; they were articulate fighters for the abolition of slavery or simple souls trying only to help other simple souls in trouble. Their only bond was the conviction that—law or no law—people with dark skins were not stray cattle or dogs returnable to their owners. Ruggles worked with them all. He also worked as a "conductor" of fugitives, and it was on such a trip that he lost his eyesight in a fight with slave catchers hunting a couple he shepherded. His charges got away, and David Ruggles, so the story went, weighed his two eyes against two lives in freedom and said, "The gain is ours."

Enfeebled and destitute, he was brought from New York to Northampton, where the members of the community cared for him and had him well again, if sightless, by the time Sojourner Truth arrived.

Sojourner had heard of abolitionism and the Underground Railroad. Everyone had. But the words, casually dropped now and then by her friends in New York or the brothers and sisters in Jesus she met on her travels, had not felt real. God had been the great reality in her life; truth had been a reality, and so had slavery, her own and Peter's. Now she saw a blind old colored man led around by white children, a free man whose eyes had brought freedom for others. Old Doc Ruggles lent a sudden stark reality to what had been mere words.

The Northampton community was deeply concerned with these words and all they stood for. They came up constantly in the talk in the factory dining room, or outdoors, in the pine grove to which the evening sessions were moved in early spring, whenever weather permitted. No real disagreement on the issues existed in the community, but they were debated and illuminated anyway, from all sides, from the moral, social, economic, and religious angle. One day Sojourner heard the young divinity student, Giles Stebbins, speak gravely and oracularly of St. Paul and Onesimus, recalling that the Apostle had sent the slave back to his master. A fierce argument ensued; no doubt, Stebbins had meant to provoke it. Some went so far as to call for denouncing the Bible along with the Constitution of the United States.

The answer seemed to come from above. "And behold the tears of such as were oppressed, and they had no comforter; and on the side of their oppressors there was power; but they had no comforter. Ecclesiastes Four, one, two . . ."

The voice came not from the sky, but from the shade of

the great pine on the hilltop. A man stood backed against its trunk.

"But the great cause of human liberty is in the hands of the One of whom is said, 'He shall not fail nor be discouraged, till he have set judgment in the earth.' "

The speaker was lean-faced, angular, with a wide mouth and eyes that burned through steel-rimmed glasses, and his voice was like a flame searing the conscience of men. "My brother-in-law Garrison," George Benson said in presenting Sojourner to the leader of American abolitionists.

William Lloyd Garrison had come to visit the Bensons in one of the frame cottages scattered around the red brick factory building. He spent several weeks at the community, for whose existence he was partly responsible—it was he who had given Benson the idea. "What say you to a little social community among ourselves?" he had asked him, some years back; "I think we must be pretty bad folks if we cannot live together amicably within gunshot of each other." When Benson and Hill had founded the Northampton Association, Garrison stayed out, but he visited often and brought his friends to lecture. "You may make your arrangements for at least one 'incendiary' meeting in your place," he would write to Benson.

To Sojourner Truth he was a revelation. No self-centered prophet like Matthias, no painstaking searcher for truth like Mr. Vale, but an apostle of the Word, whose Word was freedom. To Garrison, men's right to be free was absolute: "To invade it is to usurp the prerogative of Jehovah." Any admission of property rights in men was "a glaring violation of all the precepts and injunctions of the Gospel." Laws enforcing such rights were "therefor, before God, utterly null and void," and the Constitution, as a compact between free and slave States, was "the most bloody and heaven-daring arrangement ever made by men for the continuance and protection of the most atrocious villainy ever exhibited on earth."

About the Constitution, Sojourner only knew it was a kind of law. But the law was a tool of God; what flouted God's Word could not be truly the law. She was spared the dilemma that tried so many souls: what was here the issue—which one might honestly compromise—and what the principle, which one might not? Most men felt that preservation of the Union was the principle, with slavery the issue of the day. But some regarded liberty as one of the inalienable rights with which all men had been endowed by their Creator; they held it to be self-evident that governments were instituted to secure these rights, not as ends in themselves. These people felt one could renounce the Union, but not the freedom of man.

For Sojourner the problem did not arise. Her principle was God; she had no need to know, or to care, about issues.

Sufficient to convince her was Mr. Garrison's manner of fighting evil. "I can love even the white folks," Sojourner had cried upon discovering Jesus, and the sight of Matthias between the constables had made her fear a crucifixion. Now she heard of Garrison's ordeal when a mob had dragged him by a halter through the streets of Boston; she heard what he thought of the American Revolution, of the difference between his followers and the men of 1776:

Their principles led them to wage war against their oppressors; ours lead us to reject, and to entreat the oppressed to reject, the use of all carnal weapons for delivery from bondage. Their measures were physical resistance—the marshalling in arms—the hostile array—the mortal encounter. Ours shall be such only as the opposition of moral purity to moral corruption—the destruction of error by the potency of truth—the overthrow of prejudice by the power of love—and the abolition of slavery by the spirit of repentance.

"Resist not evil . . ." Mr. Garrison rested his case upon the Sermon on the Mount. Whenever Sojourner heard him speak under the big pine, dimly outlined against the shadowy hills, an echo would ring in herself: "Whatsoever ye would that men should do unto you, do ye even so unto them."

From one meeting in the Northampton town hall, a community member brought back a memento. It was a rock—

hurled not at Garrison, but at a speaker he had introduced with the question, "Is this a chattel or a man?" By way of reply the rock came out of the audience, missing by inches. The target, a man in his early twenties, powerfully built, with light bronze skin and a long, coarse, black lion's mane over a broad forehead and oddly aquiline nose, did not flinch. Nor did Garrison. "Frederick Douglass will now tell us his story," he closed as if nothing had happened.

The young mulatto spoke fluently, without the plantation accent of most escapees. He told of his birth in Maryland— he knew not when, to a mother unseen from his infancy, though she had served on a neighboring estate. He told of the early kindness of his master's family, of being taught the rudiments of reading and Scripture, of coming to "think too much" and being sent to a professional slave trainer named Covey, for "breaking in." Covey had a method: work and whippings, day and night, with Sundays spent "in a sort of beastlike stupor." Even so, Fred had kept thinking, always the same thought: "I have a value. Mr. Covey is supposed to break me, not to kill me. Dead, I'd be worthless. I have a value . . ."

One day he had wrested the whip from Covey, daring him to use his gun. To save his reputation, the slave-breaker had been obliged to yield and hush up the affair. "When a slave can't be flogged, he is more than half free," said Frederick Douglass.

"Is this a chattel or a man?" Garrison asked again.

"A man, a man," the echo came back a hundredfold.

Sojourner Truth saw Douglass brought in triumph to the community. The other members hailed the "swarthy Ajax," the "black hero" of the cause, the first man of color to serve the Massachusetts Anti-Slavery Society as a full-time agent; Sojourner saw a young man about Peter's age, almost white-looking in carriage and in the cut of his face. Was he his master's son, as so many others? She watched a touching scene when he met David Ruggles—it was this piteous, half-comical figure who in his seeing days had befriended the runaway slave, lodged him safely in New York, made him choose a new name, reunited him with the free woman from Baltimore who became his wife, and sent him on to New England, where slave catchers did not operate and where the abolition movement had discovered him. It was difficult now to imagine the Ruggles of old, but Frederick Douglass remembered.

Sojourner heard him converse with the community leaders and guests—with the Garrisons and the Bensons, with Seth Hunt, the lawyer from Northampton, and James Boyl, the white-bearded Bostonian doctor in Continental knee-breeches and tricorne, with young Stebbins and with Lydia Maria Child, the lady novelist whose lawyer husband was trying to make beet sugar on a near-by farm. Apart from the community, Mrs. Child disliked the region. "I have never been so discouraged about abolition as since we came into this ironbound valley of the Connecticut," she complained to all who would listen.

Douglass moved among them with self-assured modesty, as an equal save for age and formal education. His actual education astounded those who knew that it was wholly self-acquired in a few years of spending every free minute with books, quenching his thirst for knowledge. He knew a great deal more than he told his audiences. "Give us the facts; we will take care of the philosophy," his mentors advised him, and on the platform Frederick Douglass complied. In private conversation he did not hesitate to air his own views of such things as government, social reform, and anti-slavery strategy and tactics—views not always in accord with those of Garrison and other leaders of the movement.

He rather ignored Sojourner. She struck him, he explained years later, as "a genunie specimen of the uncultured Negro," and this first meeting he was far more interested in the white intellectuals of the Northampton community. He engaged them in lively discussions of their venture, inspected their plant, examined their soil, admired their dedication and the "Spartan-like simplicity" of their regime. His general reaction appeared faintly skeptical to Sojourner, if not to the rest, while his economic theories impressed the rest, if not Sojourner.

On Sunday, at the usual outdoor meeting in the grove, he quoted the strongest anti-slavery lecture he had ever heard—a lecture given to his mistress in Baltimore, after her husband caught her teaching little Fred to read the Bible. "Learning would spoil the best nigger in the world," the lady had been cautioned. "If you teach that nigger how to read the Bible, there'll be no keeping him; he'll want to know how to write, and this done, he'll be running away with himself. It would forever unfit him to be a slave.

The lesson had sunk in. Finishing in secret what the mistress had to leave undone, the boy had taught himself to read and write; then the youth, in line with his master's prediction, had escaped by means of a forged "free paper." Now the man continued to read at every opportunity, to broaden the knowledge that had freed him and would be of help in freeing others. "Knowledge," he said, "is the direct pathway from slavery to freedom. Once you know how to read the Bible, you will be forever unfit to remain a slave."

For a moment no one spoke. A motherly voice broke the silence, ringing through the pine grove. "You read," said Sojourner, "but God himself talks to me."

One side of the community remained a mystery to Sojourner. Its way of life seemed to her most natural for children of God; it would have amazed her to hear that it came not so much from Jesus as from learned men here and abroad, from French economists, American transcendentalists, and others. She never grasped details of the effort around her to "promote the further progress of society"—the unique schizophrenia, for instance, which distinguished the Northampton Association from other American Utopias of its day. This personality split, into a "stock company" and an "industrial association," was to keep capital and labor "separate, yet bound together," and both rosters were supposed to be identical. In fact, some devoted, hardworking members had joined without money, held no stock, and were simply credited with their labor and debited for their sustenance.

Sojourner was one of these but never felt the distinction. Since all were sharing in the necessary work, including the most disagreeable—"Productive labor," said Article I of the By-laws, "is the duty of every human being"—there seemed to be no such differences as she had seen on her travels, when shelter was always easier to find in a small house than in a large one, and easiest with those who had but a leaky roof over their heads. She attributed this to the sympathy that like will feel for like and noted it also in reactions to God. "I never could find that the rich had any religion," she would say. "If I had been rich and accomplished, I could have—for the rich could always find religion among the rich, and I could find it among the poor." At Northampton she could not tell one from the other.

Her attitude impressed a lady visitor: "She was working with a hearty good will, saying she would not be induced to take regular wages, believing that now Providence had provided her with a never-failing fount, from which her every want might be perpetually supplied through her mortal life.

What Sojourner believed she had found was another kingdom, one without the falsehood and sinfulness of Matthias. "In this she had calculated too fast," concluded the lady.

They met again, at George Benson's. By then the community's site—called Broughton Meadows at the time of Sojourner's arrival—had been renamed Bensonville, the Benson family had exchanged its plain cottage between a ravine and fields of mulberry trees for a home befitting the head of a large private enterprise, and the Northampton Association was in limbo. The blow had fallen suddenly, with notice that subsistence allowances to members would cease as of November 1, 1846. Benson's cotton company had bought the plant; Mr. Hill would carry on the silk production on his own; others were set to go into other lines of business, and those who prospered would look after the stranded. Benson took the "colored brethren" under his wing, gave them jobs at the cotton mill, and helped "Doc" Ruggles to set up his water cure. He also undertook to care for Sojourner Truth.

Once again she found herself amid the wreckage of a dream. Sage and sagacious reasons for the failure echoed about town and told her nothing. She knew how she had failed: she had strayed again, coming for a rest and staying, oblivious of the voice that had bidden her go. She was lost for a second time because she had neglected her Father's business, when she ought to have been up and down the land, carrying neither purse nor scrip nor bread nor two coats, to spread the Word.

What Word? There lay the rub. The religious revival had ebbed in recent years. Scarcely a camp meeting was held any more; people saw there had been a delay in the millennium, so they turned back to the world. They no longer yearned to be converted.

"Wait," said the inner voice. "Watch and pray."

At Mr. Benson's, once again half guest, half servant, she waited, wasted, rusted. One day the lady who had seen her at the community dropped in to visit and asked how she came to talk with God.

Sojourner looked feeble. The new disenchantment had sapped her resilience; she did not know her age, but whatever it was, she felt older. Yet the question somehow made the years recede, leaving a slave child on her knees beside Mau-Mau, in a dank cellar. Dutch words came back and had to be translated into English: "There is a God in the sky . . ." Names came back: Hardenbergh, Baumfree. A white-thatched old man sitting by the wayside, crying like a child.

"How he did cry!" said Sojourner. "I hear it now as if it were but yesterday—poor old man! He thought God had done it all." She talked of the auction at Stone Ridge, where John Neely had picked up his lot of sheep with a slave girl thrown in. "Now the war begun," she said with sudden vigor.

She bared her bony shoulders with the scars left by Neely's rods. "And now, when I hear of them whipping women on the bare flesh," she said, "it makes *my* flesh crawl. God, what a way is this of treating human beings?"

The lady's name was Olive Gilbert. A New Englander with Southern relations, she recalled a recent Christmas in Kentucky. At breakfast a slaveholding friend had assured her that no one there would think of abusing a slave, and at dinner he brought home the latest news: a local young matron had just personally cracked a black girl's skull before ordering her tied to the bedstead, whipped, and left to die on the day of the Lord's birth.

Olive heard the story of a black child running in the fields, crying loud enough to be heard in the sky. "And now," said Sojourner, "though it seems curious, I don't remember ever asking for anything but what I got it. And I always got it as an answer to my prayers." Then she told of the shattering "look" that had kept her from going "back to Egypt" with her old master, tempted by the frolicking that was permitted on the summer holiday.

"What holiday?" asked Olive Gilbert.

Sojourner knew only the Dutch name for Whitsuntide: "Pingster."

The lady thought of Frederick Douglass, who had termed the slave holidays "conductors, or safety valves, to carry off the rebellious spirit of enslaved humanity." Douglass was no longer in the country. Having published his autobiography, *The Narrative of Frederick Douglass*, complete with names, places, and dates—convincing any skeptic that he was indeed a former slave, but also making himself a marked man throughout the United States—he had gone to England, where funds were now being raised to buy his manumission and enable the embodiment of the rebellious spirit to return to his native land.

Sojourner's spirit did not seem rebellious. There was a glow of dogged courage in her tale that would not flare in revolt, though it burned for justice. "Do you think that's right, God?" she would keep asking. She told of begging God, "Show them that you're my helper!" when she had gone to face powerful enemies and the majesty of the law. "Oh, I felt so little! If you could have seen me in my ignorance, trotting about the streets, bareheaded and barefooted—oh, God only could have made such people hear me," she said.

The lady, watching, marveled at the change in the gaunt, aging, ailing colored woman who lived in George Benson's house and on his bounty. An hour ago she had looked like a broken scarecrow; now she made one think of Joan of Arc. If only her voice and manner could be captured in writing, to help the cause!

Olive Gilbert's abolitionism was a matter of conscience and faith. God had made man in His image; to put the divine image on a par with beasts—to be bought and sold, bred, not wed, benighted instead of enlightened—was blasphemy. It was as simple as that for Olive, a humble laborer in the vineyard. The Garrisons were her friends, and so was Amy Post who ran the Rochester terminal of the Undergound Railroad; her brother in Vineland, New Jersey, lived on its main eastern line, and her Southern trips may have involved more than met the eye. But her name appeared on no honor roll then or later. The climate in the Connecticut Valley had changed since the discouragement of Lydia Maria Child; the new Springfield-and-Greenfield Railroad was no busier than the "railroad that ran underground" as a stream of runaways en route to Canada passed through Northampton. There was a station in the old community dairy, and David Ruggles kept another at his water cure, unnoticed by forty patients taking the "course of baths." At Samuel Hill's, conductors were changed before taking the living freight to Mr. Craft's in Whately. Later, the names of all those engaged in the work were proudly recorded for posterity, but Olive Gilbert does not appear in the record.

Nor, for that matter, does Sojourner Truth. What kept her from joining in this defiance of a law that Mr. Garrison termed "a compact with hell" her friends did not know, or would not say. Her lifelong respect for law—any law—or a silence within her? "Her religion is not tinctured in the least with gloom," said Olive Gilbert; "her trust is in God, and from him she looks for good, not evil." It was different with men. Too often, as a slave and as a dupe, Sojourner had been victimized by men—white men. "She has set suspicion to guard the door of her heart," Olive explained, "and allows it perhaps to be aroused by too slight causes . . ."

The white woman felt ashamed of her race. Something must be done to help the cause and, incidentally, Sojourner. Frederick Douglass's story had produced a rash of slave narratives; there were now dozens in print, all about Southern slavery. Might it not prick Northern consciences to see that evil was not a "peculiar institution"—that the same horror had thrived in the North not long ago? Besides, the narratives all came to more or less the same end of liberation. Freedom was their be-all and end-all. Should men not learn that a freed slave could transcend the enjoyment of life, liberty, and the pursuit of happiness, that the Creator might indeed have chosen him—or her—for a greater intimacy with things unseen, an intimacy that had kept Sojourner in Olive Gilbert's mind ever since their first meeting?

"We little thought at that time," Olive said, "that we should ever pen these simple annals . . ."

It did not matter that Sojourner's voice and manner could not be captured in writing. Her words and actions would say enough. Nor did it matter that she could not write. Olive would be her pen. Olive had a passion for anonymity; she would not even let the finished work show her name. James Boyle, the quaint old community physician was to have it printed "for the author." No one but Sojourner should appear or benefit.

Into the book went more than Sojourner had to tell. There were the letters she carried with her, though she could not read them: Peter's letters, and the glowing introductions from friends to friends-to-be. There were accounts of people who had heard her preach or had been her hosts on her travels. There were experiences with slavery that Olive had gathered herself or gleaned from others. There was Vale's book, reduced to a sketch of the "Matthias Delusion" that skipped over the Sing Sing ménage, the "match spirits," and the mystery of Pierson's death. "We do not deem it useful or necessary to give particulars," Olive wrote. "Those who are curious to know what there transpired are referred to a work published in New York in 1835, entitled 'Fanaticism; its Source and Influence,' by G. Vale, 85 Roosevelt Street."

Olive had no editor, no one to check names and spellings of the long ago and far away. They went to print as she heard them. Hardenbergh turned into "Ardinburgh," Schryver into "Scriver," Squire Romeyn into "Demain," Wagondale into "Wahkendall." Peter's handwriting also was hard to decipher; his ship, the whaler *Zone,* Captain Hiller, became the "Done, Captain Miller." A slight error even mis-dated the abolition of slavery in New York State.

Except for Sojourner's kin, there were no Negroes in her story, but Olive wished to mention Frederick Douglass. He was back from England by the time the book was in the writing, a free man under the law, going his own way. Impatient of Garrison's non-resistant and non-political dogma, he had split with his mentor and moved to Rochester to found his own anti-slavery paper, *The North Star.* Not for all the world's riches would Olive Gilbert fault such a man. At the right place in her manuscript, however, before quoting from his remarks on slave holidays, she introduced him as "Frederick Douglass, who had devoted his great heart and noble talents entirely to the furtherance of the cause of his down-trodden race"—an all but imperceptible reminder that Sojourner's heart and talents had always been devoted to the Father of all mankind.

The end of the book posed a problem.

It should help the cause—and Sojourner. How? Her true loss, her true need, was bound to be misconstrued by a woman bred in the New England strain of material self-reliance. "Her heart," Olive wrote, "is now set upon having a little home of her own, where she may feel a greater freedom than she can in the house of another, and where she can repose a little after her day of action has passed by. . . . Shall she then be left to want? Who will not answer, 'No!' "

Olive Gilbert was carried away with compassion—and yet, somehow this appeal to "the charities of the benevolent" failed to satisfy her, and she put off sending the manuscript to Dr. Boyle's printer.

It was in the spring of 1849 that Sojourner got word of an illness that had stricken her eldest daughter, still living at John Dumont's. She set out for the Hudson Valley and on arrival found Diana improved and her old master alive and well, though notably aged. His hair and beard were white, and his substance, too, was reduced, but his views had become quite enlightened.

"I can see that slavery is the wickedest thing in the

world," he told his former bondswoman, "the greatest curse the earth has ever felt"—though in his days as a slaveholder he had not seen it so and thought it no more wrong than holding any other property.

Sojourner remarked that this might be true of those who were now slaveholders.

"Oh, no," Dumont replied with warmth, "it can't be. For now the sin of slavery is so clearly written out and so much talked against—why, the whole world cries out against it!—that if anyone says he don't know and hasn't heard, he must, I think, be a liar. In my slaveholding days there were few that spoke against it, and they made little impression on anyone. Had it been as it is now, think you I could have held slaves? I shouldn't have dared to. Now it's different; now all may hear if they will."

It was their last meeting. When Diana had recovered, Sojourner returned to Northampton and told Olive Gilbert about it, blessing the Lord that she had lived to hear her master speak in this vein. Then she laughed. "He taught us not to lie and steal—when he was stealing all the time himself and didn't know it!"

At Christmastime a letter came from Diana, informing her mother that Mr. Dumont had gone West and taken along, probably by mistake, some pieces of furniture that she had left with him. "Never mind," said Sojourner. "What we give to the poor, we lend to the Lord."

And Olive Gilbert sent her manuscript to the printer with an epilogue containing an account of the visit. Her closing sentence was devoted to Dumont: "Poor old man, may the Lord bless him, and all slaveholders partake of his spirit!" she wrote of the man who to Sojourner, once upon a time, had seemed like God.

O the fantastic tricks which the American people are playing before high Heaven! . . . 'Americans! We hear your boasts of liberty, your shouts of independence, your declarations of hostility to every form of tyranny, your assertions that all men are created free and equal, . . . we see your banner floating proudly in the breeze from every flagstaff and mast-head in the land—but its blood-red stripes are emblematical of your own slave-driving cruelty, as you apply to lash to the flesh of your guiltless victims. . . . We listen to the recital of your revolutionary achievements; we see you kneeling at the shrine of Freedom, as her best, her truest, her sincerest worshippers—hypocrites! liars! adulterers! tyrants! men-stealers! atheists! Professing to believe in the natural equality of the human race—yet dooming a sixth portion of your immense population to beastly servitude! . . . Boasting of your democracy—yet determining the rights of men by the texture of their hair and the color of their skin! . . . Monsters that ye are! how can ye expect to escape the scorn of the world, and the wrath of Heaven? Emancipate your slaves, if you would redeem your tarnished character—if you would obtain forgiveness here, and salvation hereafter! Until you do so, there will be a stain upon your national escutcheon, which all the waters of the Atlantic cannot wash out!'

"It is thus that as a people we are justly subjected to the reproach, the execration, the derision of mankind," continued William Lloyd Garrison—not on the platform, but in the preface to a book:

THE NARRATIVE OF SOJOURNER TRUTH:

A NORTHERN SLAVE,

emancipated from bodily servitude
by the State of New York in 1828.

With a portrait.

The year of publication was 1850, and Garrison expressed the hope that the perusal of the *Narrative* would "inspire to renewed efforts for the liberation of all who are pining in bondage on the American soil."

Eighteen hundred and fifty was no year of liberation.

It saw the Union preserved, but part of the bribe paid the South for foregoing secession was a new Fugitive Slave Law that jeopardized the freedom of every person of color,

anywhere in the United States. On the mere allegation that
he was a runaway, a free Negro was liable to arrest without
a warrant, denied trial by jury, barred from testifying in
his own defense. "On the oath of any two villains," said
Frederick Douglass, he could be made a slave for life by
a Federal commissioner whose fee was doubled if he found
for the claimant.

Terror struck the Negroes. Whole communities packed
up and moved to Canada, the freeborn and manumitted
along with the few who really had escaped. Leaders fled
to England. One of Douglass's associates on *The North
Star* went to Africa. "We're whipped, we're whipped,"
wailed Bishop Daniel Payne of the African Methodist
Church.

"We're a majority. One with God is a majority," said
Douglass and went on writing, lecturing, fund-raising, har-
boring fugitives. He spoke more of God in that year than
ever before.

In 1850 a young woman escapee stood alone on a hillside north of the Maryland border: "Oh, dear Lord, I ain't
got no friend but you. Come to my help, Lord, for I'm in
trouble." And Harriet Tubman went back nineteen times
and led out three hundred slaves while the price on her
head rose to forty thousand dollars.

"A filthy enactment," Ralph Waldo Emerson thundered
at the new law. In Boston and Syracuse, recaptured slaves
were wrested from the hands of the police, and in Northampton the townspeople made up a purse to buy the freedom of a fugitive who did the teaming for the cotton mill.

Sojourner faced the choice of her own future.

Town gossip about her forthcoming book suddenly made
her a good credit risk. When her protector Benson went
bankrupt and lost his mansion, the prosperous Mr. Hill
offered her one of the cottages he had built on the grounds
of the defunct community. Payment could wait for the
money from her book—meanwhile, "in consideration of
three hundred dollars paid by Isabella Vanwagener, sometimes called 'Sojourner Truth,'" he conveyed to said Isabella "a certain lot of land, with dwelling house thereon,
situated near Bensonville . . . containing 60 square rods,

more or less," and "whereas said Isabella Vanwagner had executed and delivered to said Hill her certain promissory note dated April 15, 1850, for three hundred dollars, payable one year after date, with interest," a mortgage was entered in the Hampshire County Record Book and signed on April 18:

> her
> Isabella X Vanwagner and Seal.
> mark

For the first time in her life she had a home of her own, a cozy, brown-shingled little house on an elm-lined road from the old factory to the Northampton highway. The neighbors, friends from community days, and everyone in town agreed that old Sojourner had earned her chance to rest in her decline, to become a local memento, a beloved relic of a past mission. Did her very name not remind one of what lay behind?

But the year was 1850, and God-given names point forward. The little house was hardly hers when Sojourner Truth was back on the nation's roads, a sunbonnet on graying hair, lugging her bundle—back on the job she called "a-testifyin' of the hope that's in me."

She was first seen at an unusual meeting held in October of that year in Worcester, Massachusetts. Delegates from nine states, proper Bostonian aristocrats, leaders of thought, luminaries of the pulpit were called to order in Brinley Hall by a local publisher's wife and presided over by a striking blonde Rhode Island woman. Messages were read, resolutions carried, committees chosen, points argued on the floor and won by women. A delicate, elderly lady received an ovation; she was introduced as Lucretia Mott, and Sojourner remembered hearing that this woman and her husband had joined Mr. Garrison in founding the Anti-Slavery Society and had since launched the woman's rights movement. The feminists of America had come to Worcester, for one of their first conventions in the land.

After the session, Sojourner peddled her *Narrative*.

It was a thin volume, and the only page that meant anything to her was the frontispiece: a drawing of a woman in a dark smock, a white kerchief on her head, looking younger and fuller than she had been looking for years. The portrait might have been drawn without seeing her, it was so much the popular image of a Negro house slave or servant. Printed on the last page were her two "certificates of character" from Dumont and Van Wagener, dating back to the Matthias affair, and two new ones of March 1850. In one, three Northampton civic leaders praised "the many social and excellent traits which made her worthy to bear her adopted name"; in the other, Garrison confirmed that he had known her for years. "Any assistance or coopera- tion that she may receive in the sale of her Narrative," he wrote, "I am sure will be meritoriously bestowed."

The sale, it had turned out, was up to her.

Each week, Boston bookstores advertised anti-slavery lit- erature in Mr. Garrison's paper, *The Liberator*. They al- ways had Frederick Douglass's *Narrative* in stock, usually those of some other fugitives, Sojourner's never. The note "Published for the author" on its title page told the literal —truth. Olive Gilbert took some copies for herself and friends; the rest was handed to Sojourner, to dispose of as best she could.

After Northampton had bought its share, she took a satchel full of books to Worcester, without knowing more about the feminist movement than that it opposed slavery. There would be some veterans of the community, and the Garrisons, and Frederick Douglass who had plunged into the woman's rights battle. In those days white Ameri- can women became aware of being governed without their consent, barred from higher education, stripped by mar- riage of property rights, of any claim to their children or the fruits of their labor—for like the clothes on her back, a working woman's wages belonged to her husband. They felt not far removed from slavery, and Douglass welcomed this chance to open a new front for freedom.

"You'd think he'd have his hands full trying to free the blacks," said the scoffers.

"When I ran away from slavery," Douglas replied, "it was for myself; when I advocated emancipation, it was

for my people; but when I stood up for the rights of wom-
en, self was out of the question, and I found a certain
nobility in the act."

In Worcester, Sojourner saw him with Wendell Phillips,
the blue-blooded "silver tongue" of abolitionism; they had
just shared the platform in Boston, and Douglass, having
done his bit for woman's rights, would hurry back to aid
a fugitive couple and to greet a visiting member of the
British Parliament. Sojourner sat quietly amid the bustle.
She had come to sell her book; at long last, she felt, it
would take her to a new destination. If Olive Gilbert had
found her suspicious, it was because she had been awaiting
orders from the one authority she knew. Now she had put
her mark on some papers, to buy a house, and like an
answer the crates had come with books about her own
way from slave child to Sojourner Truth—she had to sell
books that she could not read, to pay for a house in which
she did not want to rest, only to feel free to journey on.
Only her words and experiences were in these books, yet
they seemed to be arousing those who could read; the
voice she heard seemed to move others to action. Beyond
the Fatherhood of God, she must now bear witness to the
brotherhood of man. The switch took time.

Worcester was a step into a new world. She shook
hands, saw new faces, heard new names and the stories
behind them; even people she knew from their visits to
Northampton appeared here in a new light. Puzzled, she
sat listening to Lucretia Mott and Wendell Phillips, to
Garrison and his disciples, Abby and Stephen Foster of
Worcester and Parker Pillsbury of New Hampshire, to
Frederick Douglass who sounded as if white women were
really little better off then black slaves. At one session, the
lady in the chair suddenly mentioned the presence of Sojourner Truth and her stirring book.

"Speech! Speech!" cried some.

Sojourner got up. "Sisters, I aren't clear what ye'd be
after. If women want any rights more than they got, why
don't they just take 'em and not be talking about it?" The

deep voice rang unchanged, and yet the convention heard a new Sojourner.

When it adjourned, all the books she had brought were gone. She returned to Northampton. In the *Liberator,* her friends read her name in a brief story on Worcester, but the bulk of the issue dealt with the guest from Britain: George Thompson, M.P., was a celebrity, a hero, or a foreign meddler, depending on where you stood. He had brought emancipation to the British West Indies; a past visit of his had caused Congressional outcries and Garrison's manhandling. The *Liberator* carried pages on the projected welcome in Faneuil Hall.

Two weeks later, the same pages screamed outrage. A half proslavery, half anti-British mob had invaded the hall, shouted Thompson down, silenced Garrison, and hooted Douglass off the platform.

With the Fosters, the M.P. proceeded to Springfield, where would-be listeners could not even get near a hall that was blockaded by crowds burning George Thompson and John Bull in effigy.

The dauntless abolitionists continued westward. At Union Village, New York, Thompson, according to the *Liberator,* gave a "humorous account of the Springfield mob," and "at the close of his remarks Mrs. Foster, ever true to her duty, introduced the aged 'Sojourner Truth,' who had come from her residence in Northampton. This uneducated woman spoke for a short time in her peculiar manner and was kindly received by the audience, who pressed around her to purchase her books . . ."

The work was as new as the load of *Narratives* in her satchel. It felt strange, yet familiar; earning your "tribute to Caesar" by selling books took getting used to, but talking to people came naturally, as did calming down the excited. Reports from the next meetings, at Saratoga and Little Falls, said that the speakers had been seriously threatened, but Sojourner, "by her dignified manner and opportune remarks, would disperse the rabble and restore order."

In Peterboro, Thompson and companions were the guests of Gerrit Smith. Sojourner sat at the table and in the drawing room of one of the country's wealthiest men —one who had recently given away 3,000 forty-acre tracts of land to the poor, black and white, and had just been indicted for helping a fugitive named Jerry to escape to Canada.

In Syracuse, the party was welcomed to an anti-slavery convention by the man who had actually spirited Jerry across the border: gentle Samuel May, a former general agent of the Massachusetts Anti-Slavery Society and a friend of Sojourner's old benefactor, George Benson. Rev. May—called "the Apostle St. John of the gospel of freedom"—was also under indictment.

In Rochester, the visiting Briton was feted by the city's anti-slavery élite, largely drawn from the faculty of the newly founded university. At the parties given in his honor it was noted that the M.P. sang charming songs, told merry anecdotes, and talked wittily; as a well-mannered guest he ignored the fact that his best friend in town had not been invited. "To have Douglass here might strangle the infant university to death," someone was heard to say.

Frederick Douglass had become Rochester's controversial figure. Some viewed him as a credit to the city, some as bringing shame upon it, but no one ignored him. He owned a house near Mt. Hope cemetery, in one of the best neighborhoods; to keep his paper going, he mortgaged the house, taught his small sons to set type, and sent them out as vendors. A stream of prominent visitors from other cities and countries passed through his parlor and library. He had more than the wildest imagination could dream of, for a former slave, yet he risked it all every day, every night.

Two thousand dollars fine and six months imprisonment threatened anyone aiding a runaway, but a room in the house on Mt. Hope was always ready for arrivals. They came in carriages, bundled in Quaker capes, hidden under flour bags, or locked in crates. A few came by train. Once, conducting a small passenger in petticoats, Douglass said, "Well, my little girl"—only to hear an indignant whisper: "I'm a boy!" He never lost one. Day in, day out, he was writing, speaking, printing, traveling, fund-raising, defying the law.

Sojourner and he would now speak on the same platform, without a jarring note. In the spring of 1851, six months after final passage of the new Fugitive Slave Law, the voice she heard went well with the fruits of his reading. The newsman who had patronizingly referred to her "peculiar manner" at the outset of the tour was rather impressed now. "This woman, who can neither read nor write, will often speak with an ability which surprises the educated and refined. She possesses a mind of rare power, and often in the course of her short speeches will throw out gems of thought," he wrote from Rochester.

She was staying on Sophia Street, at the home of Isaac and Amy Post, Quakers whose name she had first heard from Olive Gilbert. Then a woman at the Worcester convention had given her the address, as one where she could rely upon a welcome if she came to Rochester. It made her feel part of a new community, somehow—one that seemed as thinly scattered as righteousness, and yet all over, like God.

"I sometimes forget the color of my skin," Frederick Douglass said that spring, in Rochester's Corinthian Hall, "and remember that I am a man. I sometimes forget that I am hated of men, and remember I am loved of God . . ."

He went to Canada with George Thompson, to see how the fugitives who had reached safety were doing. They spoke in Toronto and came back to Rochester for the most painful meeting of Thompson's tour—the urbane Member of Parliament could laugh off mobs, but squabbling abolitionists were another matter. And it was at this meeting that Douglass came to grips with William Lloyd Garrison's doctrine.

He attacked self-delusion. The slave power was growing from year to year; hopes of ending slavery by moral pressure were mirages with the new law cutting off the few rescues that had still been possible. One must face facts, he said grimly, and the facts spelled failure for an antislavery campaign that barred resistance, barred political action, and stubbornly insisted that the North dissolve the Union—which the North would never do.

The Garrisonians fought back as fiercely as abolitionists could fight in public against a former slave. "Ingratitude," they cried. "Mr. Garrison is being slandered!" George Thompson, more in sorrow than in anger, rebuked Douglass for lack of faith, for thinking the slave states could last as an isle of darkness in a forward-looking world. The world, said the Briton, looked admiringly on Garrison's watchword, "No Union with Slaveholders," as the most moral and only Christian position.

There was applause and hissing as abolitionists glared at each other all over the hall. "Sojourner Truth," the chairman said, almost pleading.

"No Union with Slaveholders!" someone shouted at Douglass, whose angry reply was drowned out by the deep voice rolling down from the rostrum.

"Oh, friends, pity the poor slaveholder, and pray for him! It troubles me more than anything else, what will become of the poor slaveholder, in all his guilt and all his impenitence. God will take care of the poor trampled slave, but where will the slaveholder be when Eternity begins?"

The meeting ended without further talk of the schism.

"Is God Dead?"

ONE NIGHT IN ROCHESTER, returning from Corinthian Hall, Sojourner was stopped in the street by a policeman looking for fugitive slaves. He demanded her name. He was a little man, seeming to shrink further as she drew herself up to her full height.

"I am that I am," boomed the great voice. The policeman vanished. Undisturbed, she walked on to the Posts' house at 36 Sophia Street.

An aura of fame had enveloped this rambling, modest-looking house when Sojourner first saw it. She had been aware of its reputation as the "central depot" of the Underground Railroad; she had since heard at the Worcester woman's rights meeting that Amy Post had opened the first such convention in the world. With a curiosity tinged with awe she had rung the bell and heard a bird-like, be-spectacled figure under a Quaker bonnet say pleasantly, "Won't thee come in?" The greeting never varied. Whoever came to the door was ushered into the parlor, introduced to Mr. Post and others, and made at home. During the conversation, Mrs. Post would sit knitting. "When we had anti-slavery fairs," she said, "the Friends sent a committee to reason with me, because I was working with the world's people. They said I could not have attended to all my family duties. I emptied my stockingbag: there were sixty-four pairs on hand."

Sojourner went to help in the kitchen. The cook knew tales about Mrs. Post: when she first came to Rochester —she had been born Amy Kirby in Jericho, Long Island —some local ladies had cautioned her against giving her help too many privileges, lest the girls become discontented. "Why?" she had asked. "I've just been thinking what I could do to improve their condition. It seems to me the workers should fare better than the idlers."

The food on the kitchen stove would have fed a dozen more mouths than Sojourner had seen. She did not hear till the next morning that twelve hunted fugitives had spent the night in the house, waiting to be embarked at dawn and sped across Lake Ontario to a free country.

Sojourner parted company with the Hon. George Thompson's team of lecturers. They continued on their tour; she stayed in Rochester. With Amy Post she went to meetings in and out of town—"myself a silent companion," said Amy, who did not fancy herself as a speaker and would sit knitting while Sojourner talked and sang. She sang the same songs and said much the same things as at the camp meetings of her past, though the groups she addressed now were not religious. Their minds were not on the end of the world, but on its betterment: by the abolition of slavery, by equal rights for women, by the promotion of temperance and education, by penal reform, by improving conditions in factories, hospitals, asylums. There was no kind of moral or social advance without some dedicated men and women—mostly women—working for it. Amy Post worked with them all, and all wished to hear Sojourner, however little she knew of their varied concerns.

Still, after two months in Rochester she moved on. "I'm to travel up and down the land," she had said once; she must not again yield to the temptation of settling. The house in Northampton was a snare to be avoided and headed away from. "I'm to go east," she had said once, walking toward the dawn; now she had to go west. It was spring, and she followed the sun along the flowering shores of the great lakes, into Pennsylvania and beyond.

At Akron, Ohio, a woman's rights convention was held at the end of May. Torrential rains poured down on opening day, but a large, generally unsympathetic crowd filled the pews of the Universalist church. The galleries were crammed with boys looking forward to the discomfiture of the weaker sex. Members of the unpopular movement shuddered at the appearance of a tall black woman

in a soaked gray dress, white turban covered by an uncouth sunbonnet. Resentment rustled alongside Sojourner
Truth, as she strode up the aisle and sat on the pulpit
steps.

She heard mutters: "An abolition affair . . . Woman's
rights and niggers—we told you so! . . . Go it, old
darkey!"

A big, strong-faced woman in the chair asked for order
and got it. The business of the convention went on with
Sojourner huddled against the side wall of the pulpit, elbows on her knees, chin in her palms. After the morning
session she got busy selling her book. Above her, she
heard voices entreating the president: "Don't let her speak,
Mrs. Gage! It will ruin us! Every paper in the land will
have our cause mixed up with abolition and niggers—"

"We'll see when the time comes," said the strong-faced
woman.

The evening session came and went, and the next morning found Sojourner back in her place. The work "waxed
warm," as Mrs. Gage put it. Methodist, Baptist, Episocopal,
Presbyterian, Universalist ministers came in to hear and
discuss the resolutions offered. Sojourner listened, scarcely
lifting her head. One of the clergymen told women to beware of selling their birthright of consideration and def-
erence for a mess of equality pottage—what man, he
asked, would help a political or business rival into a carriage, or lift her over a ditch? Another claimed superior
rights and privileges for man on the ground of superior
intellect; a third, because of the manhood of Christ. "If
God had desired the equality of women," he intoned,
"he would have given some token of His will through the
birth, life, and death of the Saviour."

The men in the pews sneered, and rude noises rang
down from the galleries, where the boys were having fun.

Sojourner got up slowly.

"Don't let her speak!" gasped half a dozen as she moved
solemnly to the front, laid down her old bonnet, and
turned her eyes on the president. Hissing greeted the an-
nouncement that Sojourner Truth had the floor, but when

Mrs. Gage asked for silence, the noise subsided. Everyone stared at the six-foot figure on the pulpit.

"Well, chillun, where there's so much racket there must be something out of kilter. I think that 'twixt the niggers of the South and the women at the North all a-talking 'bout rights, the white men will be in a fix pretty soon."

The deep voice effortlessly reached every ear in the house and in the throng outside the open doors and windows.

"But what's all this here talking about? That man over there say that women needs to be helped into carriages, and lifted over ditches, and to have the best place everywhere. Nobody ever helps me into carriages, or over mud puddles, or gives me any best place—and aren't I a woman?"

The voice reverberated in the church.

"Look at me! Look at my arm!" She bared her right arm to the shoulder, showing powerful muscles. "I've plowed and planted and gathered into barns, and no man could head me—and aren't I a woman? I could work as much as a man, and eat as much, when I could get it, and bear the lash as well. And aren't I a woman? They talks about this thing in the head—what's this they call it?"

"Intellect," whispered someone near-by.

"That's it, honey. What's that got to do with women's rights or niggers' rights? If my cup won't hold but a pint and your'n holds a quart, wouldn't ye be mean not to let me have my little half-measure full?"

Amid cheers and guffaws, her finger pointed at one of the men of the cloth.

"Then that little man in black there, he says women can't have as much rights as men 'cause Christ warn't a woman. Where did your Christ come from?"

She paused. No one answered. She repeated her question.

"Where did your Christ come from?" The voice rang like an organ with all the stops pulled. "From God and a woman! Man had nothing to do with it!"

The cheers grew deafening.

She stayed on in Ohio. There was work to be done in

the West, and a new kind of friends to work with. They lived for "the cause," and their cause was the fight against wrong—any and all wrong. "Temperance, freedom, justice to the Negro, justice to woman," said Mrs. Gage, "are but parts of one whole, one temple whose builder is God."

In Northampton, Sojourner's friends had lived on the fringe of the struggle, though some bore its scars. Through them, she had met such leaders as Garrison, Phillips, Douglass; her first speaking tour had been made with George Thompson and ler her to Gerrit Smith and Samuel May. She had entered the fray at headquarters, so to speak. Now she moved to the front.

Most of her new comrades-in-arms were women. There was Frances Gage: a pioneer's daughter descended from the Danas and Bancrofts of Massachusetts, raised on a frontier farm, educated in a lob cabin—forty now, an abolitionist lawyer's wife and the mother of eight children, but a tireless writer, speaker, organizer for the cause. There was refined Josephine Griffing, a widow with three daughters, "too benevolent ever to be rich," and always chosen to go into the most hostile towns. There was tiny Lucy Colman, whom Sojourner had met in Worcester; a railroad engineer's widow, she worked as an accredited agent of the Western Anti-Slavery Society, a self-willed, opinionated, stubborn, indefatigable wisp of valor. She weighed no more than a child of twelve and had "often smelled the tar," she used to say proudly.

There were Mary Anne Johnson and Emily Robinson, feminist wives of abolitionist husbands—a frequent division of labor. Sojourner came to Ohio as Oliver Johnson was about to leave the Salem *Anti-Slavery Bugle* to join the New York *Tribune,* and Marius Robinson, whom Mrs. Colman called "almost ethereal in his make-up," was taking over. One of the "Lane rebels," former theology students who had quit Lane Seminary in Cincinnati to practice Christianity as abolitionist agents, Robinson had been tarred and feathered and left for dead on the day his first child was born. His wife had encouraged him to continue.

And there was the shaggy stray dog that made its home in Salem, in the office of the *Bugle*. No one knew where it came from, but when an agent was sent into a new field, the big dog would trot along, never returning to Salem before the agent was well settled in a friendly home. The whole county knew the "anti-slavery dog." It had no other name.

Sojourner went to work, lecturing and selling subscriptions to the *Bugle*. The field was rough. Most rural homes were log cabins partitioned into one room and two bedchambers; some were undivided, with the sleeping loft reached by a ladder. Washbowls were rare, towels a luxury. Mrs. Colman told of children who had never seen a mirror; of a young woman teacher she had found halfnaked before a cabin, reading the *Bugle* while nursing her child; of the time when the anti-slavery dog had led her to safety through a cornfield, past the mob that was heating the tar-kettle.

The Robinsons outfitted Sojourner with a horse and buggy. That she was no longer young enough to walk from town to town was evident, although her years were shrouded in confusion. The papers usually called her "aged." Her co-workers believed her to be "nearly seventy, but as vigorous as a person of fifty"; her own guess was "gone sixty." Actually she was about fifty-five. But she wore glasses now, and carried a cane. In reply to tar-and-feather stories she would say the cane was "mighty fine for crackin' skulls," and soon a tale was afoot that she had been manhandled, hence the cane. To the embattled band of Western workers for the cause she swiftly became a legend.

For weeks at a time she traveled with her horse and buggy, getting up her own meetings all over Ohio, in Indiana, in Michigan. She did not know the country and could not read signs, so when she came to a crossroads she would let go of the lines and say, "God, you drive." He always drove her to some place, she found, where her horse was cared for and she had a good meeting.

The correspondents for the *Liberator* or the New York *Anti-Slavery Standard*, whom the effective speaking of "this unlearned woman" had so surprised on the Thompson tour, would have been still more amazed if they had heard her now. Instead of abating, her "peculiar manner" seemed intensified. Hers was not the plantation accent that Douglass had shed, yet he would have found it worse. It was common—far more so than it had sounded to her past audiences at Eastern camp meetings or in the North-ampton community. She did not try to modify her style; she responded to responses. Out West, within smelling range of the tar-kettle, she found plain language helpful, so she developed hers, just as she fanned speculation about her age. Both were accessories to gifts of God. Her voice, her appearance, her songs, the things she had to say— these came from God.

With Frances Gage she attended a meeting in Michigan, where Parker Pillsbury attacked the conduct of the churches: their Bible-quoting in defense of slavery, their trafficking in human flesh in the South, and their refusal to condemn it in the North. While he was speaking, a thunderstorm came up and a young Methodist in the audi-ence rose in alarm; he felt in imminent danger of God's wrath for listening to such blasphemies; it made his hair rise with terror—

"Chile," a voice rang out above the rain that beat upon the roof, above thunder, howling winds, and crashing branches, "chile, don't be skeered. I don't speck God's ever heard tell on ye."

"It was all she said," Mrs. Gage noted, "but it was enough."

She knew the needs of the moment, and of the hour. She never got into the political disputes that rent the movement, but one day, when a speaker had dwelled at length on the sanctity of the Constitution, she had a word about this, too. It was a year in which the weevil had destroyed thousands of acres of wheat, and she began as usual:

"Chillun, I talks to God, and God talks to me. I goes out and talks to God in the fields and in the woods. This morning I was walking out, and I got over the fence. I saw the wheat a-holding up its head, looking very big. I goes up and takes a-hold of it. You believe it, there was no wheat there? I says, 'God, what *is* the matter with this wheat?' and he says to me, 'Sojourner, there is a little weasel in it.' "

She paused and continued.

"Now I hears talking about the Constitution and the rights of man. I comes up and I takes hold of this Constitution. It looks mighty big, and I feels for *my* rights, but there aren't any there. Then I says, 'God, what *ails* this Constitution?' He says to me, 'Sojourner, there is a little weasel in it.' "

A man who was there called her "magnetic power over an audience perfectly astounding."

Marius Robinson tried to teach her to read—with her glasses, it would no longer strain her eyes—but in vain. "My brains is too stiff now," she told him. For the first time she regretted it. Wherever she went, in towns, on farms, people were discussing a book; except for the Bible, Sojourner had never heard so much talk about a book. A woman had written it, a daughter of Robinson's old divinity teacher in Cincinnati, himself a famed revivalist in the East before Sojourner's time. The woman's name was Harriet Beecher Stowe, and her book dealt with slavery and was titled *Uncle Tom's Cabin, or The Man That Was a Thing.*

This book was much longer than Sojourner's *Narrative,* too long for her friends to read it all to her. She heard parts, and some facts known in the movement: that "Uncle Tom" was really a colored preacher who had not died but escaped to Canada, and that Frederick Douglass had given the author material about life on a plantation. Sojourner cared little about the facts, but she sensed why so many who were not even in the cause would talk about the book, why they suddenly seemed to be thinking and asking themselves: what if this happened to me—not to some poor wretch, but to me? This was how Sojourner herself talked to people. It did not surprise her to hear that the whole world was reading Mrs. Stowe's book. A woman could talk to the world if she looked upon it as her own family.

Sojourner decided to have a look at Mrs. Stowe.

From town to town, walking, riding the stages, some-

times riding the trains, she made her way back east. She
saw old friends, made new ones, spent some days here,
some days there, lectured, and sold her books to pay her
way. When the last one was sold, she went to Northampton. Her house, she heard, was no longer in Bensonville—
Mr. Benson's failure had made the name unpopular, and
it had been changed to Florence. Even so, she wished to
pay her debts, and on November 1, 1852, Samuel L. Hill
discharged his mortgage on her property, "the note secured by it having been fully paid."

Mrs. Stowe proved elusive. She lived far north, in
Brunswick, Maine, but ever since the publication of her
book she had been so busily rushing to and fro that her
own friends could not keep track of her. Her husband was
joining Andover Theological Seminary, near Boston, so she
was there to supervise the remodeling of an old workshop
into a home; next, she was in Brooklyn, where her brother,
from his pulpit in Plymouth Church, sold slaves into freedom; she was in Brunswick to move her household; she was
in Hartford and New Haven and Cincinnati. In April 1853,
when Sojourner hoped to catch up with her in New York,
she had just sailed for Europe.

In the pursuit, Sojourner saw her family, found daughters, sons-in-law, grandchildren scattered over the land
and wearing different names, Caldwell and Banks, Corbin
and Schuyler. She found Dr. Boyle, the donor of her
Narrative, living in New York; told that her stock was exhausted, he arranged with his printer for a new edition.

There was a heat wave in New York in September,
when a woman's rights convention was held at the Broad,
way Tabernacle. The papers, though antagonistic, called it
"the mob convention." On the first day every speaker, man
or woman, was hissed, hooted, howled down—except for
one clergyman who berated the women and was cheered
to the echo. Despite the heat, hundreds of sweating
rowdies were in their seats for each session, at twenty-five
cents a head. The meeting's historian called this "the one
redeeming feature of the mob: it paid all expenses and
left a surplus in the treasury."

The third session opened as noisily as the earlier ones.

When Sojourner appeared on the platform, the house was Bedlam, but her voice rang above hisses and cackles. "Isn't it good," she called, "for me to come and draw forth a spirit, to see what kind of spirit you're of? I see that some of you have got the spirit of a goose, and some have got the spirit of a snake."

She sounded so amiable it made them laugh. "Hurry up that stew!" cried one. "Half a dozen on the shell," shouted another.

She grinned, peering down through her glasses. "I know it feels a kind o' hissing and tickling like to see a colored woman get up and tell you about things, and woman's rights. When she comes to demand 'em, don't you hear how sons hiss their mothers like snakes? God says, 'Honor your father and your mother.' Sons ought to behave themselves before their mothers, but I can see them a-laughing and pointing at their mothers up here on the stage. They hiss when an aged woman comes forth."

No one was hissing.

"Jesus says, 'What I say to one, I say to all—watch! I'm a-watching. I'm sitting among you to watch, and every once and a while I'll come out and tell you what time of night it is."

She walked to her seat through applause and friendly laughter. The next day's *New York Times* called the session at which the colored woman had appeared "a very jolly affair, a regular breakdown. . . . Let us be thankful," said the paper that had been thundering against the feminists, "that in such hot weather there is something to amuse us. . . . *Mem.* It was cooler in the evening."

Autumn had come to Andover, casting a mantle of red and gold over the big trees around the Stowes' house. They were back from abroad, from a triumphal but exhausting tour of Europe, and the tiny author of history's first instantaneous world-wide best seller was recovering in the transparent calm of a New England Indian summer. "I was out all the forenoon sketching elms," she wrote to her husband. "There is no end to the beauty of these trees . . ."

The calm passed. Soon a multitude of guests descended

upon the old stone house which the Stowes called their "cabin"—a spacious one, with two large floors and additional bedrooms in the attic always filled with company. Mrs. Stowe's father came; retired as president of Lane Seminary at seventy-seven, the old revivalist sat by the fire in his daughter's sitting room, dictating his memoirs and receiving more visits than Harriet. Some prominent clergymen were with him on the day the hostess got word that Sojourner Truth was calling.

The singular name brought newspaper stories to mind, about some speaker at anti-slavery meetings. It was as much as Harriet knew of the person. She resolved to keep the interview short.

Downstairs, a tall, spare figure towered above her and reminded the woman of letters of a work of art, a much-reproduced statuette called "Negro Woman at the Fountain." Sojourner was dressed in some stout, grayish stuff, neat and clean, though dusty from travel. On her head she wore a bright madras handkerchief, wound into a turban after the manner of her race; she was clearly a full-blooded African. Aged and worn with hardships, she still impressed Harriet as having once been a living embodiment of the sculpture.

She seemed self-possessed and at ease. There was a touch of unconscious superiority mixed with humor in the way she looked down on the celebrated little lady. "So this is you," said Sojourner.

"Yes," said the lady.

"Well, honey, the Lord bless ye. I just thought I'd like to come and have a look at you. You've heard of me, I reckon?"

"Yes, I think I have. You go about lecturing, do you not?"

"Yes, honey, that's what I do. The Lord has made me a sign unto this nation, and I go round a-testifying and showing them their sins against my people."

She took a seat, stooped over, and crossed her arms on her knees. Gazing upon the floor, she sank into a sort of daydream, with undercurrents of emotion working in her great, gloomy eyes and dark face. "Lord," she sighed, and now and then burst out, "Oh, Lord! Oh, the tears, and the groans, and the moans, Lord!"

Harriet found herself subtly fascinated. It almost escaped her that the woman was accompanied by a little boy of ten or so—a veritable African Puck, with a perpetual grin on his fat, jolly face—until his giggling disturbed Sojourner's reverie.

She regarded him with indulgent sadness. "Laws, ma'am, he don't know nothing about it, he don't. Why, I've seen them poor critters beat and abused and hunted, brought in all torn—ears hanging in rags, where the dogs been a-biting of them."

The little boy was convulsed by more giggles. She looked at him soberly, without irritation. "Well, you may bless the Lord, you can laugh. But I tell you, 't warn't no laughing matter."

Mrs. Stowe had changed her mind about the interview. Sojourner's manner seemed to her so original, it might be worth while to summon her friends. Old Lyman Beecher came down with his clerical visitors; together with Professor Stowe and the family, they made a roomful. No princess could have received them with more composed dignity than Sojourner. To the novelist's eye, she stood among them "as one of her own native palm trees waving alone in the desert."

Harriet presented the gentlemen, closing with her father. "Sojourner, this is Dr. Beecher. He is a very celebrated preacher."

"Bless you, dear lamb," said Sojourner, offering her hand and looking down on his white head. "I love preachers. I'm a kind of preacher myself."

"You are?" said Lyman Beecher. "Do you preach from the Bible?"

"No, honey, can't preach from the Bible—can't read a letter."

"Why, Sojourner, what then do you preach from?"

She turned suddenly solemn. "When I preaches, I has just one text to preach from, and I always preaches from this one. My text is, 'WHEN I FOUND JESUS!' "

"Well, you couldn't have a better one," one of the ministers said after a few moments. She ignored the compliment; she seemed swelling with her own thoughts before going into her recital. An audience was what she wanted, Harriet thought. High or low, learned or illiterate—she had things to say and was ready to say them at all times, to anyone. She talked of her mother and her masters, of talks with God and of things she had seen as a slave.

"And then, honey, for a while I said, 'There's the white folks that have abused you and beat you and abused your people—think of them!' But then the sun rose and something spoke out in me and said, 'This is Jesus!' And there came a rush of love through my soul and I spoke out with all my might, and I says, 'This is Jesus! Glory be to God!' Then the whole world grew bright, and the trees they waved and waved in glory, and every little bit of stone on the ground shone like glass—and I shouted, 'Praise, praise, praise to the Lord!' And I begun to feel such a love in my soul as I never felt before—love to all creatures. And I cried out loud, 'Lord, Lord, I can love even the white folks!' "

In the silence that followed, Harriet Beecher Stowe heard one clergyman whisper to another: "There's more of the gospel in that story than in most sermons . . ."

The Stowes did not let her go for days. "Come, I am dull," the professor would say of an evening, "can't you get Sojourner up here to talk a little?" And she would come into the parlor and sit among pictures and bric-a-brac in her plain gown and heavy traveling shoes, and absorb the minds of both adults and children.

They wanted to know how she had been getting on with the woman's rights advocates, and she chuckled, recalling that some of them had asked why she did not wear bloomers. "I told them I had bloomers enough when I was in bondage. You see, they used to weave what they called nigger-cloth, and each one of us got just such a strip and had to wear it width-wise. Them that was short got along pretty well, but as for me—"

She gave a droll glance at her long limbs and at the company. "Tell you, I had enough of bloomers in them days."

Left to herself, she delighted in humming hymns. Once, Harriet watched her sitting at a window, singing and fervently keeping time with her head, while the little black Puck—a grandson she called Jamie—was ornamenting her red-and-yellow turban with dandelions. He fairly split his sides laughing at their shaking and quaking in time with the song of his grandmother:

> "O glory, glory, glory,
> Won't you come along with me?"

"Sojourner," said the professor, "you seem to be very sure about Heaven."

"Well, I be," she answered triumphantly.

"What makes you so sure there is any Heaven?"

"Well, 'cause I got such a hankering after it in here," she said, thumping her breast with vigor.

For a while she dismayed the Stowes with her fondness for a melody that was not only profane but abominable to the righteous. It was a new song about the California gold rush, by a young composer whose other popular tunes were full of gay darkeys at the "old Kentucky home," or free darkeys roaming sadly, longing for "the old plantation," or loyal darkeys mourning "Massa's in de cold, cold ground." The author of *Uncle Tom's Cabin* was shocked to hear Sojourner sing Stephen Foster's "Susanna"—until she made out Sojourner's text:

> "I'm on my way to Canada,
>   That cold but happy land;
> The dire effects of slavery
>   I can no longer stand.
>
>   O righteous Father,
> Do look down on me,
>   And help me on to Canada,
> Where colored folks are free!"

Sojourner sang in a strange, cracked voice, but with all her soul and might; she mispronounced the English, but one could not fail to observe that she seemed to derive as much elevation and comfort from bad English as from good. And Mrs. Stowe listened amusedly to the new text and wrote it down, especially the final stanza about the slave's arrival in Canada:

> "The Queen comes down unto the shore
>   With arms extended wide,
> To welcome the poor fugitive
>   Safe onto freedom's side."

At length, true to her name, Sojourner departed from the house in Andover. The Stowes did not know where she went with her little Puck of a grandson; they would keep hearing about her from time to time, but they never met again. "Sojourner," Harriet wrote, "has passed away from among us as a wave of the sea."

Truth was sojourning again, mostly between the great lakes and the Mississippi and Ohio rivers. She was known and welcomed all over the East, had untold friends and a house there, yet something drew her westward. In a matter of days she was always on the move again, speaking, singing, holding meetings from town to town, back toward the West.

In the mid-fifties she visited a Michigan Quaker, Henry Willis, in one of the towns that had sprung up behind the fast-moving Indian frontier, growing out of single log cabins in a few decades. Friend Willis's town lay among forests and lakes and prairie, at the confluence of two rivers; before the government opened the land to settlers, a brawl between two surveyors and two Indians had marked the spot, and for this reason one of the rivers and the town were named, half jestingly, Battle Creek. It was a peaceful community, despite its name, but with a vein of iron. The Friends were strong there. The mayor, a Quaker merchant, ran the local Underground Railroad section, and when a band of thirty armed Southern slave catchers was reported en route from Chicago, he had handbills printed, warning them to stay out of his town. He gave the bills to a Michigan Central conductor for distribution at every stop; the Southerners got them at Niles, thought the matter over, and decided to withdraw from Michigan.

Sojourner came and left. But the next time she felt weary, she did not go to rest in Salem, as she had been doing for years. She went to Battle Creek. The Merritt family there used to entertain such anti-slavery notables as Garrison, Pillsbury, Phillips; they welcomed Sojourner regardless of local criticism of her presence at their table. Their daughter Phebe handled her correspondence, and when Sojourner sang, the younger Merritt children danced around her and climbed into her arms to feel her skin.

At her work she was growing case-hardened. The slavery issue was sharply drawn by this time, and the West from Ohio to Kansas was the battleground where audiences were not apt to be sympathetic from the outset. A meeting might burst into violence at any moment. Literate prose did not pay off here. Plain speaking did; Sojourner became a pillar of strength in the West. Time and again it was she who had to rescue her superiors in background and book learning.

She once saw a noted orator at his wit's end when a country lawyer gave the voice of reason and humanity short shrift: where, he barked, was the old tar-kettle for nigger-lovers? Were they men or mice to let a nigger-lover tell them slaves were human? Niggers were a low, lazy, lecherous tribe of baboons! The audience roared approval.

"Don't dirty your hands with that critter," Sojourner whispered into the ear of the eminent abolitionist. "Let me 'tend to him." She got up when the harangue was over.

"Chillun, I'm one of them monkey tribes. I was born a slave. I had the dirty work to do, the scullion work. Now I'm going to 'ply to this critter"—pointing her bony finger —"and of all the dirty work I ever done in the course of my time, this is the scullionest and the dirtiest. Now, chillun, don't you pity me?"

Again they roared applause, the Negro-haters as loudly as any.

After the meeting the country lawyer came up to her. "You think your talk does any good, old woman? Why, I don't care any more for it than for a fleabite."

"Maybe not," she replied. "But the Lord willing, I'll keep you scratching."

She had a new stock of books to pay her way, reprinted from Dr. Boyle's plates, but with a new frontispiece that made her look considerably older than the first, and with a new preface by Harriet Beecher Stowe, a name than probably exceeding Mr. Garrison's in drawing power. Mrs. Stowe did not express general views, as Garrison had done in the first edition; she came right to what she considered as the point of such a preface. "Her object in the sale of this little work," she wrote, evidently without bothering to ask Sojourner, "is to secure a home for her old age . . ."

Many copies of the new edition went to Northampton, where Sojourner lectured in September 1857 and stayed long enough to put her mark once more between the words "Isabella" and "Vanwagner," on a deed conveying her house and lot to one Daniel Ives for 740 dollars. It was the last time she used the name derived from her last human master. With the house in Florence, Isabella Van Wagener faded out, and by the year's end Sojourner Truth had bought one in Harmonia, a village six miles west of Battle Creek.

This house, more properly called a cabin, adjoined a spiritualist seminary. Several of her Quaker friends in Battle Creek had taken up spiritualism, founded a colony at Harmonia, and invited her. She would try anything once, and for a while she took her rest periods among the spiritualists, but she never joined the group. Her new house served a different purpose: in the 1860 census it would be listed as sheltering not only Sojourner Truth but her daughter Elizabeth Banks and two grandsons, James Caldwell—the census-taker put him down as "Colvin"—and Sam Banks. She was about to reunite her family. One by one, they drifted westward. Diana had married one Jacob Corbin and would soon come to Michigan with him. Sophia, thirty now, had married one Tom Schuyler in Medina, New York, near Rochester. Once they came West, they would have a roof over their heads.

Sojourner spent little of her own time at Harmonia. When she was not on the road, she would stay in Battle

Creek proper, usually in a barn the Merritts owned on College Street, in the heart of the town. In exchange for her board she would do housework, nurse the sick or the children, and make herself useful in other ways. The wife of Charles Merritt, who operated orchards and a strawberry patch, recalled an Eastern custom from her childhood, and the result was a sight novel to Battle Creek: Sojourner carrying a tray with pretty quart baskets of fruit on her head, calling her wares as she passed along the streets. She would deliver the fruit at the door, it was announced on printed handbills.

In 1858 she traveled more than ever. In southwestern Ohio she visited Bishop Payne of the African Methodist Church. From Tawawa Springs, where he lived, he took her to Xenia, to the campus of the new Wilberforce University which white Methodists had founded "for the benefit of the African race." Most of the students were illegitimate children of Southern planters and their slave women. "These need learning and God as much as any," the bishop told Sojourner.

God had made her "a sign unto the people" and sent her among the white people. She had God, but no learning; Frederick Douglass had learning, but she wondered whether he had God. Payne had both, and his heart was set on giving both to youngsters of color. Sojourner thought of her grandsons. James, her companion at Andover, was now a blacksmith's apprentice of fifteen, old enough to make his living, but Sammy was eight, still young enough to learn. Could the bishop's students be a sign unto Sojourner Truth?

He asked her to speak to the "Moral and Mental Uplift Society" he had established for his adult flock, and after the lecture he said, "I wish there had been a thousand instead of twenty to hear my simple and eloquent friend." He read poetry to her—some of his own, and some penned thirty years earlier by a slave in the South—and never forgot her comment. "Dan, your'n be pretty, but his'n be strong," she said and resumed her journey with a copy of the bishop's verse in her bundle and the picture of his students on her mind.

In Iowa she called on an acquaintance from Northampton, "Uncle Joe" Dugdale, a Quaker and veteran abolitionist. One cloudy day she sat in her usual position, with her cheeks in her hands, and suddenly started up as from a dream. "Friend Dugdale, poor old Sojourner can't read a word; will you get the Bible and read me a little of the Scripture?"

The Quaker opened to the fifty-ninth chapter of Isaiah. "None calleth for justice, nor any pleadeth for truth; your hands are defiled with blood, and your fingers with iniquity; they conceive mischief and bring forth iniquity; they hatch cockatrice's eggs and weave the spider's web; he that eateth of their eggs dieth, and that which is crushed breaketh out into a viper . . ."

"Is that there?" she cried, bringing her palms together like a thunderclap.

"It shall break out into a viper," Dugdale repeated.

"Yes," she confirmed, "God told me that. I never heard it read afore. Now I know it twice . . ."

The viper she spoke of daily, as the prophet of old, was the guilt incurred here and now, by a whole nation.

In the fall of 1858 she crisscrossed northern Indiana, and the opposition spread rumors that she was an imposter. At Silver Lake the United Brethren's meetinghouse was packed by pro-slavery Democrats led by one Dr. Strain. They let her talk without interruption, but when she wanted to step down, the doctor called, "Hold on," and explained that the audience had some doubt about her sex; a majority seemed to believe they had heard a man. "It is for the benefit of the speaker," said Dr. Strain, grinning broadly, "that I ask for the speaker's breast to be submitted to inspection by some of the ladies present, so the doubt may be removed by their testimony."

The pounding of Sojourner's cane quelled the uproar. "Why do you think I'm a man?"

"Your voice isn't that of a woman; it's the voice of a man, and we believe you're a man." Strain turned to the audience. "All in agreement say Aye!"

A boisterous chorus answered. Sojourner did not wait for Nays, or for lady inspectors. She unfastened her robe.

"I'll show my breasts to the whole congregation—it's to your shame I'm doing this, not to mine." Her breasts, she said into the sudden silence, had suckled many a white babe when they should have been suckling her own. Some of those infants were men now, and more manly, although they had sucked her colored breasts, than anyone here seemed to be . . . She opened her coarse shift, letting the audience see the flaccid, purplish breasts of an old Negress.

Two young men stepped up to shield her. She pushed them aside and scornfully held up her breasts to Strain: "Maybe you'd like to suck?"

Afterwards, a Democrat was heard to relish his leader's discomfiture. "Bet me forty dollars that she was a man, he did," said the member of the pro-slavery party. "And him a doctor!"

She held meeting after meeting in Indiana, Illinois, Michigan, Ohio, Wisconsin. Each town she came to had grown since her last visit. New settlers had come from the East or from overseas, some speaking strange tongues and many speaking of oppression and slavery—but not of the kind Sojourner knew. There was much talk of nation enslaving nation, of Irishmen being oppressed by Britons, Poles by Russians, Hungarians by Austrians. Here they were free, yet they differed on freedom for others. Louis Kossuth, the leader of the Hungarians, called the United States "a country without a crime"; reminded of its four million slaves, he said, "I would forget the Negro—I would forget the whole world if I could have Hungary!"

But the Irish recalled the Pope's condemnation of slavery and Dan O'Connell's exchange with an American visitor to the House of Commons: "Are you from the South?" —"Yes, sir."—"A slaveholder, I presume?"—"Yes, sir."— "Then I have no hand for you," the liberator had said and stalked away.

Sojourner met too many strangers to tell them apart— except for one line of distinction: they either sought a free life, for themselves and their children, or money and arms to fight some tyrant abroad. In a church near Salem she sang an "original song" about this, to another of the

popular new tunes about homesick darkeys, and a listener
wrote down the text because it was so unexpected.

> "I feel for those in bondage;—
> Well may I feel for them—
> I know how fiendish hearts can be
> That sell their fellow men.
>
> Yet those oppressors steeped in guilt,
> I still would have them live,
> For I have learned of Jesus
> To suffer and forgive.
>
> I do not ask you to engage
> In death and bloody strife;
> I do not dare insult my God
> By asking for their life.
>
> But while your kindest sympathies
> To foreign lands do roam,
> I would ask you to remember
> Your own oppressed at home."

She did not ask for the beam to be cast out first. She
just did not want it forgotten.

Once only, during those years, did she cross the path of
Frederick Douglass. They fought the good fight in different
roles; they moved people in different ways. Free Negroes
and whatever slaves had heard of him acknowledged
Douglass as their leader; few knew of Sojourner, and to
those few she was—and would remain to their descendants
—a lovable but minor figure. White people reacted to her
impact on the individual conscience; they reacted to Douglass's image in the public mind. They thought of him as
the spokesman for his race; they heard Sojourner and felt
as their brothers' keepers.

In a sense, she served as the American Negro's apostle
to the whites—the only abolitionist of color to spend her
life among whites, to speak almost only to whites, to influence mostly whites. Her influence was felt by people, not
by groups, classes, or parties. "I am blest and thankful
that I have held your hand in mine," they said, or, "May

our faith be like yours, and our duty as well done." None ever thought of linking her with events, of greeting her, perhaps, as Lincoln greeted Harriet Beecher Stowe: "So you're the little woman who wrote the book that made this great war!" Sojourner's way to freedom led through the hearts of those she met. It was no way of historic action.

Frederick Douglass lived for action. He was seeing much, in those days, of a man who spoke of God in terms unlike Sojourner's. "God cries out for blood," said this man, a one-time wool merchant named John Brown. Douglass had met him back in 1847, a lean, graying, hawk-nosed, eagle-eyed figure from the Old Testament, who wore the plainest of clothes and a military leather stock, had sworn war to the death against slavery, and believed neither in Garrison's non-resistance nor in Gerrit Smith's political designs. The slave power seemed triumphant. In 1854 it had put through a law that opened the Great Plains to the "peculiar institution"—by territorial option, to be sure, but the slaveholders took no chances. In Kansas, they set up a government by fraud and maintained it by terror; for the first territorial election, five thousand border ruffians came in from Missouri under orders from a U. S. senator to "shoot, stab, or beat any abolitionists seen at the voting places." In Washington, Charles Sumner of Massachusetts denounced "the crime against Kansas" on the Senate floor; on the next day, a Southern congressman entered the chamber with a cane, trapped Sumner in his seat, and beat him to a pulp.

John Brown and his sons went to Kansas. They went by covered wagon, with rifles concealed and surveying tools prominently displayed on the trip through Missouri, and set themselves to "do the work of the Lord." It was bloody work. Douglass, back East, could not suppress a shudder: "To call out a murderer at midnight, and with-out warning, judge or jury, run him through with a sword is a terrible remedy for a terrible malady." Brown became the terror of pro-slavery men, an avenging angel in the torn, faded summer clothes he wore through the campaign. Later, asked if he had gone out under the auspices of the abolitionist Emigrant Aid Society, he answered, "I went out under the auspices of John Brown, directed by God."

Kansas was saved. But it had no sooner been declared free than the Supreme Court stepped in to quash the victory. No one, it held in denying freedom to a slave named Dred Scott, had the power to bar slavery from U.S. territories.

Impotent rage swept the North. At a protest rally in Boston, a huge crowd packed floor and galleries of Faneuil Hall, stood in the narrow staircases and in the lobby, round the Corinthian pilasters. Douglass was the main speaker. He recounted the wrongs done to his race —a fearful catalogue. He reviewed the struggle: the friends of freedom had won in debate, only to face mob violence; they had beaten the street mobs, only to meet armed terror; they had put the terrorists to flight, only to confront the august power of the courts. For each head they cut off, slavery had grown one more formidable. "It must come to blood," Douglass prophesied, and the blood drawn in the land must no longer be colored blood only. Black men must fight for themselves, and redeem themselves, or it would never be done!

Sojourner, black-clad as usual, white turban on her head, sat in the front beneath the speakers' platform, watching Douglass grow more and more excited. There were few other Negroes in the audience, but many veteran abolitionists; no dissenters or hecklers, only people as outraged as Douglass. Still, they were white. Sojourner saw Wendell Phillips, who had shared a bed with Douglass more than once in poor anti-slavery homes, look at him as though an utter stranger were shouting his people's frustration.

"They have no hope of justice from the whites, no possible hope except in their own right arms . . ."

The hall was deathly still. A tall, dark woman had risen in the front row, facing Douglass.

"Frederick," she asked, "is God dead?"

anti-slavery Emigrant Aid Society, he answered, "I went
out under the auspices of John Brown, directed by God."
Lincoln was asked how Judge ...... had been declared
insane. "Sojourner Truth .... at the Supreme ......

War and Peace

THE TURN WAS NEAR. John Brown took the
sword and perished by the sword, and Frederick Douglass,
having tried in vain to dissuade the old man from his
suicidal raid on Harper's Ferry, barely escaped arrest for
complicity and had to flee abroad once more. But the
year was 1859; the tide of events rushed on to Lincoln's
nomination and election, to secession and war. John
Brown's body lay a-mouldering in the grave, but his soul
went marching on. Anti-slavery men quivered with impa-
tience. Now, would the monster be cruched? Their press
chided Lincoln for temporizing on emancipation, on the
use of Negro troops. Douglass, back from England, joined
in the strictures.

"Wait, child," counseled Sojourner. "It takes a while to
turn about a great ship of state."

Waiting was hard, after so many years of it, and when
the longed-for word finally came, it called for more patience. An emancipation proclamation was issued in September, 1862, but not to take effect for a hundred days;
even after the New Year it should apply only to the states
"then in rebellion." The oft-disillusioned could scarcely believe that the New Year might bring freedom. What if the
war ended sooner? If the rebels quit before the year's
end, would they keep their human chattels next year, and
forever?

"Seek ye first the kingdom of God, and his righteousness, and all these things shall be added unto you," Sojourner answered from Scripture. Sufficient unto her day
was the evil thereof.

That fall, with Josephine Griffing, she held meetings in
the northern counties of Indiana. Indiana was Copperhead
country, so livid with anti-war and anti-Negro feeling that

the legislature had barred non-resident colored persons from the state. Sojourner was arrested repeatedly, but Mrs. Griffing convinced every judge that the law was unconstitutional. Their associates were prosecuted for encouraging Sojourner to remain. Arriving in Steuben County for a meeting in the town hall of Angola, she was yelled at, "Down with you! We think the niggers have done enough! We won't have you speak! Shut your mouth!"

"The Union people will make you shut your mouths," she yelled back.

She stayed with a family in Pleasant Lake, five miles from Angola. On the eve of the meeting her host was arrested for entertaining her, and two ladies hurried to warn Sojourner. She got into their chaise, expecting to be driven to their home; when they headed for a hide-out in the woods, she balked. "I'd sooner go to jail," she said, and indeed, a constable promptly appeared with a warrant for her arrest.

On his heels came a captain of the Union home guard. "She is my prisoner," he announced, producing orders to take her into custody. The fife and drum of a home guard unit was heard down the street.

The constable looked disgusted. "I ain't going to bother my head with niggers; I'll resign my office first," he said and vanished as the handful of guardsmen marched up, cheering lustily for Sojourner and the Union. The captain promised to escort her to the meeting—if there was a meeting. It seemed doubtful, for the Copperheads had threatened to burn down the town hall if she tried to speak in it.

"Then I'll speak on the ashes," said Sojourner.

The ladies thought she had better wear uniform. They found her a red, white, and blue shawl with apron to match and put a cap with a star on her head, and a star on each shoulder. "I could scare myself," she said after a glance at the mirror. She refused to take a sword or pistol: "The Lord will preserve me without weapons. The truth is powerful and will prevail."

In the street she found a carriage waiting. The captain and some gentlemen got in with her, the home guard marched alongside, and the Loyal League of Pleasant Lake brought up the rear. Sojourner gripped a white satin banner the ladies had given her, with the inscription, "Proclaim Liberty Throughout the Land," and as the procession entered Angola, she saw the town hall ringed by a huge crowd. "I felt I was going against the Philistines," she said later, "and I prayed God to deliver me out of their hands. But when the rebels saw such a mighty host coming, they fled, and by the time we got there they were scattered over the fields like a flock of scared crows, and not one was left but a small boy who sat on the fence crying, 'Nigger, nigger!' "

After the meeting her friends took her to the squire's home for safety, but in Angola she had no more trouble. She was threatened, heckled, and arrested elsewhere—"at all our meetings," Mrs. Griffing wrote to the *Anti-Slavery Standard,* "we have been told that armed men were in our midst and had declared they would blow out our brains." No meeting was canceled, and Sojourner's banner waved at every one.

"What business are you now in?" she was asked once, by a man who knew her from New York.

"In New York," she told him, "my business was scouring brass door knobs; now I go about scouring copperheads."

She scoured them until winter, when she fell ill. The long wait was drawing to a close, and Freedom Day came near enough to grasp. On New Year's Eve, Negro churches and lodge halls were crowded all over the land; in Boston's Tremont Temple William Lloyd Garrison sat in the balcony, weeping, while Frederick Douglass led the singing on the floor: "Blow ye the trumpets, blow! The year of jubilee has come . . ."

Battle Creek, too, saw rejoicing by the fugitives who had settled in shacks at the ends of the streets. There was "Old Agnes," who owed her life to the mercy of her master's hounds; there was "Old Nancy" whose growing son had no wish to join the Union army; there were a mother and daughter whom chance had reunited in Battle Creek, after long years. Singing paeans, they marched through the frozen town.

Sojourner was at the Merritts' again—bedridden, unable to help in the house, feeling hopelessly dependent. She thought of the aged who were now to go free, and she wondered about the lucky ones who had been cared for by kind masters rather than set adrift like Mau-Mau and Baumfree. Free people worked or paid for their keep, and the oldsters had no money, nor had they strength left to work. The Merritts were kindness itself, but every trifle Sojourner had to accept nowadays reminded her painfully of old age in bondage.

A young woman sat by her bedside, writing a letter. "From Phebe M. Stickney"—the Merritts' daughter had married the year before—"to Joseph A. Dugdale, Mount Pleasant, Iowa . . ."

"At the request of our dear friend, Sojourner Truth," Mrs. Stickney wrote to the Quaker who had been Sojourner's host on the prairie across the Mississippi River, "I write to thee and thine to solicit a little assistance for her. She is now with us, and has many friends, and all are trying to do a little for her. She is this winter quite feeble, not able, by selling her book, to supply herself with the many little comforts that an aged and feeble person needs . . ."

She could not explain her reluctance to take what the friends in Battle Creek were so persistently offering. The voice she had heard all her life had work for her still—yet how to do it, so dependent upon white people as if she had never been free? She thought of her friends elsewhere. "Uncle Joe" Dugdale and others would surely help pay for her needs till she could work again; there was a world of difference, to Sojourner, between asking friends for assistance and inflicting your infirmity upon them like an outworn slave. "Help me live a little longer to praise God and speak to the people in this glorious day of 'mancipation . . ."

Mrs. Stickney put the exact words into her letter. "I write this with Sojourner at my side," she concluded,

"and at her request. She is very poorly, and probably will
not live long."

"You sent the ravens to feed 'Lijah in the wilderness;
now send the good angels to feed me while I live on thy
footstool . . ."

Alone in her barn, Sojourner talked to her God. One
day, Phebe Stickney came with mail. One by one, she
opened and read the letters. Friend Dugdale's reply, "I
never remember to have regretted more that I had so little
at command to bestow," was accompanied by greenbacks,
and his Iowan neighbors had followed his example.

Sojourner lifted her weary eyes. "Lord, I knew thy laws
was sure, but I didn't think they'd work so quick!"

To everyone's surprise, the next week's *Anti-Slavery
Standard* contained Phebe's letter to Dugdale. It was not
her doing; friends from Pennsylvania had responded to
her plea and sent it in. Contributions could be addressed
to the Stickneys in Battle Creek, the editor added. It sufficed to keep them coming from East and West.

"I tell you, child, the Lord manages everything," Sojourner explained to the young woman. "You see, when
you wrote that letter you didn't think you was doing
much; but I tell you, dear lamb, when a thing is done in
the right spirit, God takes it up and spreads it all over
the country."

Among the senders were Oliver Johnson, the *Standard*
editor who had welcomed Sojourner to Ohio, and Samuel
Hill who had befriended her in Northampton, and Mrs.
Griffing who was now in Washington, working for Freedmen's Aid. "Sojourner," wrote Gerrit Smith, "the God
whom you so faithfully serve will abundantly bless you; he
will suffer you to lack nothing either in body or soul . . ."

She threw up her hands. "The Lord bless the man! His
heart is as big as the nation—if he hadn't sent a penny, his
words would feed my soul, and that's what we all want."

The surprises mounted. When the *Standard* of March
25 arrived, Mrs. Sitckney brought it to the barn with all
signs of excitement. Spread over the whole back page was
an article that said, "From the Atlantic Monthly for

April," over the title: "Sojourner Truth, the Libyan Sibyl," by Harriet Beecher Stowe! Almost ten years had gone by since their first and last meeting, but Mrs. Stowe had not forgotten anything. Word by word, as Phebe read from the printed page, the colloquies at Andover came back, from the moment of arrival to Sojourner's departure "as a wave of the sea."

"Her memory still lives in one of the loftiest and most original works of modern art," continued Mrs. Stowe who had visited Rome, some years back, and there told Sojourner's history to the American sculptor, William Wetmore Story. The marble statue inspired by her account had been judged the most impressive word at the 1862 World's Exhibition in London. It was called *Sibilla Libica*, the Libyan Sibyl.

Sojourner shook her head. Could she be that? Nowhere in Scripture was mention made of a sibyl. She pronounced it, "symbol," and when Phebe wished to read the article over, she became impatient: "Oh, I don't want to hear about that old symbol. Read me something that's going on now, something about this great war!"

Hearing her grandson described as an "African Puck" did not please her, either. James was no longer the giggly child of Andover. Grown up into a tall, able-bodied lad, he had gone to answer a call sounded by Frederick Douglass: "MEN OF COLOR, TO ARMS!" At last, the nation had unchained "her powerful black hand." On every highway men were making their way eastward to join the new colored units, and the nineteen-year-old from Battle Creek had just enlisted in the 54th Massachusetts Volunteer Infantry, Colonel Robert Gould Shaw commanding.

"We are the valiant soldiers who've enlisted for the war," Sojourner hummed to the tune of "John Brown's Body." Whatever she sang now would fit itself to this tune that was sweeping the land. Her voice regained its vigor. Her careworn face lit up on hearing names she knew. "They're appointed to God," she said of abolitionists commanding Negro troops, of feminist ladies gone south to care for slaves escaping through the lines—"contrabands," the Army termed them. She was aglow with her old fire.

If only she were younger and as strong as when Olive
Gilbert had been sitting in Phebe Stickney's place! What
had Olive said she might have been? "Another Joan of
Arc"—that was it. "I'd be on hand as the Joan of Arc,"
she told Phebe, "to lead the army of the Lord. For now
is the day and the hour for the colored man to save this
nation."

She asked the young woman to tell her friends that her
health was better than ever. "I've budded out with the
trees," she put it. The flow of gifts began to embarrass
her. When Samuel May and his wife forwarded donations
from Dublin, Ireland, she was baffled. Who had heard of
her in Ireland? "I'm sure," she said, "the Lord never sent
his angels from so far off even in 'Lijah's day."

Phebe proposed writing to the *Standard* to thank all the
donors at once, but Sojourner would thank the Lord only.
A newspaper had other functions. She wanted her friends
to know of her grandson's enlistment: "He's gone forth,"
she dictated, "to redeem the white people from the curse
that God has sent upon them." The boy was drilling at
Camp Read, near Boston; two sons of Frederick Douglass
were with him in Company H. "She wishes you to print
the name of her grandson, James Caldwell, of the 54th
Mass., thinking that someone may go and see him," Phebe
wrote to the editor of the *Standard*.

Another letter to the editor came from Frances Gage,
Dated Freedmen's Camp, Beaufort, South Carolina. Beaufort was a beachhead precariously shielded by naval guns,
a forward base of operations and a haven for countless
runaways. Their needs occupied Mrs. Gage from dawn to
dusk, yet she found time to reminisce about Sojourner,
who had so often "taken us up in her strong arms and
carried us safely over the slough of difficulty . . ."

The *Standard* ran both letters in the same issue, a week
after the 54th embarked from Boston for the Carolinas.
When the paper reached Beaufort, and Mrs. Gage read of
Sojourner's wish, it was too late to go and see Private
Caldwell; the regiment had left the base to join the as-
sault force deploying against the forts of Charleston.

By then Sojourner was up and around town again, wash-

ing people's laundry for her keep and talking to them for
the good of their souls. God was all over, she told them:
"We live in him as the fish live in the sea." She thought of
resuming her travels. Her stock of books had run low, but
another means of paying her way presented itself in time.
A photographer was in town, and the little images drawn
by his magic box struck her as probably easier to sell
than books had been. "I'll sell the shadow to support the
substance," she quipped.

Her first "shadows" went to New York, to the *Anti-
Slavery Standard* which promptly announced that "a card
photograph of that noble woman, Sojourner Truth," was
available to the public. The editor's own reply had to wait,
for in mid-July—right after Gettysburg and Vicksburg—
mobs took over the big city. The wrecking of a draft
office set them off: "To hell with the draft! To hell with
the war! To hell with the niggers!" they howled while an
orphanage sheltering a hundred colored children burned
down. A Negro was hanged from a tree, his body burned
in a bonfire in the street where Isabella had lived with
Matthias.

"The Copperhead Mob," the *Standard* headlined its
two-page report on July 25. On the 27th Mr. Johnson
finally wrote to Sojourner, as reassuringly as possible. He
acknowledged her pictures, complimented her on likeness
and workmanship, and added:

The mob did not disturb the Anti-Slavery office, nor me.
. . . A good Providence seems to have watched over us.
. . . Many of the colored people were dreadfully abused,
but a very healthful reaction has already set in; and I believe the condition in this city will be better than before . . .

This city! It was twenty years since Sojourner had been
called from the new Sodom. She remembered the days
of Matthias, the hate-filled glances and whispers and mut-
terings—but she also remembered the trial of her slander
suit, and she asked what news the *Standard* had this week

about the colored soldiers. Now it was they who had the power of a nation in them.

In the draft riot issue there were two lines on the 54th Massachusetts: its attack on a rebel fort on July 18 had failed for lack of support, not for lack of valor . . . Sojourner was glad. She told Old Nancy, the laundress—another Battle Creek woman whose only link with her boy was the *Standard's* weekly column "Negroes in the Army."

Next week, it carried excerpts about the 54th from the daily press dispatches. The unit had received its baptism of fire on July 16, in a successful skirmish on James Island, and on the 18th, picked to lead the assault on Fort Wagner, it had kept pressing forward bravely, regardless of losses. "Thank God," said Nancy, never ceasing to rub the clothes in her tub, "he didn't run. Thank God."

Not until August 8 could one tell by the *Standard* what had really happened down there, three weeks before. An editorial eulogized the heroic young white commander of the black regiment, and on the front page an eyewitness told how it had been wiped out. On a narrow sandspit, through a curtain of fire from three forts that pinned down supporting units, the 54th had kept going. A ditch turned into a death trap for half the men; the others kept going. Colonel Shaw, leading the remnants up the glacis, was last seen atop the parapet, and the next day a request for his body brought the reply, "We have buried him with his niggers."

Two messages from the Adjutant General of Massachusetts arrived in Battle Creek. "Died gloriously on the field of battle," someone read to Old Nancy, "among the defenders of his country . . ."

"Praise the Lord," sobbed the one-time slave woman, "I done raised a son to be the defender of his country. Praise the Lord."

The second message named Private Caldwell as "missing in action on James Island, 16 July, 1863." He had not even come as far as the charnel house of Fort Wagner! Family and friends clutched at the word "missing." He might be alive, they told his grandmother.

She nodded, "God told me," and went to join Nancy in prayer.

The colored youths from Battle Creek who had enlisted since were encamped in Detroit. In the fall, Sojourner began knocking on doors and accosting strangers in the street: "How about sending the boys a dinner?" Few refused; only one used rude language about the war and the nigger. For a moment she was put out. "Who are you?"

"I'm the only son of my mother," the man jeered.

"I'm glad there's no more," Sojourner said and passed on.

On Thanksgiving Day, at eleven, a carriage piled high with boxes pulled up by the quarters of the colonel commanding the 1st Michigan Regiment of Negro Volunteers. By noon the soldiers had been ordered into line "in their best" and were cheering Sojourner as she made the presentation of the fattened turkey. Afterwards s spent an hour in motherly conversation with the boys.

On Sunday afternoon she came back for another speech, but when she arrived there were so many white visitors in the camp that the troops had to pull far back, almost out of earshot. Only scattered words were audible as she began to speak. The ranks grew restless. The colonel proposed telling the men that she would address them some other time.

Sojourner shook her head. She knew what carried farther than the spoken word, and suddenly a song soared over the heads of the white crowd:

"We are the valiant soldiers who've enlisted for the war;
We're fighting for the Union, we are fighting for the law;
We can shoot a rebel farther than a white man ever saw,
            As we go marching on!"

A Sabbath School convention was held in Battle Creek, that year, and the children's meeting at the Methodist Church had dozed through some long-winded speeches when a voice rang out: "Is there an opportunity that I might say a few words?"

The moderator hesitated. A local clergyman brought the audience to its feet by presenting Sojourner.

She said the spirit of the Lord bade her use this occasion to talk to so many children at once about the sin of prejudice. She would be brief. "Chillun, who made your skin white? Warn't it God? Who made mine black? Warn't it the same God?" She paused. "Now, chillun—remember what Sojourner Truth told you, and learn to love the colored children, that you may all be children of your Father in heaven!"

"Perhaps the most telling anti-slavery speech ever delivered in Michigan," somebody called those few words to a children's meeting.

She had a child with her again. Daughter Elizabeth had remarried recently; with her new husband, a mechanic named Bill Boyd, and a new baby to care for, she did not mind at all if her thirteen-year-old, Sammy Banks, was to be her mother's companion. Sammy could read and write. He had gone to school since Sojourner's return from her visit to Bishop Payne, the man of God and learning. Every time Sammy read to her, Sojourner thanked God who provided for all his children, talking to some and having others educated by his chosen instruments.

In Micnigan the instrument was a woman familiarly known as "Aunt Laura." Everyone had heard of Laura Haviland's Underground Railroad exploits, of the 3,000 dollars put upon her head in Tennessee, of her withdrawal from the Quaker meeting in the days when Friends would free their slaves but frowned on fighting slavery in the world. When no school in Michigan would admit Negroes, Mrs. Haviland had founded one of her own for any child of good character, regardless of sex or color. Her brother had sold his farm to pay for the simple buildings in the valley of the Raisin river—"Friends' Valley," people called it. They had named their school Raisin Institute.

Others talked of "the nigger den." They allowed it was a good school and might be the state's most popular if Mrs. Haviland would just forget about taking in Negroes. But she had no use for prudent advice. There was a tale of a young lady who wept at finding colored children in her class; she asked to be taken home, but her father was too busy to come before Christmas, when black and white children in unison read the message of peace and good will—and then he found his daughter sitting happily beside a little colored boy who helped her parse sentences. She would no longer leave the school for anything.

Throughout Michigan, school children of color knew Aunt Laura as their guardian angel. "God bless her," Sojourner said, patting the head of her grandson.

God had sent her a new travel companion, as James had been before going off to war. At Sammy's age, James had been an "African Puck," laughing merrily at her old tales of horror. "He don't know nothing about it," she had explained to Mrs. Stowe. But Sammy now, he could read the book into which Olive Gilbert had put all that James had not known, and he understood that it had been no laughing matter.

Where James was now, would he be laughing still? Or had he learned better? She added a new stanza to her song for colored soldiers, the boys who went marching on and knew why. Sergeant Lewis Douglass knew why he had followed Colonel Shaw up the glacis of Fort Wagner, owing his life to the bullet that had struck his sword sheath and knocked him back down the slope. His father knew why: "The iron gate of our prison stands half open. One gallant rush will fling it wide, and four millions of our brothers and sisters will march out to liberty!" Sojourner knew why. She had heard what Mr. Lincoln, days before her Thanksgiving in Detroit, had said about "the unfinished work . . . that this nation, under God, shall have a new birth of freedom . . ."

She sang:

"Father Abraham has spoken, and the message has
    been sent;
The prison doors have opened, and out the prisoners
    went
To join the sable army of African descent,
            As we go marching on!"

Spring returned to Battle Creek, and this time she had no need to "bud out with the trees." Her friends in the East sent her newspaper clippings mentioning her; they gave her age as eighty, which she did not mind, but it annoyed her to be written up as dying. With little Sammy by her side she felt as young as ever. One day in June, come to do a family's washing, she remarked that she must get everything done today. "Why?" asked her employer.

"I got to go to Washington," she said, "to see Mr. Lincoln afore the four years is up."

She finished the washing as she had once finished spinning her master's wool, and by nightfall she was on her way with Sammy, her grandson.

Their first stop was Detroit, where they stayed with friends and made themselves useful. In the morning Sojourner caught rain water, to give the baby in the house a bath, and held him while his mother got ready to wash him; Sammy took the older children for a walk. He came back excited: a lady had given him flowers. Later in the day, a spry little woman walked in. Sammy beamed. "God bless thee, Sister Sojourner," said Aunt Laura.

They talked like friends of long standing. Raisin Institute, most of whose students had been old enough to enlist, was closed for the duration; the Freedman's Aid Society would use it as an orphanage for needy colored children. Mrs. Haviland had just returned for a tour of military hospitals and was now going to take a carload of food to Kansas, lately plagued by rebel raiders. She carried a special pass from President Lincoln and was glad to hear that Sojourner would see him . . . They did not run out of subjects.

In the afternoon, with Mrs. Leggett, her hostess, Sojourner drove to the barracks of the colored regiment, the fifth or sixth to drill there since Thanksgiving—the boys who had enjoyed her turkey dinner were with Grant before Petersburg or Sherman in Georgia, and many had fallen, and some had been buried alive at Fort Pillow by a one-time slave trader who had become a Confederate hero. In the evening the ladies called on Sojourner's friends in town, on Giles Stebbins from the Northampton com-

munity, now a rising preacher, and on others who were as
eager to see her and Aunt Laura. Mrs. Haviland had much
to tell. "You have observed troop movements on the eve
of battle," she had been warned by a general, "and these
you are not to report; but the wrongs you have met you
may proclaim from the housetops . . ."

Sojourner and Sammy spent a week at the Leggett home
in Detroit. After their departure, the younger Mrs. Leggett opened a diary she kept, for her baby boy to read in
the future. "I was to tell you of Sojourner Truth," she
wrote. "She has a superior mind, and her abiding faith in
God is beautiful. She talks of Him and to Him as familiarly
as your father and I talk to each other. She is now on
her way to Washington to see the President . . ."

The way was long and led into the past. By slow stages
Sojourner retraced her steps of decades, through Ohio,
Pennsylvania, Upper New York, through the Hudson Valley, where she had been a slave, and the city of New
York, from which God had called her to sojourning. She
traveled from friend to friend, from lecture to lecture.
One Saturday she spoke in New York's Unitarian Church
at Lafayette Avenue and Shelby Street, ferried to Brooklyn,
heard Henry Ward Beecher's opening sermon of the season
on Sunday morning, found it "a feast for her poor old
soul," and spoke from his pulpit. She visited the newspapers—the *Standard*, the *Independent*, the *Tribune*, any
that stood for the right—to confound the rumors that she
was dying. She had not been sick for months, she declared,
and having run out of her *Narratives*, she was now carrying
with her a "Book of Life" whose pages were still mostly
blank, though she hoped in time to fill them with the
names of friends all over the country.

Thus, at the end of summer, she left New York with
Sammy and continued on her journey, looking up her
friends in Orange and Vineland, New Jersey, in Philadelphia, and in other places on the way.

The leaves on the Maryland hills had yellowed when
Sojourner and her grandson came to Washington. She had
never seen it before. In all her travels she had not set foot

in slaveholding territory, and the capital had not long been free soil. But what impressed her was not what impressed other visitors: the Capitol dome, the ankle-deep mud on Pennsylvania Avenue, or the prevalence of uniforms and the grim ring of forts. Victories—Sherman's in Georgia, Sheridan's in the Shenandoah Valley—were the talk of the town, but Washington still felt as if one could see the front.

Sojourner saw her people.

In her born days she had not seen so many. There were few colored soldiers in Washington and vicinity, no colored regiments in camps such as she had been visiting, but here a colored host roamed the city. Decently clad or in rags, in the faded finery of some master or mistress or in the coarse, sweat-stained togs of the field, dark faces seemed to be everywhere. Only a fraction were Washington Negroes. The bulk were "contraband of war." The ingenious label, devised to free the early wartime runaways for trench-digging, had stuck to the deluge that followed. All through the war they kept pouring into the city where "Massa Linkum" lived and they were free—free to live in shanty towns, to be herded into camps, to be locked up in the "Blue Jug," the dismal county jail. Sojourner could soon tell the contrabands. They had a dreamy unawareness of time as if a pause had come in their lives, as if they were facing an abyss and dared not look. They were strangers in a strange land, hungry, thirsty, ragged, homeless.

She saw bands of children prowl the streets, children who pilfered and robbed to live, were caught, jailed, released, and went back to stealing. She saw what was called "home" by the contrabands who had come early during the war: teeming shacks, often built atop one another—near the Washington Canal a hundred families, three to ten persons each, lived in a space 50 yards square. The rooms were windowless, some accessible only through others, so no light at all got in. The roofs leaked. The stench from beneath the few rotten floor boards was worse than in the cellar of Sojourner's childhood. The filth was indescribable. Washingtonians knew the spot as "Murder Bay."

Sojourner stayed with a friend, a feminist and abolitionist from way back; in the old days a mob had wrecked

Jane Swisshelm's paper in Minnesota, and after the outbreak of war she had nursed in field hospitals until the Army Nurse Corps came into being. At fifty she was busier than ever. The veterans of the great cause did not rest after emancipation. Frances Gage, back from South Carolina, had left on a speaking tour for Freedman's Aid; Laura Haviland was trouble-shooting in Louisiana; Lucy Colman, Sojourner's companion in Ohio, served as a gadfly to Washington bureaucrats—"Somehow," she boasted, "if anything was to be done for any special colored person, everyone knew I was the one to do it." And Josephine Griffing was the freedmen's angel in the capital, the one who organized relief, the one who found work. Week after week she took small groups to Philadelphia or New York, paying their fare and feeding them until they started in their jobs as free people.

As the stream of contrabands swelled, camps were set up on North Tenth Street, on Mason's Island in the Potomac, finally at Arlington Heights across the river, where the men were put to tilling the farms around the pillared mansion of Robert E. Lee. The Arlington camp was named Freedman's Village. Many called it Freedom Village. The superintendent, Captain Carse, a man as dedicated as the women volunteers, arranged for crafts to be taught and a school, a church, a hospital, a home for the aged to be set up—the camp, laid out around a small park, could have been a model miniature city if the incoming tide had not continually overflowed its bounds and overtaxed its facilities. Bewildered, uncertain, without possessions other than their bodies, without resources other than hands and legs accustomed to move only at a master's bidding, the freedmen poured in. Young men went into the Army; the women and children, the crippled and the aged remained. They kept coming and coming.

Sojourner moved out of Mrs. Swisshelm's. After a week on Mason's Island, holding meetings for the people there, she went to Arlington and found she was needed. The contrabands at Freedman's Village were not the strong and the strong-willed, those who had escaped in former years and had since had a taste of the free world. These, until now, had never left a plantation except to be sold to another plantation; their world was the cotton field, the cabin, and the coffle. Their habits were dirty. Their children wallowed naked in the mud. But the word God, on Sojourner's lips, still had a sound all its own.

It was Sunday; she held a meeting. From all over the camp they came to listen, to look at the tall woman who stood on the platform wearing a turban of spotless white, who was one of them and yet so different. She preached on cleanliness. "Be clean," she demanded as a start. "Cleanliness is next to godliness!"

They flocked about her after the sermon, to hear more, listening as to an oracle.

The superintendent asked her to stay at the Village. She had of course, come to Washington to see Mr. Lincoln, but this proved to be more difficult than she had thought. One did not simply call on the President. One needed an appointment, and Captain Carse was unable to get one for her. The war, the government, and the election that was only a few weeks off kept Mr. Lincoln too busy. The captain advised asking Mrs. Colman. If anyone in Washington could wangle it, she was the one.

In mid-October Sojourner saw the President, but at a distance. The State of Maryland had abolished slavery, and the colored people in Washington and environs were celebrating. Sojourner was one of the speakers. Afterwards, when a torchlight procession with banners marched behind a brass band to the White House lawn, she went along. The crowd cheered itself hoarse until the French doors opened and a man came out on the portico.

In the flickering light of the torches Sojourner saw a gaunt figure—not unlike her own, but taller—and a drawn, deeply lined face. "I have to guess, my friends, the object of this call which has taken me quite by surprise this evening," said the President.

"The emancipator of Maryland, sir," someone shouted.

Lincoln smiled. "It is no secret that I have wished and still do wish mankind everywhere to be free."

"God bless Abraham Lincoln!" The cheers rose to the portico, and Sojourner kept looking at the doors that had closed behind the gaunt man. Freedom, like God, must be all over . . .

It was for 8 A.M. on Saturday, October 29, that Mrs. Colman finally obtained a White House appointment for herself and Sojourner. The two arrived to find about a dozen callers waiting, among them two other colored women. The door to the President's room was open. Waiting her turn, Sojourner enjoyed hearing him converse with others, and it occurred to her that he was as friendly to his colored visitors as to the whites—indeed somewhat friendlier. One of the colored women, a soldier's wife, was sick and due to be evicted for being behind in her rent. The President listened attentively, and there was kindness and concern in his voice as he told the woman where to turn for help and asked Mrs. Colman to assist her.

Lucy Colman gave the woman some instructions and turned back to the President. "I am happy to say to you, sir, that I haven't come to ask any favor. My business is simply to present Sojourner Truth, who has come all the way from Michigan to see you."

Abraham Lincoln rose and gave Sojourner his hand, with a bow. "I am pleased to see you."

"Mr. Lincoln," she said, "I'd never heard tell of you before they put you up for president."

"But I had heard of you," he said, smiling.

"And when you took your seat," she went on, "I feared you'd be torn to pieces. I likened you unto Daniel, who was thrown into the lions' den—and if the lions didn't tear you to pieces, I knew it would be God that saved you. And I said if he spared me, I'd see you before the four years expired, and he'd done so, and now I'm here to see you for myself."

He congratulated her on being spared. When she called him "the best president who's ever taken the seat," he replied that she was probably referring to his Emancipation Proclamation, but his predecessors, Washington in particular, had been just as good and would have done just as he had, if the time had come. "If the people over there," he said, pointing across the Potomac, "had behaved themselves, I couldn't have done what I have; but they didn't, which gave me the opportunity to do these things."

"Thank God," she said with fervor, "that you were the instrument chosen by him and the people to do it."

He opened a silver-mounted box and showed her a book, which she recognized as a Bible even though the gold plate on the cover bore a slave with the shackles dropping off his hands in a cotton field. Lincoln turned the book around; on the back cover was another gold plate, with an inscription.

Mrs. Colman rushed to read it aloud: "To Abraham Lincoln, President of the United States, the friend of universal freedom, by the loyal colored people of Baltimore, as a token of respect and gratitude. Baltimore, July 4, 1864."

Sojourner examined the gift and had to think of the laws that made it a crime to teach the givers to read it. "And for what?" she asked. "Let them answer who can."

As if to answer, the President reached for her "Book of Life." The hand that had signed the death warrant of slavery wrote a few words, and she heard him say, writing "For Aunty Sojourner Truth, October 29, 1864. A. Lincoln." Then he rose, took her hand, and told her that he would be pleased to have her call again.

Her time had run out. And so, before she had a chance to call again, would Mr. Lincoln's.

A week after the election, Sammy took down a letter for his grandmother, to friends up north. "Abraham Lincoln, by the grace of God President of the United States for four years more," she began a detailed description of her White House visit. And she summed up: "I must say, and I am proud to say, that I never was treated by anyone with more kindness and cordiality than by that great and good man. I felt I was in the presence of a friend."

She was now at Freedman's Village and had found things as well as expected. "I think I can be useful and will stay. The captain in command of the guard has given me his assistance, and by his aid I have got a little house, and will move into it tomorrow. Will you ask any of my friends to send me a couple of sheets and a pillow?"

Her job was to keep the new arrivals out of the filth and crime and degradation of their predecessors in the slums of Washington. The job began in the home, and the women who would have to make the homes did not know how. They had been taught to pick cotton, not to keep house; they could handle a hoe, but not a needle or a skillet. Yet Sojourner, walking about the camp to instruct them in domestic duties, found them eager to learn. "They want to learn the way we live in the North," she reported. "I am listened to with attention and respect, and from all things, I judge it is the will of both God and the people that I should remain."

She wanted the *Standard* sent to her in care of Captain Carse, for the freedmen like to hear what was happening in the new world they had entered—how the war was going, and what would be done for them. "Sammy, my grandson, reads for them. We are both well and happy, and feel that we are in good employment," she assured her friends.

In December a document came from up north.

New York, Dec. 1, 1864

This certifies that The National Freedman's Relief Association has appointed Sojourner Truth to be a counselor to the freed people at Arlington Heights, Va., and hereby commends her to the favor and confidence of the offices of government, and of all persons who take an interest in relieving the condition of the freedmen, or in promoting their intellectual, moral, and religious instruction. . . .

"They have to learn to be free," Sojourner put it. The need was obvious. Daily she found women in tears or stony grief, or rattling the bars of the guardhouse—women whose children had been spirited off to Maryland. The law abolishing slavery in Maryland was still being fought in the courts, and in the meantime many of her slaveholders felt entitled to make up for their absconding property. As grown blacks might cause trouble, they preferred the children playing in the fields about the camp. They took what came to hand; one could not tell the pickaninnies apart, anyway. If the dams squawked, one locked them up for disturbing the peace.

Captain Carse shrugged: his authority was confined to Freedmean's Village. There he had to keep order. He pitied the women, but they must not make a fuss in his camp.

Make a fuss! Voices from the past rang in Sojourner's ear—Mrs. Dumont's, Mrs. Gedney's. Then her own son had been sold away, and the law had brought him back. She told the mothers that they were free and had rights; they could bring the robbers to justice. "The law is with you," she insisted.

The freedwomen gaped. They knew there was no more selling down the river, no more toiling for masters—but the law? They knew about the law. Where they came from, it was called the Black Code. It set less store by a free Negro than by a slave. Bring white men to justice? They shuddered at the idea.

Sojourner talked to some soldiers she knew as good anti-slavery men, and the next time the kidnappers struck, a posse pursued them. Caught, they denied that the cowering little blacks in their company came from the camp. Sojourner recalled the Kingston courthouse, the book she had sworn by, without knowing what it was, that her son was her son.

She rounded up the frightened mothers. "The law is with you; get behind it!"

Trembling, they swore out warrants and received their children.

The exasperated Marylanders turned upon Sojourner. "We'll have you put in the guardhouse, you old . . ."

"If you try to put me in the guardhouse, I'll make the United States rock like a cradle," she threatened back.

She had been five months at Arlington Heights when the war ended. A half million lay dead, but the young leaves were sprouting green as ever on the Palm Sunday of Lee's surrender at Appomattox, and his vacant mansion on the Heights glittered with lights on Tuesday night, when a delirious host from Freedman's Village celebrated on the lawn, chanting "Year of Jubilee."

The following Tuesday found the White House lawn

thronged as never before, yet more silent than ever. In two hushed columns the masses filed through the French doors to the East Room, past an open coffin under a canopy of black crape and silk. A silver-plated shield bore the legend: "Abraham Lincoln, 16th President of the United States, born February 12, 1809, died April 15, 1865."

They filed in, looked, moved on. Veterans who had left arms or legs on the battlefield came out of hospitals for a last look at the commander in chief. A Negro woman, graven-faced like a bronze figure, bowed over the lips that had told her, "I'll be pleased to have you call again . . ."

The lips were closed now. Tears ran down Sojourner's furrowed face as she moved on with the crowd.

In May the armies came to Washington for the Grand Review. Four of Sherman's corps bivouacked south of the Potomac, their Negro camp followers mingling with the freedmen at Arlington, swapping escape stories, telling of the fighting they had seen and of the hundred men, women, and children who had once been caught asleep and sabered down by rebel cavalry.

The signs of mourning vanished from the capital. The skies were blue for the pageant, so were the streets— Union blue, and full of flags and happy faces. There was anxiety, too, on this last day of now-or-never. The scales would now tip for the missing, on the side of life or of death; but hope died hard—except for Negroes. No one held much hope for missing Negroes. "The river was dyed with the blood of the slaughtered," said a Confederate general's report on the disposition of colored prisoners. "I regard captured negroes as I do other captured property," another had explained.

Sojourner watched and prayed.

The parade took two days. Washington's own Army of the Potomac, under Meade, the victor of Gettysburg, marched on the 23rd, cheered for six solid hours. On the 24th, one hailed the Army of the West. The crowds lined Pennsylvania Avenue, piled up on doorsteps, hung out of windows to pelt the heroes with flowers. Sojourner and her grandson stood on a jammed sidewalk as red-bearded Sherman, flanked by a young officer with one arm, rode at the head of the troops he had led two thousand miles through enemy country—troops partly ragged or shoeless, but with the rough look of frontiersmen and the bold, rolling stride that had brought them over mountains and through swamps, fighting as they went. Companies were trailed by captured horses or mules loaded with cooking utensils and captured chickens. Cows, sheep, goats, dogs, raccoons came down the Avenue with the contrabands who had followed Sherman and were now sharing his triumph, often with three or four children packed upon one mule. "Hurrah! We bring the jubilee!"

Sojourner watched the black pioneers marching two abreast ahead of each division, armed with picks and spades—the only colored soldiers in the parade, yet far too many to pick out an individual.

The men scattered all over Washington after the review, got drunk, found women, lined up for mustering-out pay. At Freedman's Village, Sojourner sang the song that had always been her own: "It was early in the morning . . ."

One colored soldier, big, burly, and gay, his uniform faded and torn beyond recognition, told a story so simple it made people gasp. Taken prisoner on James Island, held for twenty months, paroled this March, he was now headed for Boston, to be mustered out and go back home to blacksmithing in Battle Creek.

But, they asked, was that all? Had he bluffed the rebels? Had some officer taken him for a servant? What had saved him?

"God saved him. He told me," said Sojourner, happy, thankful, but not surprised at her grandson's safe return.

Her song echoed over Arlington Heights. It welcomed newcomers and piloted the forlorn; it was the trumpet of the new life, now that the bugles of war had ceased blowing. "When he rose—when he rose . . ."

The one-armed officer who had ridden with Sherman walked through the camp, talked to her, listened carefully. Oliver Otis Howard had lost his arm at thirty, at Fair Oaks, and commanded the Army of Tennessee at thirty-two; he had just been appointed to head the new Freedmen's Bureau. There followed an interview with a young colonel who had been President Lincoln's aide and was now General Howard's deputy, and an official document bearing his signature:

WAR DEPARTMENT

BUREAU OF REFUGEES, FREEDMAN, AND ABANDONED LANDS

Washington, September 13, 1865

Sojourner Truth has good ideas about the industry and virtue of the colored people. I commend her energetic and faithful efforts to Surgeon Gluman, in charge of Freedmen's Hospital, and shall be happy to have him give her all facilities and authority so far as she can aid him in promoting order, cleanliness, industry, and virtue among the patients.

John Eaton, Jr.
Col. and Assistant Commissioner.

Her hospital work did not take up all her time. She held meetings in Washington, spoke in churches, kept making friends, and was asked once to find a congressman to present a feminist petition drawn up by a new associate editor of the *Standard,* a young woman named Susan B. Anthony. The burning issue of the day was Negro suffrage —"I hear so much about colored men getting their rights," she said, "but not a word about the colored women." She went to a New York equal rights convention, as Elizabeth Cady Stanton's house guest, and addressed the fashionable audience at the Church of the Puritans as "chillun," like everybody else.

"I call you chillun, because you are somebody's children, and I'm old enough to be the mother of all that's here. I want women to have their rights, and while the water is stirring I'll step into the pool. Now that there's a stir about colored men's rights is the time for women to get theirs. I'm sometimes told, 'Women ain't fit to vote;

don't you know a woman had seven devils in her?' Seven devils ain't no account. A man had a legion in him."

The hall roared.

In Mrs. Stanton's parlor she explained her reasoning. "You never lose anything by asking everything. If you bait this suffrage hook with a woman, you'll surely catch a black man." She gathered up her bag and shawl. "There's a great deal in that philosophy, chillun. Now I must go and take a smoke . . ."

She smoked a pipe and blamed the habit on race prejudice: on railway trains she had been sent into the smoking car so often, she had taken it up in self-defense. She now traveled much for the purpose of placing freedmen in jobs. Families wanting to go north were sent to her, as were requests for young, strong, willing workers, trained domestics in particular. But matching supply and demand was no easy task. There was the red tape of Bureau regulations to be overcome, and the natural fear of dispersal in a strange environment, and the politicians' desire to keep the newly enfranchised where their votes would do the most good.

"I wish we could send a hundred men," she heard from Josephine Griffing; "they stand idle everywhere and will not go in any considerable numbers till after the first of June, when they will vote. We have been trying to get some to go the last week, but all who go incline to go to Providence, Battle Creek, or some place where already several have gone."

In the winter of 1867, it took Sojourner three trips to the Deep South to find the laborers wanted in the region of Rochester. Mrs. Griffing was almost losing heart. "I am so thronged with applications from all parts," she wrote, "that I cannot finish any day's work. I always go to bed tired, leaving much undone. As to sending you people, it is impossible to promise anything. We will make one desperate effort . . ."

In Rochester, Sojourner saw Frederick Douglass again and had him write some friendly lines into her "Book of Life." She stayed with the Posts again, at the old Underground Railroad terminal which was no longer needed, thank Heaven. Time never stood still. There were new needs, new railroads.

One day, without warning, she quit her jobs in Washington and left the capital as she had once left New York. She was busy, beloved, yet more and more discontented. The "sable host" in the camps would not diminish. Hundreds were placed by her, thousands by others—it made hardly a dent. For the old and infirm, for the children growing up in wickedness, there was no chance, no hope of learning "the way we live in the North." The Bureau fed them, but they had no future. In the South she had seen them living in their old cabins, toiling for their old masters, cowed as before, torn between a longing to leave and the dread of a lonely, friendless new life on their own. Some day, too, the government was bound to tire of supporting those in Washington. Where could they go?

Sojourner went home with Sammy. He was nearly eighteen; James had been a full-fledged blacksmith at that age, but Sojourner could not bear to be without her "reading eyes." Her family had grown in her absence. The Boyds' little William was six, and so was the Corbins' boy, Frank —Diana and her husband had settled in Battle Creek, with Jake Corbin working as a cook at the local hotel and Diana keeping house on South Street, near the Kalamazoo River dam. James lived with them now, as a boarder. And the Schuylers had arrived and moved into a cabin at Harmonia, where Sophia had since borne a son, two years old now, whose name was Sojourner Schuyler.

For the first time since the day she had carried the infant Sophia out of New Paltz, Sojourner Truth had her whole family together. It made her feel the need of a proper home, a place for them to keep while she was sojourning. She decided to buy the College Street barn from the Merritts, who would let her have it on credit— in exchange for putting her mark on a mortgage, as in the case of the Northampton house. The Merritts also furnished her with lumber for remodeling the barn, but it was slow work; only two rooms could be finished in time for the winter. The first city directory of Battle Creek, due next year, would still say: "Truth, Mrs. Sojourner (col'd), lecturer, boards 10 College."

There was sad news, too, that winter. Young Phebe Stickney fell ill and was not expected to live. Her friend Frances Titus took over the handling of Sojourner's affairs, promptly repeating the error that Olive Gilbert and Mrs. Stowe had made before her. "She is anxious to have a little home of her own," Mrs. Titus broadcast all over hte country, "where she can be comfortable and can make her friends comfortable . . ."

Sojourner stayed home less than six months.

In these months on the prairie, a plan had ripened in her. What did white folks do who had no chance in the East? They went west. What was done about the Indians? They got government land in the West, sometimes with housing. The railroads got land in the West every day, to create new wealth for the country. Why should the freedmen not have this chance to enrich the country by supporting themselves, to escape from slavery's backwash without being scattered all over?

She left children and grandchildren in Battle Creek and took to the road once more, to proclaim her idea.

"Don't you want to write your name in the Book of Life?" she asked everyone she told it to, high or humble. Slowly the blank pages filled up with a cross section of America. In Detroit her hostess, Nannette Gardner, signed on a note of triumph, having just cast the first vote for a state office deposited by a woman in an American ballot box. In Erie County, New York, a Phebe Merritt—a cousin of the one in Battle Creek—drove Sojourner from town to town. In Syracuse, Samuel May gave her a note thanking any who would assist her at the Courtland depot. In Peterboro she stayed at Gerrit Smith's mansion, and when she became ill in Rochester, Mrs. Smith sent her a note full of love and hope that she would soon be well enough to come again.

Mail kept following her. "You asked me if I was of your race," wrote a Connecticut girl to whom she had sent her picture. "I am coloured, thank God for that; I have not

the curse of God upon me for enslaving human beings."
From Brooklyn, Elizabeth Tilton, wife of the editor of the
Independent, sent an invitation to Livingston Street, with
assurances that the guest would be met at the depot. Laura
Haviland, from Toledo, detailed her own travel plans and
signed her letter, "Yours for the poor and needy."

It was in Brooklyn that Sojourner's idea evolved into a
project. Theodore Tilton explained to her why those who
would like it lacked the power to carry it out, while those
who had power were apt to view it with indifference. A
petition, with signatures enough to impress the politicians,
was the answer.

Sojourner had put her mark to many petitions. After all,
what were they but prayers—prayers to human authority?
She had always stood on praying ground. Mr. Tilton helped
her with the wording:

To the Senate and House of Representatives, in
Congress assembled:

Whereas, From the faithful and earnest representations
of Sojourner Truth (who has personally investigated the
matter) we believe that the freed colored people in and
about Washington, dependent upon government for support, would be greatly benefited and might become useful
citizens by being placed in a position to support themselves: We, the undersigned, therefore earnestly request
your honorable bodies to set apart for them a portion of
the public land in the West, and erect buildings thereon
for the aged and infirm, and otherwise legislate so as to
secure the desired results.

The crusade began quietly, in the homes of friends in
Philadelphia. Lucretia Mott, the grand old lady of the
cause, signed the petition and offered encouragement. Anna
Dickinson, a young woman whose wartime speeches as a
teen-ager had set the North ablaze, signed and replenished
Sojourner's supply of "shadows." A doctor promised to
forward her back pay, which General Howard had finally
pried out of the Treasury—fifteen dollars a month for

two years—to William Merritt in Battle Creek on account of her mortgage. She traversed New Jersey: "On Saturday, January 1st, 1870, our house received a new baptism through Sojourner Truth," wrote her hosts at Vineland. She went on to New England, and in February, at a mass meeting in Providence, she took her petition to the public.

In plain Quaker garb, bent only slightly with age, her voice first husky, but clearing fast, she pleaded the cause of her people. They could not take care of themselves, she assured her listeners: "Why, you've taken that all away from them. They've got nothing left." They were doomed in the South: "I know the good people in the South can't take care of the Negroes as they ought to, 'cause the rebels won't let them." But the nation had grown wealthy on the Negroes' toil. They had earned help. "We've earned land enough for a home, and it would be a benefit for you all, and God would bless the whole of you for doing it. How can you expect to do good to God, if you don't learn first to do good to each other?"

The whole audience signed.

Wendell Phillips was present; he had lately opened some of his own speeches with a line heard from Sojourner: "Children, I've come here tonight like the rest of you, to hear what I've got to say . . ." And he inscribed her book: "Blessings on thee, my good old friend."

Flushed with success, she headed straight for Washington, to let the government go to work on her program. "I thank my God that I have met Sojourner Truth," wrote someone along her way.

A letter from Leeds, Massachusetts, caught up with Sojourner.

My dear friend: A line from my brother, received this afternoon, speaks of your being at Vineland, so I must send you a few lines. . . . How strange are the events of our lives! You and I seem to move around as easily as soap bubbles—now here, now there—making our mark, I suppose, everywhere, though mine is a very quiet mark compared to yours. I did not think you were laying the founda-

tion of such an almost world-wide reputation when I wrote
that little book for you . . .

Olive Gilbert! A reply was dicated at once, and a second
letter from Olive, "fervent, fresh, and warm from the
heart," was not long in coming. It mentioned Sojourner's
calls on Mrs. Stowe and "our dear, sainted president," her
work in Washington, and everything else that had got into
the papers and thus enabled Olive to "observe you at your
old vocation of helping on and doing good to your fellow-
creatures. . . . I have written more than a sheet," she
wrote,

and have not spoken of what has been in my mind all the
time, of the great deliverance of your people from the
house of bondage, the wonderful work of the Lord, accomplished only through a cruel and bloody war. . . .
Oh! it makes me almost speechless when I contemplate the
hosts of men that were thus sacrificed to Moloch. There is
but one reconciling thought, and that is, The Lord is all-
wise and reigneth over all . . .

The second letter was signed only "O.G." Olive was
withdrawing into her anonymity of so many years.

In mid-March Sojourner arrived in Washington. The first
man she went to see was the Commissioner of the Freedmen's Bureau, and she left his office with his warm wishes
and a letter:

Washington, D.C., March 17, 1870.

Gen. U.S. Grant,
President, U.S.

Sojourner Truth, quite an aged and distinguished colored
woman, earnestly working for years for her people, desires
to see the president. She will pray for him surely; but
more heartily if she sees him.

Yours respectfully,
O. O. Howard.

The appointment came through for the 31st—a big day, it turned out: on the 30th, ratification of the Sixteenth Amendment had pledged the right to vote to all Americans regardless of color. Friends accompanied Sojourner to the White House. The news of her coming had preceded her; she was known wherever she went. "I recollect having seen you at Arlington Heights," said a gentleman in the anteroom. "How old do you call yourself now?"

She had a ready answer, "I get five dollars for telling my age."

The gentleman smiled and asked her to call on him at the city hall. After he left, her friends told her she had been talking to Washington's Mayor Bowen.

The visitors were ushered into the reception room. One of them—"a free and easy sort of fellow," in Sojourner's view—stepped right up: "President Grant, is it? Your picture looks older than you do."

"I am not so very old," said the President.

"Well, how old do you call yourself, anyhow?"

Forty-nine years, said the President.

"No older than that?"

"No, sir."

"You look older," the man insisted, waiting for the President to say more. "Goodbye," he said finally.

"Goodbye, sir," said the Chief Executive.

Sojourner was next. Ulysses Grant shook her hand, and when she told him how happy she was that her people had won the vote, he said he was, too. He signed her book; the major impression she retained was of his courtesy in telling his age.

She promptly called on the mayor to apologize for her bad manners, but he replied that it was he who should apologize, it being improper to ask a lady her age, and he invited her to spend a day at his home, with Mrs. Brown and their family.

She visited the Capitol. The corridors rustled with subdued excitement. Pages stared in disbelief. Wide-eyed clerks peered out of office doors along her way to the Chamber. The stir had nothing in common with the hostile mutters of old; what she felt around her, what she felt herself, was wonder at the change that had come to pass in ten years.

"It was an hour not soon to be forgotten," a Washington Sunday paper said of the scene that ensued,

for it is not often even in this magnanimous age of progress that we see reverend senators—even him that holds the second chair in the gift of the Republic—vacate their seats in the hall of State, to extend the hand of welcome, the meed of praise, and substantial blessings, to a poor negro woman. . . . It was as refreshing as it was strange to see her who had served in the shackles of slavery in the great State of New York for a quarter of a century before a majority of the senators were born now holding a levee with them in the marble room, where a decade ago she would have been spurned from its outer corridor by the lowest menial. . . . Truly, the spirit of progress is abroad in the land, and the leaven of love is working in the hearts of the people, pointing with unerring certainty to the not far distant future, when the ties of affection shall cement all nations, kindreds and tongues into one common brotherhood . . .

The two senators from Michigan, one a millionaire merchant from Detroit, hovered about her like guardian angels. Fourteen, all told, signed her book, and when the names were read back to her, she could count one from her native New York, one from Indiana, where she had been jailed so many times, and five from the South—including one who had inscribed himself, "H. R. Revels, Senator, Miss., Colored."

Only one asked about her plan for the freedmen. It was a man as tall as she, with a mane of white hair over a lined, leonine face, who invited her to his office to discuss her ideas in more courtly fashion than she had ever seen a gentleman treat a lady. He signed her book not like the rest, with name and state only, but wrote:

Equality of rights is the first of rights.

Charles Sumner,
Senate Chamber, April 26, 1870.

Sojourner knew the tall man. The senior Senator from Massachusetts was a familiar figure in Washington; she had seen him in Lafayette Square, faultlessly dressed, walking to or from the simple home on the corner of Vermont Avenue in which no one suspected the art treasures massed inside. She had seen him walk—he never rode—to Capitol Hill, though she had no clear picture of what he was doing there as chairman of the Committee on Foreign Relations. But she knew he had borne the brunt of the battle against slavery for twenty years, had fought it wherever he found it, in every form, under every disguise, on any issue. In Massachusetts she had not known either that he, more than any one man, had welded the state to the cause, that he had broken up the alliance between Southern cotton planters and Northern cotton manufactures, "the lords of the lash and the lords of the loom." She had known only a story people told about him: when someone said he was forgetting the other side of the question, Sumner thundered, "There is no other side!"

His friendly concern with her plan came as no surprise to Sojourner. He advised her, as others had, to get a great many more signatures to her petition than she had gathered thus far, and even then he seemed not to hold much hope for an effort to aid neither veterans nor industries nor railroads, only former slaves. But he did not discourage her. Prospects of failure never daunted the man of whom a friend would soon say, "I don't suppose Charles Sumner knew what fear was."

He went on to talk of his own fight of the time: for a civil rights bill that would achieve his goal of "absolute human equality, secured, assured, and invulnerable." His chances were not too good, either. There were not votes enough to pass the bill as written, but he would not have it watered down—in fact, he had to die before it could become law in 1875, in a form that even Southerners ad-

mitted they could "live with." While Sumner lived, he preferred to keep "his bill" unpassed but unweakened, as a
goad to the national conscience.

Meanwhile, he worked to better things piecemeal. Sojourner's visit was an occasion for reminiscing, for they
had been comrades-in-arms in a skirmish of the great campaign: in the fight over the streetcars in the nation's
capital.

Wartime Washington had restricted Negroes to special
Jim Crow cars. Whites often occupied the seats in these,
too, leaving the colored with standing room only—a situation accepted by the newly freed, but not by Sojourner.
She complained to the president of the street railway, and
Senator Sumner used her complaint to get Congressional
action banning segregated public transport in the District
of Columbia.

But the law did not enforce itself. It had to be made
effective in the streets, and local Negroes feared to test
its power. Sojourner "got behind it." Her every trip to
Washington was marked by running fights with streetcar
drivers, conductors, and infuriated passengers. When a
driver ignored her signal, she yelped, "I WANT TO
RIDE!" in a voice that stopped traffic. Or she got on by
surprise, resisted attempts to eject her, and rode farther
than she had to, so as to make the most of her experience.
"Bless God! I've had a ride," she would exclaim when she
got off.

One day, returning from Georgetown with Laura Havi-
land, she kept walking as her friend signaled to a streetcar.
The driver stopped. Mrs. Haviland got on slowly. Suddenly
Sojourner wheeled and jumped aboard also.

"Conductor! Do niggers ride in these cars?" a man
bristled.

The conductor tried to put Sojourner off, dislocating her
shoulder in the process, but she held fast. Mrs. Haviland
protested. The conductor shouted at her, "Does she belong
to you, lady?"

"No," said the lady. "She belongs to humanity."

A Woman Remembered

COLLEGE STREET, where Sojourner made her home, still runs through the heart of Battle Creek. The white and colored people of her town have never lived apart. The ancient trees may have stood in the days when she would walk down the street to meetings, or to do a family's washing, or to sell the berries she carried on her head in baskets, on a large tray. The rest of College Street has changed, down to the house numbers. Sojourner's converted barn used to be Nr. 10; it has made way for Nr. 38, a two-story frame building, no longer new but definitely of the twentieth century. When the old barn was torn down, some thought it should have been preserved as a landmark. Today some feel there ought to be a marker on the spot where "Battle Creek's first national figure" lived.

There is a marker on her grave, also in the heart of what is now Greater Battle Creek. The broad mall, the well-kept gravel paths and lawns and giant trees make it appear like a shady town park—only far quieter. The paths lead into solitude. No children play on the lawns, in the shade of the old trees.

The dead of Battle Creek sleep in the shade of the trees, some seventeen thousand of them. Ellen White, the prophetess of Seventh Day Adventism, has her grave there; so has John Harvey Kellogg, the medical genius of the Adventist-founded Sanitarium; so have two unknown soldiers of the Civil War; so has C. W. Post, who came to Battle Creek as a Sanitarium patient and stayed to found its world-wide health food industry. The place where he was buried in 1914 is designated by the cemetery's outstanding memorial, a huge marble mausoleum.

Behind it stands a modest white stele of arresting simplic-

ity. Visitors bound for the Post mausoleum see first the
rear of the slim little monument and can make out no
more than a cross on it. Approaching, they find the cross
formed by letters darkly graven into the white stone:

```
                      I
                      N
          M E M O R I A M
                      S
                      O
                      J
                      O
                      U
                      R
                      N
                      E
                      R
                      T
                      R
                      U
                      T
                      H
```

On each side two dark-green cypresses cling in tender
vigilance to the marble. The base tapers off into the lawn.
Roundabout, as though scattered at random, gray slabs
without inscriptions mark the graves of Sojourner's kin.
The stone that says so was not set until 1961; previously
her chosen name stood alone among nameless relatives and
unknown Civil War soldiers, shining darkly on a white
background in the sign of her Master, Truth. Timelessly it
rises to the crossbeam—IN MEMORIAM.

Her grave, too, was unmarked at first, identifiable only
by the lot number. But memory then was as fresh as the
earth on the grave, and all the Battle Creek knew where to
find it. Thousands of all ages and conditions had walked
there with Sojourner, regardless of race or creed—the
first time in America for a black and white multitude to
join in prayer at a Negro grave.

No one now living remembers her. Her children died

about the turn of the century; her grandchildren have vanished. But the townspeople react with smiles of proud familiarity to the name Sojourner Truth, as to a famous relative's. "I'm a little too young to have known her myself," say the septuagenarians. A white-haired lady speaks of her older sister who passed away: she could recall Sojourner's singing. A younger woman has heard from her mother how she loved to sit on the stoop of Sojourner's house as a child, listening to stories that were always new and beautiful. A librarian at the Willard Library is descended from the Merritts who move through the "Sojourner Truth file" in her care: Charles, who shipped his strawberry crop to the Chicago market, but would keep some for Sojourner to sell in town; William, who held her mortgage; Merritt Woods, source of the lumber for her home; Merritts who helped their friend, Frances Titus, with material on Sojourner's life.

"I sell the shadow to support the substance . . ." Her shadow lingers in the streets of Battle Creek. "Lincoln's friend" is her title in town. Once the last witness to the facts departs, legend is free to thrive on what might have been. Some traced her descent to royalty in Guinea; others credited her with a Mohawk grandmother. There is testimony in stone to the effect that Sojourner lived to be "about 105," and testimony in print that she grew new teeth, and new black hair in place of her own white hair, after passing a hundred.

She did live to be eighty-six, give or take a year, as we can calculate from the reference Dumont gave her at the time of the Matthias trouble. He then wrote that in 1810, when he bought her, she had been "between 12 and 14 years"—an age that would seem to leave little margin for error. But Sojourner did not calculate. "I done quit telling people my age," she said in the eighteen-sixties. Later she came to enjoy being called a hundred.

Dr. Kellogg became her physician and friend when he took over the Battle Creek Sanitarium in 1876, as a young man in his twenties. When he asked how old she was, a twinkle came into Sojourner's eyes. "Why should I tell you?" she countered. "It might spoil my chances."

The Sanitarium still looks from its hilltop over the roofs
of Battle Creek. Dr. Kellogg's portrait greets you in the
lobby; the kindly, wise, bearded face seems about to talk
to you, as he often talked to Sojourner. The Sanitarium
used to have another picture: a life-sized oil painting of
Lincoln with "Aunty Sojourner." This was destroyed in a
fire in 1904, and there is a story that a boy ran into the
flames, trying to save the picture, and barely was saved
himself. Reproductions of the double portrait have traveled
far—one, for instance, into Carl Sandburg's *Lincoln Collector*. A copy hung in Dr. Kellogg's office. After his
death it passed into private hands, and its present whereabouts are unknown even at the Sanitarium.

"I hope he's just been anticipatin'," Sojourner remarked
when a rumor of her death moved a friend to write that
she could now rest in heaven. Far from resting, she was
on the road with her resettlement petition, speaking day
after day, often in half-empty halls, to lethargic audiences.
She had been so confident at first, when Sumner and
others said she needed more signatures. She had fifty petitions printed at her own expense and expected to fill them
in a matter of weeks. It took years. It took coaxing, pleading, scolding. "With all your opportunities for readin' and
writin' you don't take hold and do anything. My God, I
wonder what you are in the world for?" she cried in a
hall in New York.

Her friends encouraged her to go on, to talk to the
people, to stir them up. "Why don't you stir them up?"
asked Sojourner. "As if an old body like myself could do all
the stirring!"

For four years she toiled, speaking in twenty-one states
and the District of Columbia, until her petitions were
covered with names and could be presented in Washington.
With luck, she heard there, Congress might act. It must
act! It needed one more push . . . At that moment
Sammy fell ill. Sojourner had to take him home to Battle
Creek, where he lingered and died, early in 1875, and her
own health declined so that hope for her recovery was
given up. Then Dr. Kellogg came to town, and the next
spring found her rejuvenated. She walked straighter than

before, and friends noted that "from this time onward her eyes never grew dim, as is often the case in old age." She even discarded the spectacles she had worn so many years. "The Lord," she said, "put new glass in the windows of my soul."

She was urged to give up the pipe she had been in the habit of smoking. "No unclean thing can enter the kingdom of heaven," one reminded her, "and what could be more filthy than a smoker's breath?"

"Child," she answered, "when I go to heaven I expect to leave my breath behind me." Warned of the effect on her life span, she said, "I'll quit if I die."

Coming to feel, however, that she could not well chide people for imbibing liquor while she indulged in tobacco, she quit, and lived. "It ought to be proclaimed far and near," her friends rejoiced over her effort, "to strengthen others to cast aside the abomination."

Dr. Kellogg did not see her for weeks at a time, but one day she came to his office with her chronic leg sores worse than ever. "Why, Aunty, what have you been doing?" he inquired.

She said she had thought his ointments were too mild for one as tough as she, so she had asked the horse doctor for "something real strong. But I guess it's made it worse," she added sheepishly.

By then she was ready to believe that she was a hundred and had the constitution of a horse. Even so, the claims of new teeth and a new crop of black hair were probably due to confusion with Diana, whom strangers more and more often mistook for her mother. The Corbins still lived near the river dam, but Diana spent most of her time with Elizabeth Boyd at 10 College Street, tending their mother's garden, caring for her house, and keeping it always in readiness for her return from her lecture tours.

She was lecturing again, often three times a week. In 1878 she spoke in thirty-six towns in Michigan and at a woman's rights convention in Rochester. What she spoke of was still God, faith, and love. What she spoke for now was woman's rights, temperance, penal reform—all the causes once allied with anti-slavery—but her heart re-

mained in the one she had brought to the verge of success
when her breakdown after Sammy's death had ruined
everything. She made a fresh start now, concentrating on
the new fugitives who came to Kansas from the post-
Reconstruction South with its night riders and "Regulators."
She spoke for the Kansas Relief Association which Laura
Haviland had set up; she traveled once more to Kansas, to
see for herself. "These colored people," she told the whites,
"are going to do right among you. You think God had
them scourged all the days of their lives for nothing?"

She liked to joke about herself: "I have a white skin
underneath. Just scratch deep enough." In the end she
acquired some white skin on her surface. It happened when
Dr. Kellogg had to operate on her leg ulcer: to make the
lesion heal over, he decided on a skin graft, then one of
the newest medical techniques. He called her daughters and
asked that one of them give him a piece of her skin for
their mother, but the poor women, scared to death by this
request, ran screaming into the street.

There was no time to lose, so Dr. Kellogg stripped off
some of his own skin and applied it to the raw surface on
Sojourner's leg. The operation was technically successful,
although the doctor himself expected his graft to last only
for a year or two.

Sojourner did not care. "My good Master kept me," she
said each time she recovered. "He still has something for
me to do."

She had to give up travel, but she kept trotting up to the
Sanitarium, where she always found an audience, however small for one accustomed to addressing crowds. Soon
even this was too arduous. Her strength dwindled. Only
the light within remained and gave a strange, mystical
radiance to the eyes in the withered face. When a last
reporter came to call, she perked up once more. "Her
face was drawn and emaciated," he wrote in the *Grand
Rapids Eagle,* "and she was apparently suffering great pain.
But her eyes were very bright and her mind alert, although
it was difficult for her to talk."

She would talk of death now. She had long known just

how it would be: like stepping out of one room into another. "Stepping out into the light," she said. "Won't that be glorious!"

Watching through the nights, her three daughters—Diana, Elizabeth, and Sophia Schuyler from Harmonia—remained at her bedside. Before the break of day, at 3 A.M. on November 26, 1883, they saw her go out as she had said she would, "like a shooting star."

She did not lie in state in the Zion African Church of Battle Creek, though some will now have it so. The records leave no doubt: she was buried from the Congregational and Presbyterian Church on Main Street. On the third day after her death, the family and Mrs. Titus received her friends at her home, and some of the town's leading citizens carried the casket in procession to the church, where a crowd of a thousand was waiting. In the lobby the lid was removed to allow the crowd to file past and bid Sojourner farewell.

Black-clad as always, but robed for her last journey in a nun's veiling, she lay in the coffin. As always, she wore the white bonnet, the white kerchief folded around her shoulders. A woman from Kalamazoo, at whose home she used to stay, had placed a bunch of exquisite flowers in her right hand. Flowers shaped other emblems: a crown, a sheaf of ripened grain, a sickle of death.

The coffin seemed borne by a wave of flowers and wreaths. A basket of ferns had a card attached: "In memory of my father and mother, who loved Sojourner's race. Lucia E. F. Kimball, Chicago, Ill." Another basket came from "The Band of Hope, Battle Creek." No one in Battle Creek seems to know more about the Band of Hope; it is remembered for having remembered Sojourner.

The short November day was drawing to a close as the black-plumed hearse approached the grave. It was the day before Thanksgiving, and there were many who could think back twenty years to the Thanksgiving at Camp Ward, where Sojourner had sung for the First Michigan Negro Volunteers:

We are the valiant soldiers who've enlisted for the
  war;
We're fighting for the Union, we are fighting for the
  law—

Now her lips were closed. The fight was over. The sky
was cloudless, and the sun a red ball lying low on the
horizon. The waiting grave resembled a rent in the red
and golden carpet of leaves over the dead of Battle Creek.
The trees spread naked boughs. Only the maples still clung
to the gold of Indian summer, as on the day when Sojourner Truth had gone to look at Harriet Beecher Stowe.
Never, the author of *Uncle Tom's Cabin* said afterwards,
had she met anyone who possessed more of "that silent
and subtle power which we call personal presence."

Silently the casket was lowered into the ground. The
Reverend Reed Stuart led the mourners in prayer: rows
upon rows of kin and friends, neighbors and followers—
all those who had come to see Sojourner laid to rest, black
or white as the same God had made them.

"Our Father which art in heaven . . ." Thus the slave
child who was to become Sojourner Truth had learned to
say after her "Mau-Mau" in the Hardenbergh slave cellar.
"Thy will be done in earth, as it is in heaven . . ."

The sun went down while the Lord's Prayer came from
the young, blond minister's lips. "And forgive us our debts,
as we forgive our debtors . . ."

All heads were bowed, all hands folded. The children
stood next to the grave, with Frances Titus and Giles Stebbins, whose path had kept crossing Sojourner's from Northampton to her last resting place. Only the trees rustled.
Suddenly voices rose—a few, a hundred, a thousand—and
Sojourner's favorite song soared over the hills.

"It was early in the morning,
Just at the break of day,
When He rose—when He rose . . ."

Through the tears in her eyes Mrs. Titus saw distant
crimson and golden clouds drift over the western horizon,

like messengers from the departed sun. Once more Sojourner seemed to lead the choir.

"And went to heaven on a cloud."

The crowd stood waiting, as if listening in the silence for the irretrievably stilled voice that had talked to God.

The country's newspapers carried appreciations of Sojourner. "Most singular and impressive figure . . . We shall not look upon her like again . . . There was a native nobility about her, which broke down all barriers . . ."

In New York, the *Telegram* interviewed T. Thomas Fortune, editor of the largest Negro paper, the *Globe*. He said such events should remind the colored people that eternal vigilance was the price of liberty, and that "while we had many noble white women who sacrificed their time and talents to the suppression of human slavery," Sojourner stood out "conspicuously as the one woman of her race who did valiant battle." As an afterthought, almost, Mr. Fortune added: "Although the name of Sojourner Truth is familiar to many people, not more than one colored person out of ten knows who she is."

She was one of them, and no other Negro's voice in America had been more widely heard. She had crisscrossed the North before the war and spent the post-war years at the reception center for the hosts pouring into Washington from the slave pens of the Upper South. Surely, the mothers of the children abducted from Freedman's Village must have remembered the woman who recovered them. Yet the editor of the *Globe*, who was in a position to know, thought her name meant nothing to nine out of ten of her people.

The name of Douglass was a byword. He had done most of his work with the pen, in language far over the heads of former slaves, but even the illiterates knew all about him. They knew about Harriet Tubman, whom they called "Moses," the Maryland girl who escaped and went back time and again, leading hundreds to freedom. Theirs was a fame likely to spread among the downtrodden, to nourish hope on every sorrowing day.

Sojourner had not been active in the Underground Railroad. One of its main western routes passed through Battle Creek; her friends included conductors and terminal agents, outstanding violators of the Fugitive Slave Law, some who had spent years in Southern jails, one who had "SS," for "Slave Stealer," branded on his hand—but the only slave she ever freed was her own child, and that in a court of law.

The law was a controlling force in her life. If the law served God, it meant freedom. If the law was just, it was one with God. Some day this image of the law would sway Sojourner's people; but in her time, when the bulk could hardly believe that they had indeed ceased being things under the law, that day was not yet.

From Boston, one whose wizardry with words had served the anti-slavery cause from its infancy sent a message unlike Mr. Fortune's. Silver-tongued Wendell Phillips had known Sojourner well. A few words from her, he used to say, could move an audience as he had never seen people affected by another. He liked to follow her on the platform, to pick up the threads of thought she had scattered before and weave them into the fabric of his own speech.

At her death, too, the renowned orator thought naturally in the terms of his vocation. He characterized her as the movement's "only speaker who had once been a slave in a Northern state," mentioned her "natural wit and happiness in retort," her "rich, quaint, poetic, and often profound speech," and did not forget the effect of her towering figure. "I once heard her describe the captain of a slave ship going up to judgment, followed by his victims as they gathered from the depths of the sea, in a strain that reminded me of Clarence's dream in Shakespeare, and equaled it," the man of letters ventured to say of the illiterate. He summed up by quoting Sojourner: "You read, but God himself talks to me . . ."

The news of her death reached Frederick Douglass in Washington, at the office of the Commissioner of Deeds for the District of Columbia. Douglass was the Commissioner. Earlier, he had been U.S. Marshal for the District—the first man of color in America to be honored with such appointments. He was a power in politics and lived in Anacostia, in a splendid house with servants, horse and closets full of suits he ordered from New York. His forceful mind, his device, "Knowledge makes free," had brought the "black hero" a long way in the forty years since he had met Sojourner.

Now, from his desk in Washington, Commissioner Douglass issued a statement. "In the death of Sojourner Truth a marked figure had disappeared from the earth. Venerable for age, distinguished for insight into human nature, remarkable for independence and courageous self-assertion, devoted to the welfare of her race, she has been for the last forty years an object of respect and admiration for social reformers everywhere."

He spoke as a social reformer, not as her friend. Yet both of them had come out of bondage to serve the same cause of freedom, although from different ends. At Northampton, Douglass had winced at Sojourner's lack of culture, and in the pre-war years he had mocked her as "one of the Garrison school of non-resisters." In wartime he had chided Lincoln in print for dawdling on emancipation; Sojourner had faced Copperhead mobs time after time but trusted the President to turn about the ship at the right moment. And after the war, when she wanted the human wreckage of slavery made independent of government and former masters—when she packed her bundle and went barnstorming again, telling what she had seen in Washington, foretelling what was ahead in the South, begging people, "Please help me with these petitions!"—by then Douglass opposed any migration of freedmen. Migration, he held, was no cure for their ills. Numbers gave them weight in the South. They must fight for their rights where they were.

Thousands went west, anyway; hundreds of thousands did not make it. Withdrawal of federal troops doomed their rights in the South; before they knew it, they were "put back in their place." His people's fate for the half-century to come was settled by the time Douglass wrote his formal farewell to the late Sojourner.

His informal comments differed. "My quaint old sister," he called her. "She seemed to feel it her duty," he complained, "to trip me up in my speeches and to ridicule my efforts to speak and act like a person of cultivation and refinement." He never forgot the scene she had stolen from him simply by asking whether God was dead.

"We were all for the moment brought to a standstill, just as if someone had thrown a brick through the window," Douglass admitted years later, in his memoirs. But he gave himself the last word: " 'No,' I answered, 'and because God is not dead, slavery can only end in blood.' "

Eyewitnesses said soon after the event, however, that Sojourner's question "thrilled through the whole house," that "as by a flash" it changed the feeling of the audience, that a spell was broken. "Not another word she said or needed to say," Wendell Phillips reported. "It was enough."

It took a hundred years and a young, college-bred, world-conscious Negro generation to make Sojourner's road to equality ready for mass travel. In 1957 a gathering of Southern Christian leaders coined the watchword "Love, Law, Liberation" for a new, militant pursuit of freedom in our time—for desegregation suits and registration drives, bus boycotts and prayer marches, sit-ins and "wade-ins" and "jail-ins" and other forms of nonviolent action against injustice. "Christian love can bring brotherhood on earth," Reverend Martin Luther King told the Negroes of Montgomery from the bombed porch of his parsonage. Asked if his model was not in fact the non-Christian Gandhi of India, Dr. King said, "Jesus Christ showed us the way, and Gandhi showed us that it would work."

Sojourner Truth was no mass leader, and "Love, Law, Liberation" was no device for people just out of bondage. It could not even be put into words until Sojourner had been buried for generations. But she had lived the device, and she, too, had shown that it would work.

The first marker on her grave was a simple headstone
set by her friends. In black paint it carried the legend:

IN MEMORIAM

SOJOURNER TRUTH

Born a slave in Ulster County,
New York, in the 18th century.
Died in Battle Creek, Nov. 26,
1883, aged about 105 years.

"IS GOD DEAD?"

When thirty years of sunshine and rain had made the
words illegible, the local D.A.R. chapter restored the inscription and pledged itself to look after the grave. Then
the Negro community of Battle Creek formed a "Sojourner Truth Memorial Assoiciation" and started raising
funds for a "huge boulder" as an appropriate monument. They found the boulder, but the project fell through.

In the nineteen-thirties, Sojourner lent her name to a
housing development in Detroit and, through the development, to a race riot. She was not present to turn the
goats into sheep, as she had done at so many meetings.
But the rioting ceased, and the housing remained.

Today's chaste marble monument in Oak Hill Cemetery,
behind the Post mausoleum, was not erected until 1947.
Higher and higher, the dark-green cypresses grow on each
side of the slim, six-foot shaft. Sojourner's name forms a
cross on its back; engraved in the front is the inscription
that was painted on the earlier stone. "Aged about 105
years . . ." A legend is perpetuated.

By a lake near Battle Creek lives a local historian, a
lecturer herself, who has set out to save "the truth about
Sojourner Truth" before it fades. A curious urgency per-
vades her search for data, her analyses of "the intermin-
gling of fact and fiction which constitutes reminiscences."
A folder of pictures reminds her of the many who had
Sojourner and her daughter Diana mixed up: "It has hap-

pened to me, too," she admits. Diana copied her mother,
sold her pictures like her mother, sang like her mother,
though her voice was not so deep and not so moving.

The pictures show two gaunt women, both wearing white
bonnets and white shawls over dark robes. Diana has her
mother's large, luminous eyes, but not her high cheekbones;
her face looks narrower, lighter than Sojourner's, and her
nose longer, slightly aquiline. No doubt, Diana was beautiful, but she lacked her mother's magic. Poor Diana finally
died in the County Home.

A reproduction of the double portrait with Lincoln ap-
pears from the folder. The familiar figures, one bewhisk-
ered, the other bespectacled, look at you—not at each
other, nor at the Bible between them. Sojourner and Lincoln were dead when a Battle Creek artist painted the
picture for the 1893 World's Fair; Diana, at seventy-five,
posed for her mother's figure.

The setting sun casts a golden sheen on the lake, like a
swaying westward trail. "At first I wanted to write about
this lake and the Indians," sighs the historian of Battle
Creek. "Then Sojourner took hold of me . . ."

Pilgrimages are now made to the cemetery, and wreaths
laid on the marble steps between the cypresses. At memorial observances held by the National Council of Negro
Women, Sojourner's people throng the walks under the old
trees. Once upon a time she won a law suit and felt as if
the power of a nation was in her.

A chapel not far from the grave, lovely to look at, is
unfinished and full of rubbish; only through the stained-
glass windows a dimly celestial radiance falls. The broken
rays transfigure the dirt on the floor. Some day it may be
swept out.

Sojourner's grave is well cared for. The lawn is cut and
rolled. The cypresses are neatly pruned, lest they over-
grow her question, "Is God Dead?"

Of her earthly relics nothing is left but the dress she
wore to lecture. It is a print inset with black silk, with
long sleeves that are beginning to fray. The Titus family
has presented it to the local museum, where the dress is
carefully kept on a hanger in a special room; there are

rumors that it came from England, sent as a gift by Queen Victoria, who had heard about Sojourner Truth. A tall, ebony-skinned girl wore the dress at a recent local ceremony, and people seeing the young girl in the old dress thought Sojourner Truth was walking again in the streets of Battle Creek.

God is not dead, and neither is his faithful daughter. She lives as a sign unto the people, and in the heart of her town.

Acknowledgments and Sources

This is a note of thanks to the many people whose generous assistance made this book possible.

In New York City I am especially grateful to the staff of the Schomburg Collection of the New York Public Library, where I took up Sojourner's trail years ago; in Ulster County to Kenneth E. Hasbrouck, New Paltz, and Harold Harris, Ellenville; on Long Island to the Cold Springs Harbor Whaling Museum and the Huntington Historical Society of my home town; in Massachusetts to Mrs. Thomas Shepherd and Dr. Sidney Kaplan, Northampton, and to the staffs of the Forbes Free Library, Northampton, and the Lilly Library, Florence.

In Michigan invaluable help and information came from Miss Helen L. Warner and Mrs. Corinne J. Wascher of the Willard Library, Battle Creek, from Mrs. Elleine H. Stones of the Burton Collection, Detroit Public Library, from Ross H. Coller and, above all, from Mrs. Berenice Lowe of Battle Creek, without whose tireless efforts and unflagging devotion to Sojourner's memory her full story would still lie buried.

Finally I want to thank my friend Bettina Peterson for her travel companionship and research aid, and for innumerable other things she has done for this book.

The publications to which I am indebted are too numerous to list in full. The following contain specific details on Sojourner Truth or background material corroborating her story.

Anthony, Stanton, and Gage, *History of Woman Suffrage*. Rochester, 1887.

Brockett, L. P., *Woman's Work in the Civil War*. Philadelphia, 1867.

Colman, Lucy N., *Reminiscences*. Buffalo, 1891.

Cromwell, J. W., *The Negro in American History*. Washington, D. C., 1914.

De Witt, William C., *People's History of Kingston, Rondout and Vicinity*. Kingston, N. Y., the author, 1944.

Douglass, Frederick, *Life and Times of, written by himself*. Boston, 1892.

————, "What I found at the Northampton Association," in Sheffeld, Charles Al, *A History of Florence, Massachusetts*. Florence, 1895.

Drake, W. E., *The Prophet! A full and accurate report of the judicial proceedings . . .* New York, 1834.

Fauset, Arthur Huff, *Sojourner Truth, God's Faithful Pilgrim*. Chapel Hill, University of North Carolina Press, 1938.

Galvin, Corinne B., "Sojourner Truth, the Libyan Sibyl." *New York Folklore Quarterly*, Spring 1950.

Gilbert, Olive, *The Narrative of Sojourner Truth, a Northern Slave*. Boston, 1850.

————, *The Narrative . . .*, reprinted with an introduction by Harriet Beecher Stowe. New York, 1853.

————, *The Narrative . . .*, reprinted by Frances W. Titus, with additions from Sojourner Truth's "Book of Life." Boston, 1875.

————, *The Narrative . . .*, reprinted with further additions. Battle Creek, 1878, 1881, 1884.

Gilbertson, Catherine, *Harriet Beecher Stowe*. New York, D. Appleton—Century Co., Inc. 1937.

Johnson, James Weldon, *Black Manhattan*. New York, Alfred A. Knopf, 1930.

Leech, Margaret, *Reveille in Washington*. New York, Harper & Brothers, 1941.

Lowe, Berenice, "Michigan Days of Sojourner Truth." *New York Folklore Quarterly*, Vol. XII, Summer 1956.

————, "The Family of Sojourner Truth." *Michigan Heritage*, Vol. III. Summer 1962.

Massachusetts Soldiers, Sailors, and Marines in the Civil War, published by the Adjutant General. Norwood, Mass., 1932,

McBee, Alice Eaton, *From Utopia to Florence*. Northampton, Mass., Smith College, 1947.

Miller, Lillian M., " 'Aunt Laura,' the Story of Laura Haviland." *Northwest Ohio Quarterly*, Vol. XXIV, Autumn 1952.

Nye, Russell B., "Marius Robinson, a forgotten abolitionist leader." *Ohio State Archaeol. and Histor. Quarterly*, Vol. 55, 1946.

Olde Ulster. Kingston, N. Y., 1905-14.

Osborn, Gardner, *The Streets of Old New York*. New York, 1939.

Redding, J. Saunders, *The Lonesome Road*. New York, Doubleday & Co., Inc., 1958.

Sandburg, Carl, *Abraham Lincoln; The War Years*. New York, Harcourt, Brace & Co., Inc., 1939.

———, *Lincoln Collector*. New York, Harcourt, Brace & Co., Inc., 1949.

Schoonmaker, Marius, *The History of Kingston*. New York, 1888.

Sheffeld, Charles A., *A History of Florence, Massachusetts*. Florence, 1895.

Stegman, H. M., *Battle Creek; Its Yesterdays*. Battle Creek, 1931.

Stone, William L., *Matthias and His Impostures*. New York, 1835.

Vale, Gilbert, *Fanaticism, Its Source and Influence*. New York, 1835.

Of periodicals, the *Anti-Slavery Standard*, the *Liberator*, the *Anti-Slavery Bugle*, and the *Battle Creek Journal* have provided much new information, also daily and weekly newspapers of almost all the places touched by Sojourner Truth.

Index

CAMELOT BOOKS **FOR YOUNG READERS**

CAMELOT BOOKS FOR YOUNG READERS